AF770311

Getting Started

With

Microsoft PowerPoint 4.0

For Windows

Getting Started With Microsoft PowerPoint 4.0 For Windows

Lynn Marie Bacon
Pace Computer Learning Center
School of Computer Science and Information Systems
Pace University

Babette Kronstadt
David Sachs
Series Editors
Pace Computer Learning Center
School of Computer Science and Information Systems
Pace University

JOHN WILEY & SONS, INC.
New York / Chichester / Brisbane / Toronto / Singapore

Trademark Acknowledgments:

Microsoft is a registered trademark of Microsoft Corporation
Excel for Windows is a trademark of Microsoft Corporation
Word for Windows is a trademark of Microsoft Corporation
PowerPoint for Windows is a trademark of Microsoft Corporation
Microsoft Office is a trademark of Microsoft Corporation
Windows is a trademark of Microsoft Corporation
Microsoft Access is a registered trademark of Microsoft Corporation
1-2-3 is a registered trademark of Lotus Development Corporation
WordPerfect is a registered trademark of WordPerfect Corporation
IBM is a registered trademark of International Business Machines Corporation
Paradox is a registered trademark of Borland International, Inc.
Microsoft Encarta is a registered trademark of Microsoft Corporation

Portions of this text were adapted from other texts in this series and from Pace University Computer Learning Center manuals.

ISBN 0-471-14059-7

Printed in the United States of America

10 9 8 7 6 5 4 3

Preface

Getting Started with Microsoft PowerPoint 4.0 for Windows provides a step-by-step, hands-on introduction to *PowerPoint*. It is designed for students with basic PC and Windows skills who have little or no experience with *PowerPoint 4.0 for Windows*. Basic skills are taught in short, focused activities which build to create actual presentations.

Key Elements

Each lesson in *Getting Started with Microsoft PowerPoint 4.0 for Windows* uses eight key elements to help students master specific concepts and skills and develop the ability to apply them.

- **Learning objectives**, located at the beginning of each lesson, focus students on the skills to be learned.
- **Project orientation** allows the students to meet the objectives while creating a real-world application. Skills are developed as they are needed to complete projects, not to follow menus or other artificial organization.
- **Motivation** for each activity is supplied so that students learn *why* and *when* to perform an activity, rather than how to follow a series of instructions by rote.
- **Bulleted lists of step-by-step general procedures** introduce the tasks and provide a handy, quick reference.
- **Activities with step-by-step instructions** guide students as they apply the general procedures to solve the problems presented by the projects.
- **Screen displays** provide visual aids for learning and illustrate major steps.
- **Independent projects** provide opportunities to practice newly acquired skills with decreasing level of support.
- **Features reference** at the end of the book allows students to have a single place to look for commands to carry out the activities learned in the book.

Stop and Go

The steps for completing each *PowerPoint* feature introduced in this book are covered twice. First they are described in a bulleted list, which can be used for reference. Then the same steps are used in a hands-on Activity. **Be sure to wait until the Activity to practice each feature on the computer.**

Taking Advantage of Windows

Getting Started with PowerPoint 4.0 for Windows provides a balanced approach to using a Windows application. The use of the mouse, buttons, and icons for carrying out commands is emphasized. However, familiarity with the menus is developed so that students can take advantage of the greater options often available in menu commands.

Shortcut methods are introduced when appropriate. The convenient **Features Reference** at the end of the book summarizes menu commands and mouse and keyboard shortcuts for each of the features covered in the lessons. Students can use this both to review procedures or learn alternate ways of carrying out commands.

Taking Advantage of The Internet and Multimedia

The resources for research that are available today because of the advancing technologies of telecommunications and multimedia are quite extensive. There is a wealth of continually changing information out on The Internet. The information for the presentations created in *Getting Started with Microsoft PowerPoint 4.0 for Windows* was found using The Internet and *Microsoft ® Encarta (The Complete Multimedia Encyclopedia)*. Specifically, the information for presentations for Kaleidoscope Rain, the Browning Museum, and Julie's Travel Agency was found on The Internet and the information for the Ellis Island presentation came from *Microsoft ® Encarta.*

Flexible Use

Getting Started with Microsoft PowerPoint 4.0 for Windows is designed for use in an introductory computer course. As a "getting started" book, it does not attempt to cover all of the possibilities for creating presentations. Rather, it introduces and reinforces the basic methods of creating a presentation that students will be likely to find valuable. While designed to be used in conjunction with lectures or other instructor supervision, concepts are explained clearly enough so that students can use the book in independent learning settings. Students should be able to follow specific instructions with minimal instructor assistance. Also, the lessons are designed to build on each other to finally view the presentations in Lesson 6. It is suggested that the first four sections, Introduction, Lesson 1, 2, and 3 are worked through in order. There is more flexibility with the last three lessons. If you choose to omit lessons or work through the last three lessons in a different order, you will need to make minor adjustments. There are notes in the book when sequential information will be needed.

Data Disk

There is no data disk for *Getting Started with PowerPoint 4.0 for Windows*. The activities are designed so that the student will create presentations from the beginning of the process to the end. The saved file from each lesson will be used in the following lessons.

Acknowledgments

Getting Started with PowerPoint 4.0 for Windows would not have been possible without the support and effort of many individuals and organizations. Babette Kronstadt provided energetic leadership and orchestrated the production of not only this book but all of Pace's books in the Getting Started series. Matthew Poli performed his usual miracles with the layout and text formatting. Joseph Knowlton did just as amazing a job with the annotations for the screenshots. Katherine Scherer and Nancy Treuer worked diligently to ensure accuracy in the activities, projects, and screenshots. Lynnette Murnane was a tremendous help by creating the table of contents. Sylvia Russakoff, Janet Smith, and Henry Gaylord shared their expertise unselfishly.

We received enormous institutional support from Pace University and the School of Computer Science and Information Systems (CSIS). In particular, much personal support and personal leadership for our work as come from the Dean, Dr. Susan Merritt. Additionally the faculty, staff, and students of the Office Information Systems Department including Professor Nancy Hale and Dr. Judy Caouette have provided their support and expertise generously.

From another perspective, this book is also a product of the Pace Computer Learning Center, a loose affiliation of approximately 15 faculty and staff who have provided more than 7,000 days of instruction to over 60,000 individuals in corporate settings throughout the United States and around the world during the past nine years. Our shared experiences in the development and teaching of these non-credit workshops, as well as credit bearing courses through the Pace University School of Computer Science and Information Systems, was an ideal preparation for writing this book. In addition none of our books for John Wiley would have been possible without the continuing support of Dr. David Sachs, the director of the Computer Learning Center.

We have received many invaluable comments and suggestions from instructors at other schools who were kind enough to review earlier books in the *Getting Started* series and offer their suggestions for the current books. Our thanks go to Jack D. Cundiff, Horry-Georgetown Technical College; Pat Fenton, West Valley College; Sharon Ann Hill, University of Maryland; E. Gladys Norman, Linn-Benton Community College; and Barbara Jean Silvia, University of Rhode Island.

Our thanks also go to the many people at John Wiley who provided us with support and assistance. Our editor, Beth Lang Golub, and editorial program assistant, Christopher Actis, have been very responsive to our concerns, and supportive of all of the Pace Computer Learning Center's writing projects. Andrea Bryant was invaluable in her management of all aspects of the production of this book.

Last but not least, I would like to thank my friends and family for their encouragement and patience. Specifically, my grandmother, Emile Sillery, who has waited patiently for a ferry ride across Long Island sound since the beginning of the summer.

Lynn Marie Bacon

August, 1995
White Plains, New York

Contents

2 EDITING A PRESENTATION 51

3 FORMATTING A PRESENTATION 83

4 INSERTING OBJECTS IN A PRESENTATION 107

Students and Instructors

Before Getting Started Please Note:

WINDOWS INTRODUCTION

Getting Started with Microsoft PowerPoint 4.0 for Windows assumes that students are familiar with basic Windows concepts and can use a mouse. If not, instructors may consider using the companion book, *Getting Started with Windows 3.1*, also published by Wiley. Windows has a tutorial which can also help students learn or review basic mouse and Windows skills. To use the Windows Tutorial: 1) turn on the computer; 2) type: **win** or select Windows from the menu or ask your instructor how to start Windows on your system; 3) press the **ALT** key; 4) press the **H** key; 5) when the **Help** menu opens, type a **W**; and 6) follow the tutorial instructions, beginning with the mouse lesson if you do not already know how to use the mouse, or go directly to the Windows Basic lesson if you are a skilled mouse user.

STUDENT DATA DISKS

Unlike other books in the *Getting Started* series this book does not contain a Data Disk. Each lesson uses the saved file from the previous lesson. Therefore this book assumes that students will have their own blank formatted disk and know the name of the disk drive that they will be using it from. When using a network, students must know the name(s) of the drives and directories which will be used to open and save files.

SETUP OF WINDOWS AND POWERPOINT 4.0 FOR WINDOWS

One of the strengths of Windows and *PowerPoint* is the ease with which the screens and even some of the program's responses to commands can be customized. This, however, can cause problems for students trying to learn how to use the programs. This book assumes that Windows and *PowerPoint* have been installed using the default settings and that they have not been changed by those using the programs. Some hints are given about where to look if the computer responds differently from the way it would under standard settings. If your screen looks different from those in the book, ask your instructor or lab assistant to check that the defaults have not been changed.

VERSION OF THE SOFTWARE

All of the screenshots in this book have been taken using Version 4.0 of *Microsoft PowerPoint for Windows*. If you are not using version 4.0, the appearance of your screen and the effect of some commands may vary slightly from those used in this book.

Microsoft PowerPoint

Introduction

Objectives

In this lesson you will learn:

- The uses of a presentation
- How to start *PowerPoint*
- The parts of the *PowerPoint* screen that are common to Windows programs
- The parts of the *PowerPoint* screen specific to *PowerPoint*
- Terminology used in presentations
- How to use the toolbars
- How *PowerPoint* follows Windows procedures for using menus and dialog boxes
- How to use Help
- How to exit from *PowerPoint*
- The typographical conventions used in this book

PURPOSE OF THE INTRODUCTION

In all of the other lessons in this book you will develop a specific project. This introduction is designed to teach you the basic concepts, terminology, and techniques that you will need to use *PowerPoint* successfully to complete the projects that follow. This introduction will quickly review basic Windows concepts and terminology, but it will also indicate areas in which *PowerPoint*'s procedures may differ from those used in other Windows applications.

The last section in this lesson describes the typographical conventions used in this book. In this lesson, more explicit instructions will be given. Most commands that you are to follow are given using the mouse unless a keyboard combination is particularly easy. However, the task list in Appendix A includes shortcut keys for most tasks that you will do in this book.

WHAT IS *POWERPOINT 4.0 FOR WINDOWS*?

PowerPoint is a presentation graphics package. With *PowerPoint* you can create and manage simple or complex presentations. A *presentation* is a collection of *slides*, *handouts*, *speaker's notes*, and an *outline*, all in one file. When designing your presentation, you will select one background or format that will be carried throughout the whole presentation.

Slides are the individual "pages" of your presentation. Slides can have titles, text, graphs, tables, drawn objects, shapes, clip art, and visuals created with other applications. To support your presentation, you have the option of providing handouts for your audience. *Handouts* consist of smaller, printed versions of your slides. You will be able to print two, three, or six slides to a page. If you want to, you can also print additional information such as your company name, the date, and the page number of each page. For the presenter, you can create and print speaker's notes. A *speaker's note page* shows the slide at the top of the page with room for notes at the bottom of the page. Finally, you can create an outline of your presentation. An *outline* consists of the text of your presentation including titles and main text.

There are several types of output available in *PowerPoint*. Printouts can be created in black and white or color depending on your printer. Black and white or color transparencies can be created also either by using your printer if this option is supported or by having the originals copied onto transparencies. 35mm color slides can be created by sending your *PowerPoint* files to a film or service bureau such as Autographix or Genigraphics. *Slide shows* are presentations that can be projected through your computer to a projection system or an LCD panel that sits on top of an overhead projector.

GETTING STARTED

Since *PowerPoint* runs under Windows, the appearance of the *PowerPoint* window plus the methods of starting *PowerPoint*, selecting commands from menus, completing dialog boxes, and performing basic file commands like opening, closing, and saving files are the same as those used for any other Windows application package. This introductory lesson will review these procedures briefly, but it is assumed that you are familiar with Windows and that you know how to use the mouse.

STARTING *POWERPOINT*

Since *PowerPoint* runs under Windows, it is started in the same way as any other Windows application.

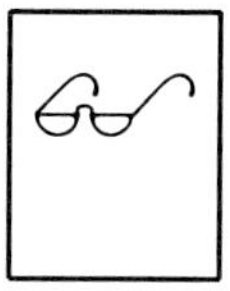

The steps for completing each *PowerPoint* feature introduced in this book are covered in two ways. First, they are described in a **bulleted** list, that can also be used for reference. The steps are used in a hands-on *Activity*. Be sure to wait until the **numbered** instructions in the *Activity* to practice each feature on the computer.

To start *PowerPoint*:

- Turn on your computer and start Windows.
- Open the *Microsoft Office* program group if it is not already open.
- Double-click on the *PowerPoint* icon.

Activity I.1: Starting PowerPoint

1. Turn on your computer and start Windows.
2. If the *Microsoft Office* program group is open (Figure I - 2), go to step 4.

3. If the *Microsoft Office* program group appears as an icon (Figure I - 1), point to the program group icon and double-click the left mouse button.

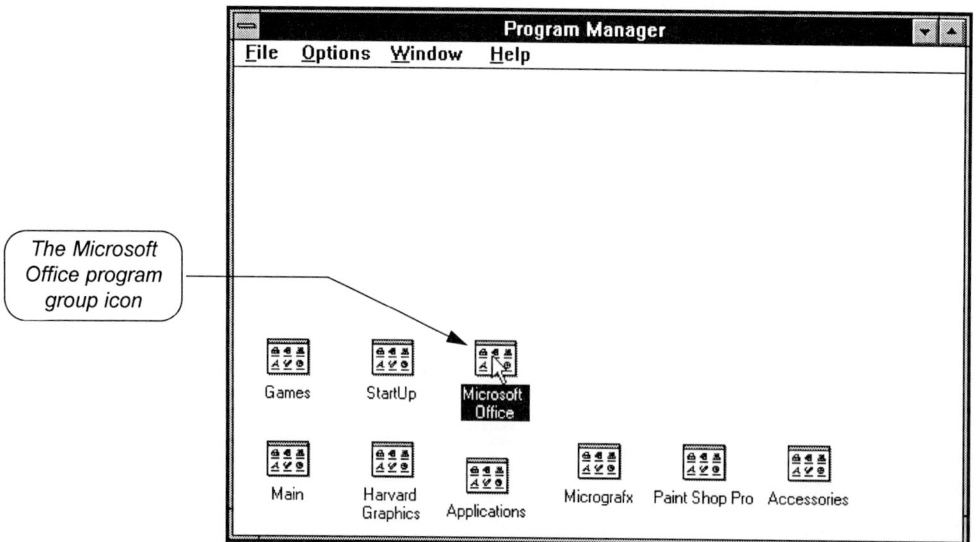

Figure I - 1

If the program group icon is not visible on the screen, click on the ***Window*** *menu. Click on* ***Microsoft Office*** *in the drop-down menu. If* ***Microsoft Office*** *is not listed, but* ***More Windows*** *is, click on* ***More Windows****, click on* ***Microsoft Office****, and then click on* ***OK****.*

PROBLEM SOLVER: *If you are having trouble double-clicking the mouse button, point to the application icon, click the mouse button once, and press* ***ENTER****.*

PROBLEM SOLVER: *If your computer does not have a program group called Microsoft Office, look for one called Microsoft PowerPoint or PowerPoint or ask your instructor or lab assistant for help.*

4. Point to the *Microsoft PowerPoint* application icon (Figure I - 2) and double-click the left mouse button.

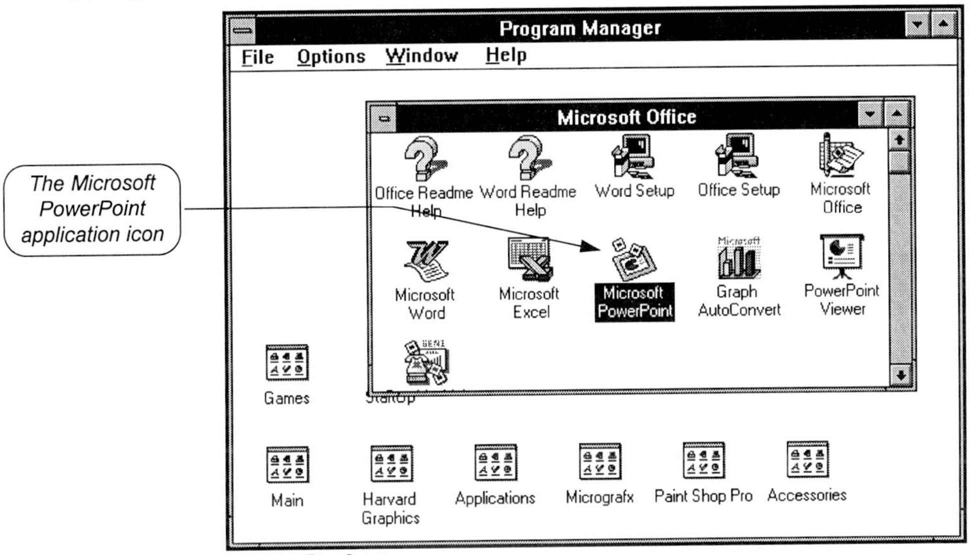

Figure I - 2

The Microsoft PowerPoint ***Startup*** *dialog box should be displayed (Figure I - 3).*

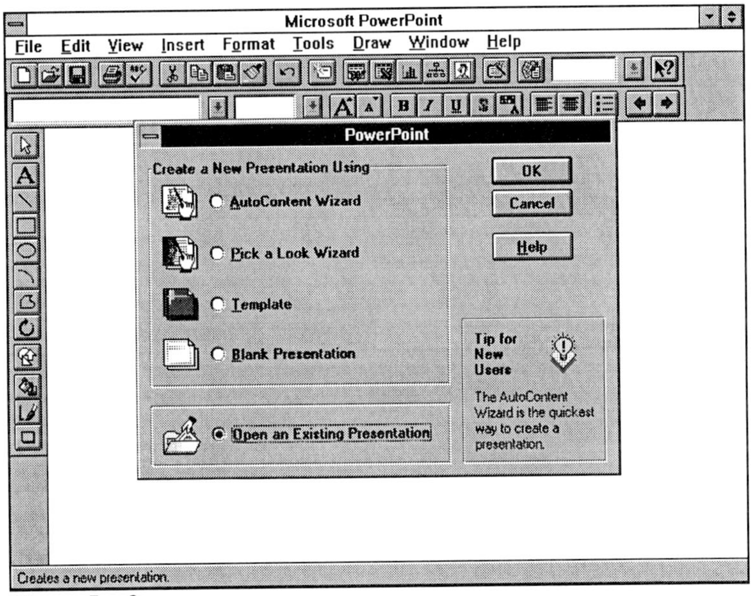

Figure I - 3

CAUTION: *If the* ***Tip of the Day*** *dialog box appears on the screen, click on the* ***OK*** *button to go to the* ***Startup*** *dialog box (Figure I - 4).*

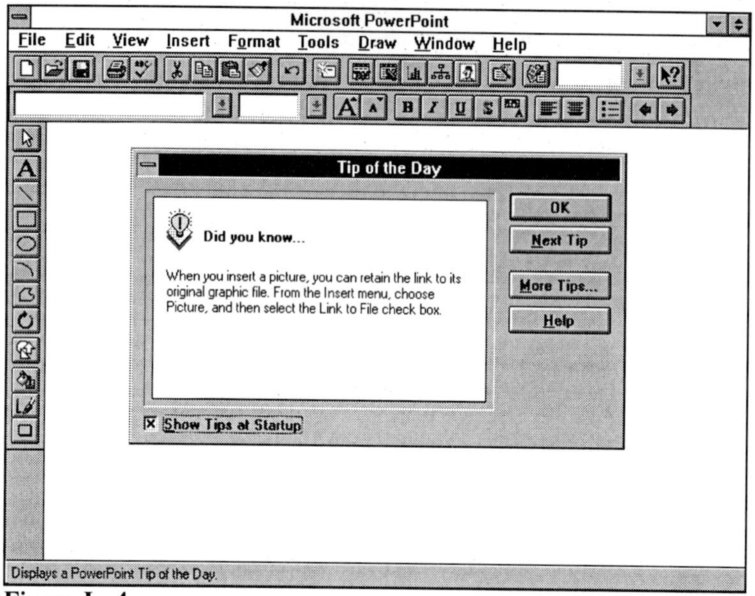

Figure I - 4

5. To have access to any of the options we will talk about in the rest of this lesson, it is necessary to have a presentation open. For the purposes of the exercises in this lesson, you will create a blank presentation.
6. At the **Startup** dialog box, click on the **Blank Presentation** button, and then click on the **OK** button. The **New Slide** dialog box appears on the screen (Figure I - 5).

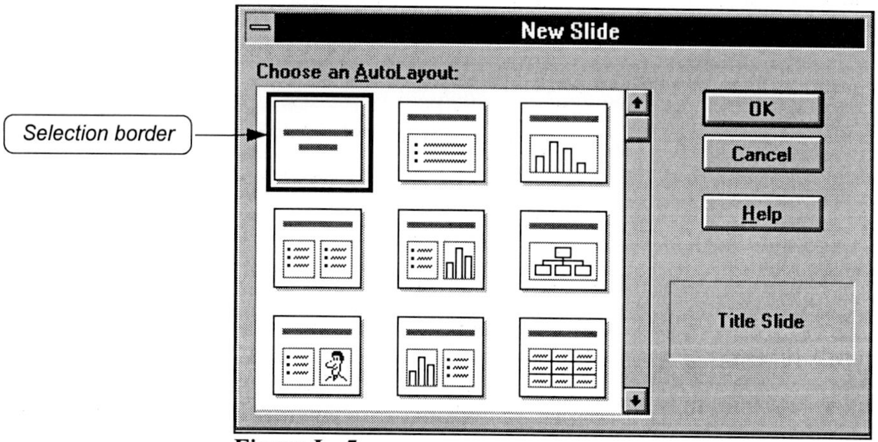

Figure I - 5

7. The selection border appears around the default slide style, **Title Slide**. Click on **OK** to accept the default. A blank Title slide will appear on the screen. (Figure I - 6).

THE *POWERPOINT* SCREEN

Most of the *PowerPoint* screen is made up of components that are familiar to you from other Windows applications. Other elements may be less familiar because they are specific to working with presentations or with *PowerPoint.*

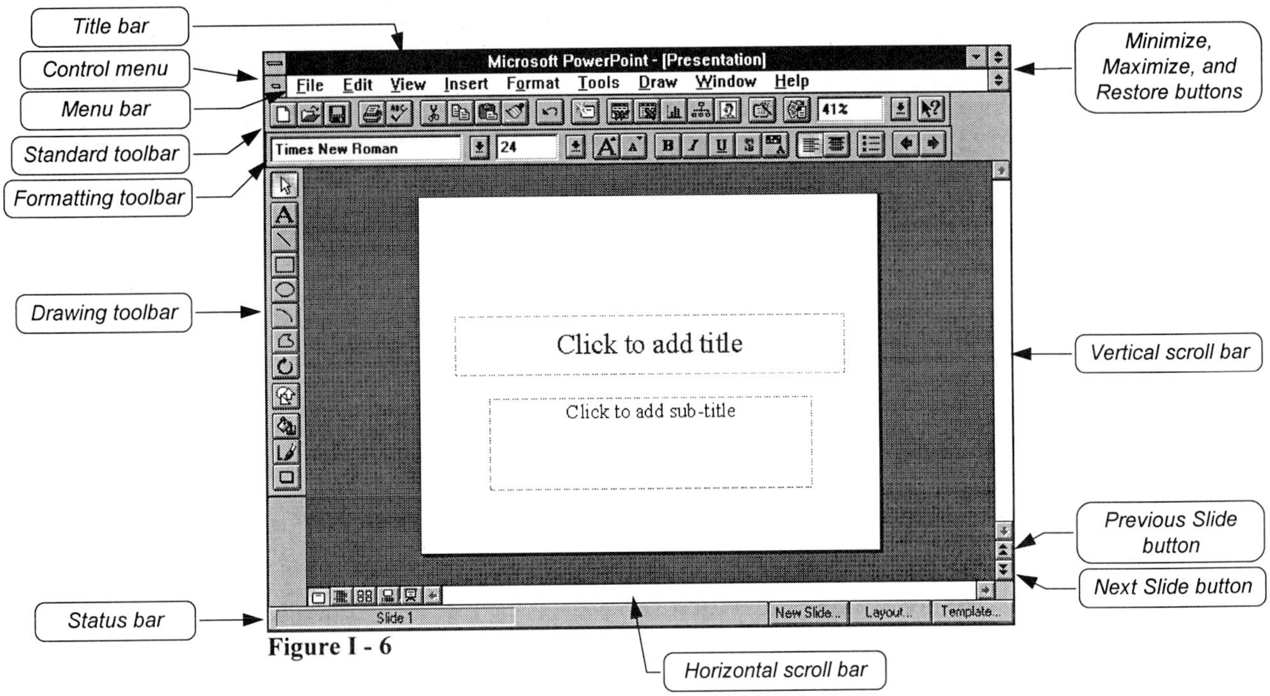

Figure I - 6

Typical Windows Components

Figure I - 6 shows the screen components that appear when *PowerPoint* is first installed according to a standard setup. As is true with all Windows applications, your screen may look somewhat different from Figure I - 6 if someone has changed the default settings. Some of the more common changes, and ways of changing the appearance of your screen to match those used in this book, will be discussed in this lesson. As you work through this book if your screen differs from those in the book even after you have tried the techniques described in this lesson, check with your instructor or lab assistant.

The Title Bar

As in all Windows applications, *PowerPoint* may have two title bars—one displaying the application name (*Microsoft PowerPoint*), and one displaying the name of the document, or *presentation*, that you are working on. If your presentation has been maximized, your screen will look like Figure I - 7.

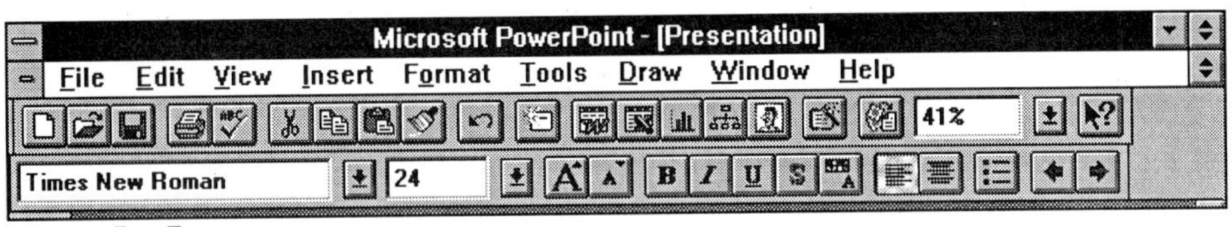

Figure I - 7

The right side of the title bar in Figure I - 7 contains the *minimize* and the *restore* buttons. The *minimize button* is used to shrink the *PowerPoint* window to an icon. The presence of the *restore button* indicates that the window is already maximized. The *restore button* is used to return a maximized window to its previous size and location. Once a window is restored, the restore button is replaced by the *maximize button*. The *maximize button* is used to enlarge a window to its maximum size. Notice also the second restore button that appears below the title bar. This restore button is for the presentation window, while the restore button on the title bar is for the application window. If the title bar on your screen does not resemble Figure I - 7, complete Activity I.2. Otherwise skip to the next section on the Menu bar.

Activity I.2: Maximizing the PowerPoint and Presentation Windows

Do this activity if your title bar(s) resemble(s) Figure I - 8, Figure I - 9, or Figure I - 10.

1. If the **Maximize** button appears on the *Microsoft PowerPoint* Title bar, as in Figure I - 8 or Figure I - 9, then the application is *not* maximized. To maximize it, point to the **Maximize** button on the right side of the *Microsoft PowerPoint* Title bar and click once with the left mouse button.

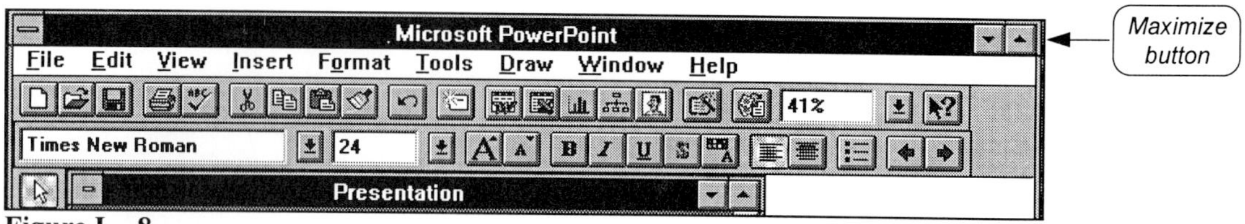

Figure I - 8

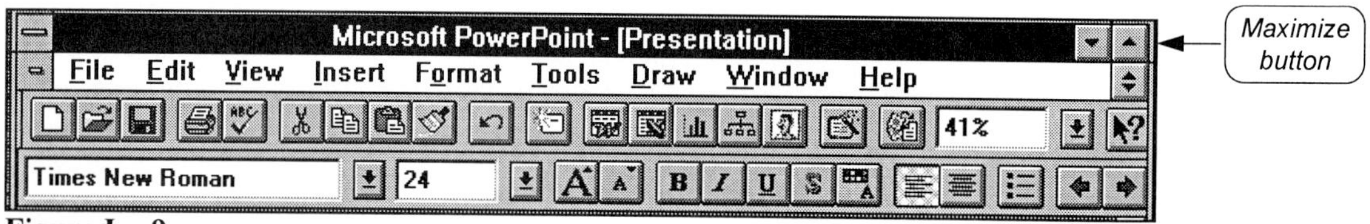

Figure I - 9

2. If **Presentation** has its own title bar (Figure I - 10), point to the **Maximize** button on the right side of the Presentation Title bar and click once.

   The presentation (Presentation) and PowerPoint title bars are now combined and the title bar should resemble Figure I - 7.

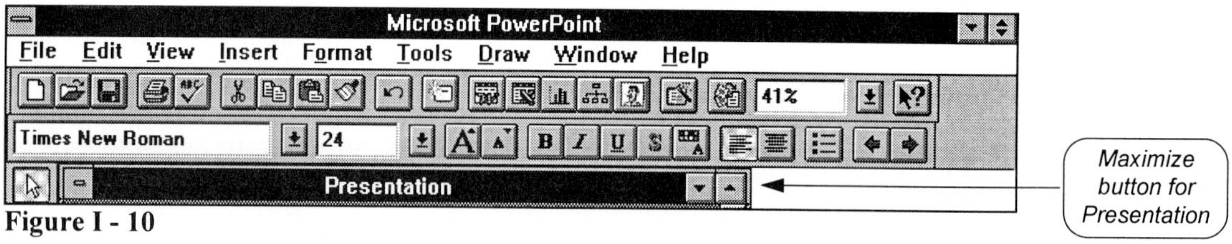

Figure I - 10

The Menu Bar

Immediately under the title bar is the Menu bar (Figure I - 13). The Menu bar contains the names of the menus from which you choose *PowerPoint* commands. If you have used *Microsoft Word 6.0* (Figure I - 11) or *Microsoft Excel 5.0* (Figure I - 12), you may notice that all the menu names except for **Draw** are the same as those in *Word* or *Excel*.

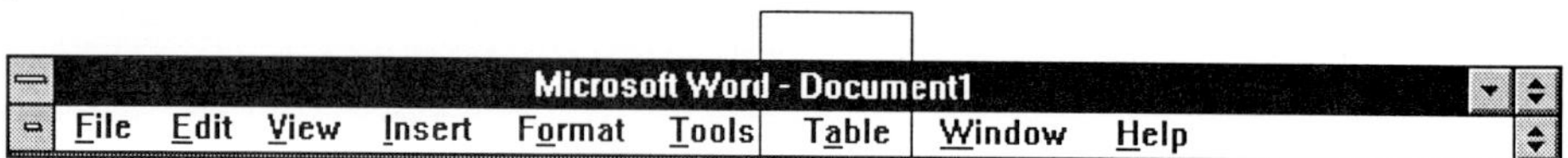

Figure I - 11

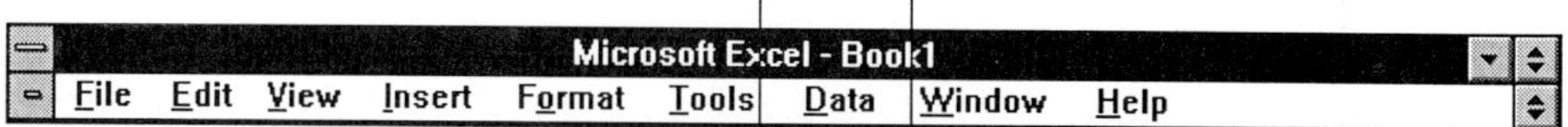

Figure I - 12

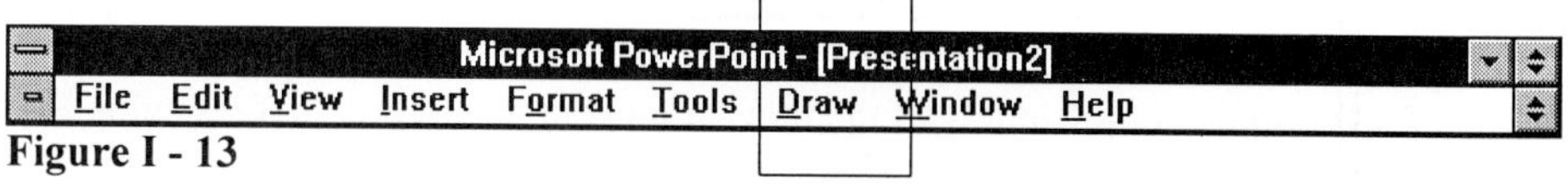

Figure I - 13

The Toolbars

Immediately under the Menu bar are the Standard and Formatting toolbars (Figure I - 6), unless the person who previously used *PowerPoint* on your computer has chosen to hide one or both of them or to display additional toolbars. *PowerPoint* comes with seven toolbars, some of which are automatically displayed when you issue certain commands. Additional customized toolbars can be created. You will learn how to display the toolbars of your choice in a few pages. Each toolbar contains a set of buttons that perform related actions more quickly than if you used the menu commands they replace. If you have used *Microsoft Word 6.0* or *Microsoft Excel 5.0,* you will notice that many of the buttons on the Standard and Formatting toolbars are identical to those used in *Word* and *Excel.*

The Drawing toolbar appears on the left side of the screen. The Drawing toolbar has buttons for tools used in drawing objects such as free-floating text, lines, rectangles, circles, arcs, and polygons.

Any of the toolbars can be dragged to a different location on the screen.

Scroll Bars

PowerPoint, like all Windows packages, includes *scroll bars* (Figure I - 6), shaded bars along the right and bottom sides of a window, allowing you to move rapidly around a magnified page or through a long presentation.

Use the horizontal scroll bar to move quickly from the left side of the page to the right side of the page. Use the vertical scroll bar to move quickly from the top to the bottom of the page. Located at the bottom of the vertical scroll bar are the **Previous Slide** and **Next Slide** buttons. These buttons will move you quickly from slide to slide. When you have many slides in your presentation, you will be able to use the scroll box that appears in the vertical scroll bar to move quickly from one slide to another.

Status Bar

The Status bar (Figure I - 6) is the shaded bar along the very bottom of the screen that displays information about what you are currently doing. It is very important to get into the habit of looking at the Status bar. When you are working with menus or toolbar buttons, the left side of the Status bar gives you information on what actions the menu commands or toolbar buttons carry out. At other times the left side of the Status bar gives a general description of the type of task you are performing, or even instructions for completing a task. When no task or operation is being completed, the left side of the Status bar displays the current slide number. The right side of the Status bar has shortcut buttons to add a new slide to the presentation, select a new layout for the slide, or select a new template for the presentation.

PowerPoint Components

Figure I - 14 labels the parts of the *PowerPoint* window that are specific to *PowerPoint.* In this section we will take a look at the Slide Work Area and the different Views that are available in *PowerPoint.*

The Slide Work Area

In *PowerPoint 4.0* each new file is called a *Presentation.* Each new page is called a *slide.* The blank slide that appears on the screen is the *Slide Work Area* (Figure I - 14).

Views in *PowerPoint*

There are five different views that you can work with in *PowerPoint.* The view that you will probably work in the most is *Slide View.* The **View** buttons are located at the bottom left of the Slide Work Area, above the Status bar. The Views include *Slide View, Outline View, Slide Sorter View, Notes Pages View,* and *Slide Show.*

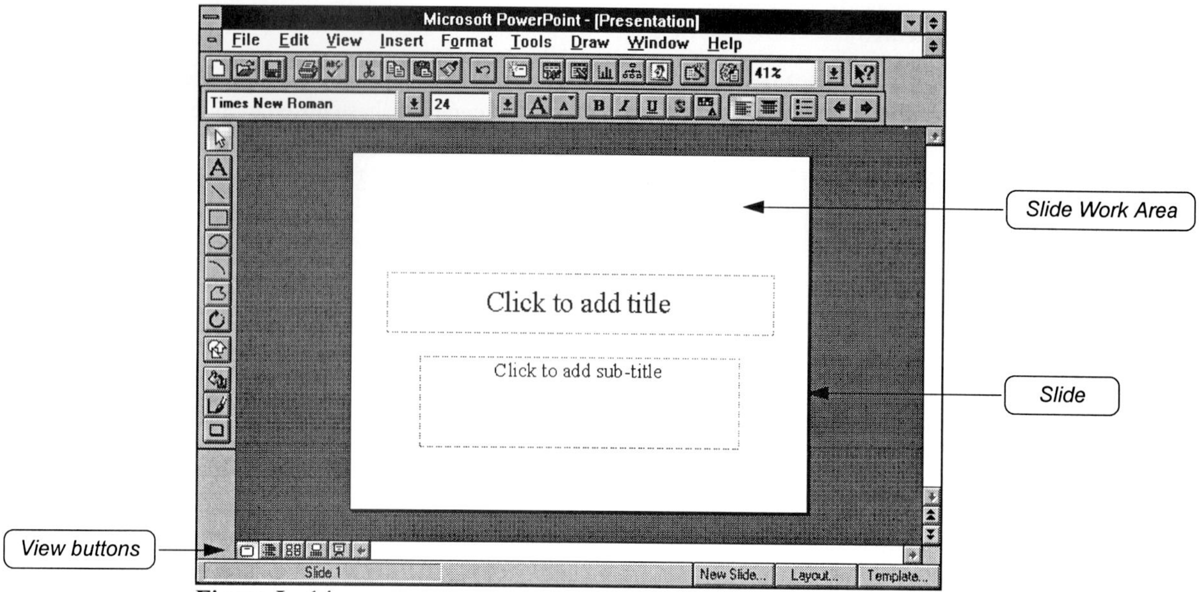

Figure I - 14

The presentation used for Figures I - 15 through I - 19 illustrate these different views using the General choice from the AutoContent Wizard.

- ## Slide View

Slide View is the view used to make editing changes to a single slide. In Slide View you will be able to type, draw, add clip art, insert pictures, and edit text and objects (Figure I - 15).

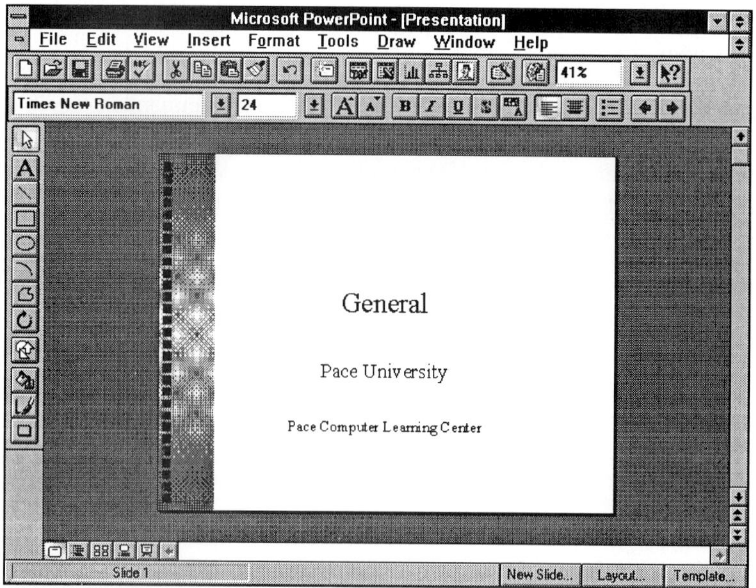

Figure I - 15

- ## Outline View

Outline View is the view used to make editing changes to the text of the whole presentation. For example, the headings of the slides are presented as Level 1 of the outline. Any bullets are shown indented below Level 1. Because the text for the whole presentation is available in Outline View, you will easily be able to make changes from slide to slide. For example, moving a bullet line from Slide 2 to Slide 8 is as easy as dragging the bullet line down in the outline (Figure I - 16).

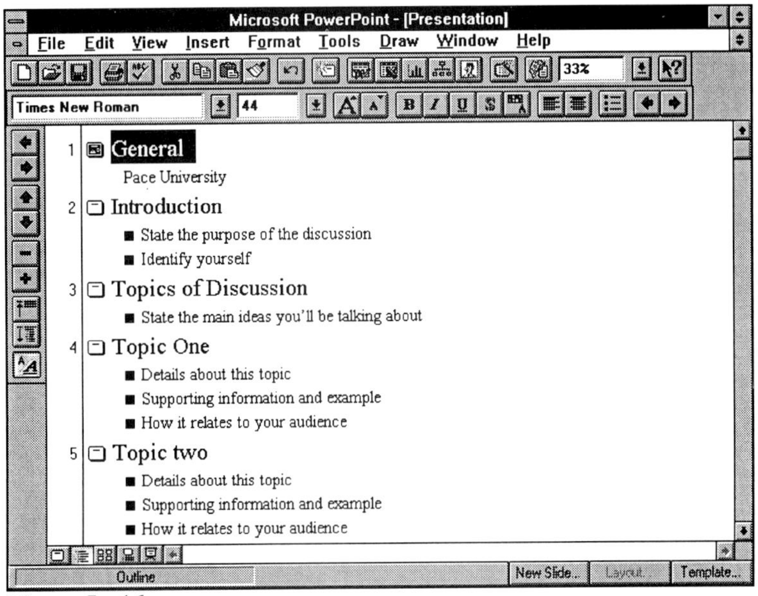

Figure I - 16

• Slide Sorter View

Slide Sorter View is the view used to make editing changes to the order of the presentation. In Slide Sorter View you will see a miniature of each slide. Here you can copy, move, or delete slides. Slide Sorter View is also where you will add *transition effects* to your presentation. Transition effects are used to change the way each slide comes on the screen in On-screen presentations (Figure I - 17).

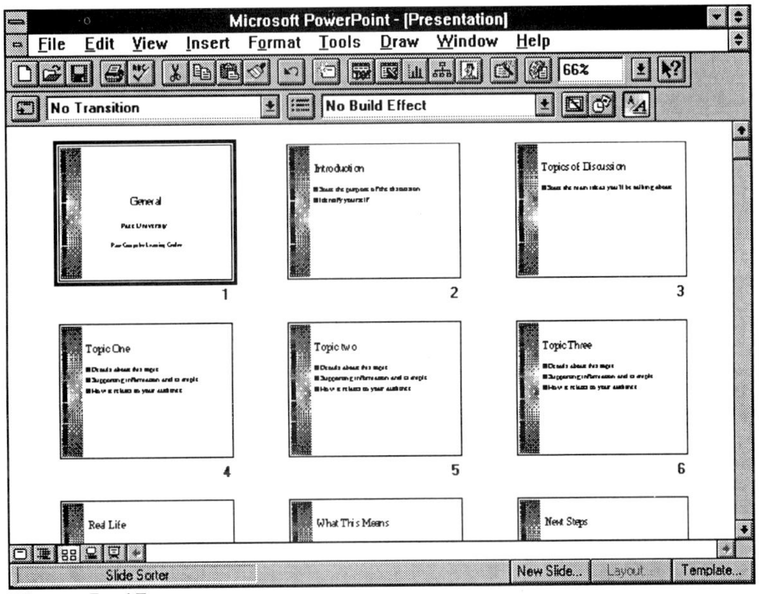

Figure I - 17

- **Notes Pages View**

Notes Pages View is the view used to make editing changes to speaker's notes. In Notes Pages View you will be able to add notes on the same page below the slide thus creating speaker's notes. You can also use the Drawing toolbar to enhance the page around the actual slide. The drawing tools will only appear in Slide View and Notes Pages View (Figure I - 18).

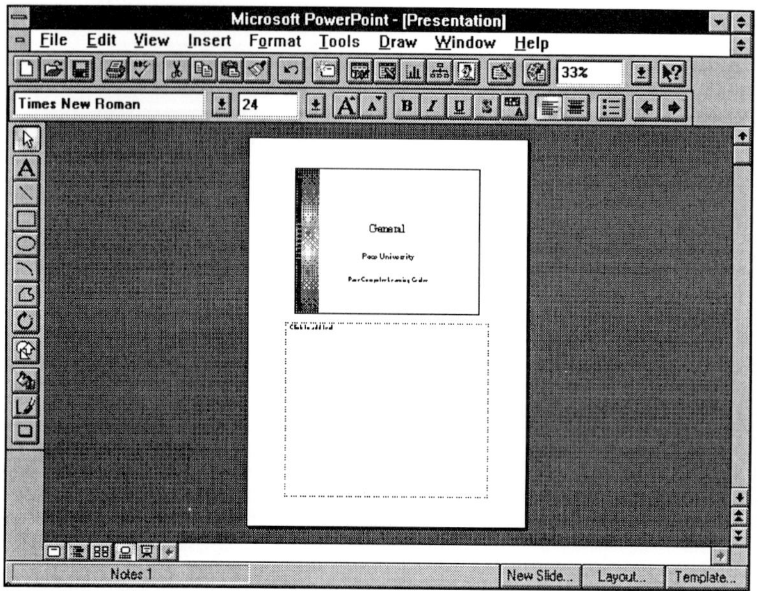

Figure I - 18

- **Slide Show**

Slide Show is the view that shows the presentation. Each slide fills the screen. You will see the results of the transition effects that you added to the presentation in Slide Sorter View. You also have the ability to draw while showing the On-screen presentation using the pencil that appears in the bottom right corner (Figure I - 19).

Figure I - 19

THE MOUSE POINTER

As you move the mouse, a mouse pointer moves across the screen. The shape of the pointer changes depending on the part of the screen to which it is pointing. For example, the mouse pointer is an  when you are pointing to items on the Menu bar, toolbars or Status bar, but changes to a + when drawing objects.

As you follow the activity instructions in this book, look for descriptions of the shape of the mouse pointer and make sure the mouse pointer on your screen is the correct shape.

GIVING COMMANDS IN *POWERPOINT*

Commands in *PowerPoint* can be given through the use of the main menus (and their related dialog boxes), toolbar buttons, shortcut keys, and shortcut menus. Instructions in this book will focus on the use of menus and toolbar buttons. Shortcut keys will be mentioned occasionally. Keyboard shortcuts for the main tasks covered in this book can be found in Appendix A. The menus and dialog boxes in *PowerPoint* work the same way as in other Windows packages. Features that may not be common to all Windows packages will be introduced when first used.

To use the menus to give commands:

- Open the menu by pointing to the menu name and clicking the left mouse button.
- Choose a command by pointing to the command name and clicking the left mouse button.
  - If the command name is followed by an ellipsis (…), a dialog box will be displayed. Follow the instructions in Table I - 1 to complete the dialog box.
  - If the command name is preceded by a check mark, choosing the command will turn it off.
  - If the command name is followed by a triangle, choosing the command will display a submenu. Choose the submenu command the same way you choose the menu commands.
  - If the command name appears in light print, it cannot be used at that time. Choosing it will have no effect.

KEYBOARD ALTERNATIVES: *To open a menu using the keyboard, press the **ALT** key and then type the underlined letter in the menu name. To choose a command from the menu, type the underlined letter in the command name.*

KEYBOARD SHORTCUT: *Key combinations that appear to the right of a menu command can be used as shortcuts for the command. They must be used, however, before the menu is opened.*

To close a menu without choosing a command:

- Point to the menu name or a blank part of the screen outside of the menu and then click the left mouse button.

KEYBOARD ALTERNATIVE: *Press the **ALT** key to close an open menu.*

Task	Mouse	Keyboard
Text Box (Figure I - 21)	Double-click in the text box; then type the new information	Press **ALT** and the underlined letter in the text box name; type the new information.
Option (radio) Button (Figure I - 20)	Point to the option button and then click the left mouse button.	Press **ALT** and the underlined letter in the option button name.
Check Box (Figure I - 20 and Figure I - 21)	Point to the square preceding the box name and then click the left mouse button to toggle the box on or off.	Press **ALT** and the highlighted letter in the check box name.
List Box (Figure I - 21)	Point to the list box item and click the left mouse button. If the item is not visible, click on the scroll arrows to move the list up/down one item at a time; click on the list item once it is displayed.	Press **ALT** and the underlined letter in the list box name; use the **UP** and **DOWN ARROW** keys to select the list item.
Drop-down List Box (Figure I - 20)	Click the ↓ to the right of the list box and then follow directions for list boxes.	Press **ALT** and the underlined letter in the list box name to open the drop-down list.
Spinner (Figure I - 20)	Click the **UP** and **DOWN** arrows to the right of the box until the number you want appears in the box, or type the new number.	Press **ALT** and the underlined letter in the spinner name; press the **UP** or **DOWN ARROW** keys to change the numbers by the default amount or type the new number.
Command Button (Figure I - 20 and Figure I - 21)	To execute or cancel the command, or display another dialog box, click on the appropriate command button.	Press **ESC** to cancel a command, **ENTER** to execute a command, or **ALT** and the underlined letter.

Table I - 1

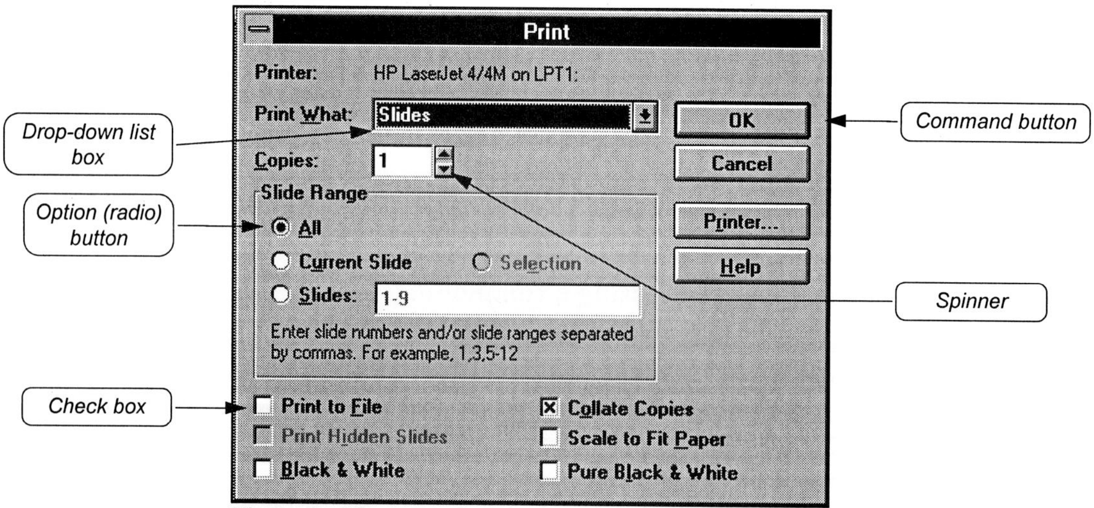

Figure I - 20

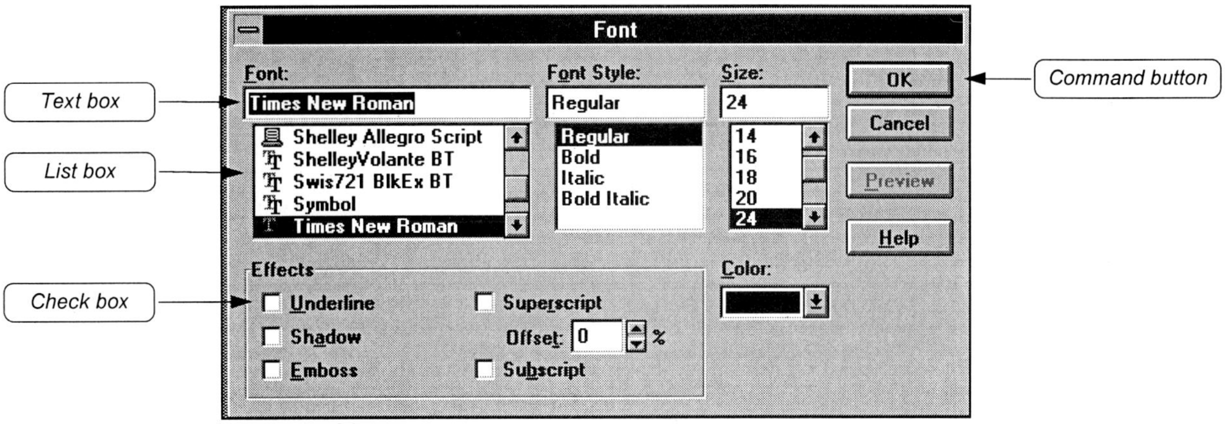

Figure I - 21

THE VIEW MENU

The **View** menu controls the appearance of the screen and allows for movement between the different Views (previously mentioned in this lesson) or work areas available in *PowerPoint*. If your screen does not contain all the components described previously, the **View** menu is the first place to go to change the display.

To display/hide toolbars:

- Open the **View** menu.
- Point to **Toolbars** and click on it with the left mouse button.
- In the **Toolbars** dialog box, a toolbar preceded by a marked check box is displayed. Click on empty check boxes to display additional toolbars; click on marked check boxes to hide already displayed toolbars.

To display/hide the ruler and guides:

- Open the **View** menu.
- Point to **Ruler** or **Guides** and click on it with the left mouse button.

  If there is a check mark next to Ruler or Guides, the option is turned on. If a check mark does not appear next to Ruler or Guides, the option is turned off.

To change Views:

- Open the **View** menu.
- Point to the desired View and click the left mouse button. Notice the current view is preceded by a circle.

TIME SAVER: *A quicker way of changing the Views is to use the **View** buttons located at the bottom left of the Slide Work Area.*

Activity I.3: Using the View Menu to Change the Appearance of the Screen

1. To open the **View** menu, point to **View** on the Menu bar and click the left mouse button (Figure I - 22).

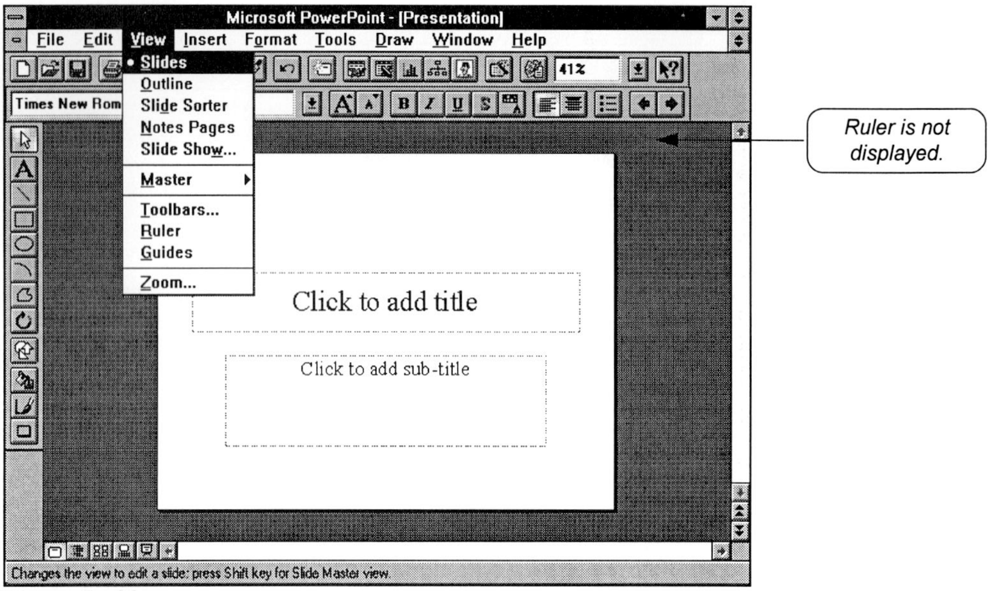

Figure I - 22

2. In Figure I - 22 **Ruler** and **Guides** both do not have check marks preceding them, indicating that they are not displayed. If **Ruler** is not preceded by a check on your screen, point to **Ruler** and click the left mouse button.

3. Open the **View** menu again. If **Guides** is not preceded by a check on your screen, point to **Guides** and click the left mouse button. Now when the **View** menu is opened again, check marks precede **Ruler** and **Guides**, indicating that they are showing on the screen (Figure I - 23).

   ***Ruler** and **Guides** work like toggle keys — selecting them changes their state from on to off and vice versa. If the Ruler was previously displayed, it will be removed as in Figure I - 22. If it was not previously displayed, it will now be displayed.*

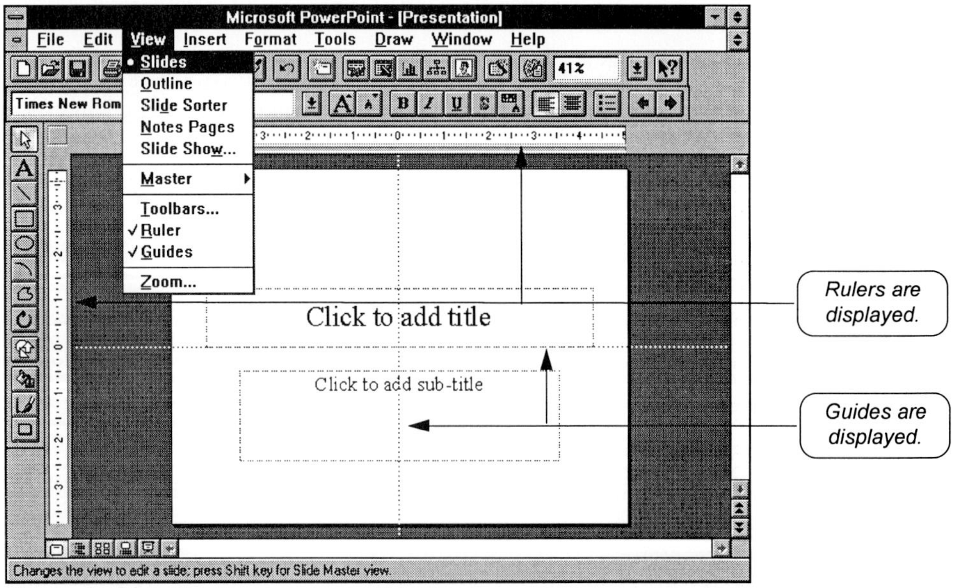

Figure I - 23

4. Open the **View** menu again.

5. Choose **Toolbars** by pointing to it and clicking the left mouse button.

   *The **Toolbars** dialog box (Figure I - 24) is displayed.*

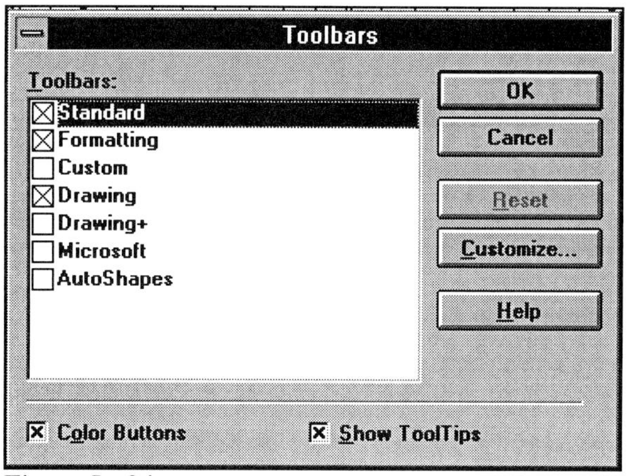

Figure I - 24

6. The **Standard, Formatting**, and **Drawing** check boxes should be marked as in Figure I - 24. If any are not checked, click on them to check them. If any other check boxes in the **Toolbars** section of the screen are checked, click on them to unmark them.
7. Make sure that there is also an **X** in the **Color Buttons** and **Show ToolTips** check boxes at the bottom of the dialog box. If not, click in the check box so that an **X** appears.
8. To return to the Slide Work Area, click on **OK**.

   Now let's add the Drawing+ toolbar to the screen.

9. Open the **View** menu.
10. Click on **Toolbars**.
11. Place an **X** in the **Drawing+** check box, then click **OK** to return to the Slide Work Area.

   *Your screen should resemble Figure I - 25. Use the **View** menu through this book anytime the Ruler, Guides, or Toolbars are missing from your screen.*

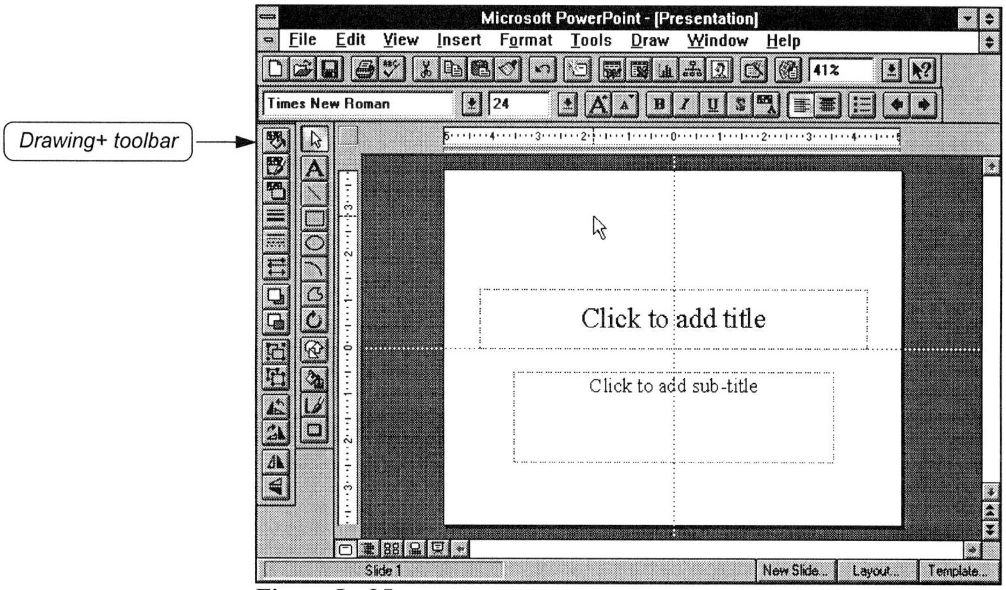

Figure I - 25

12. Open the **View** menu.
13. Click on Outline.

    Your screen should now resemble Figure I - 26.

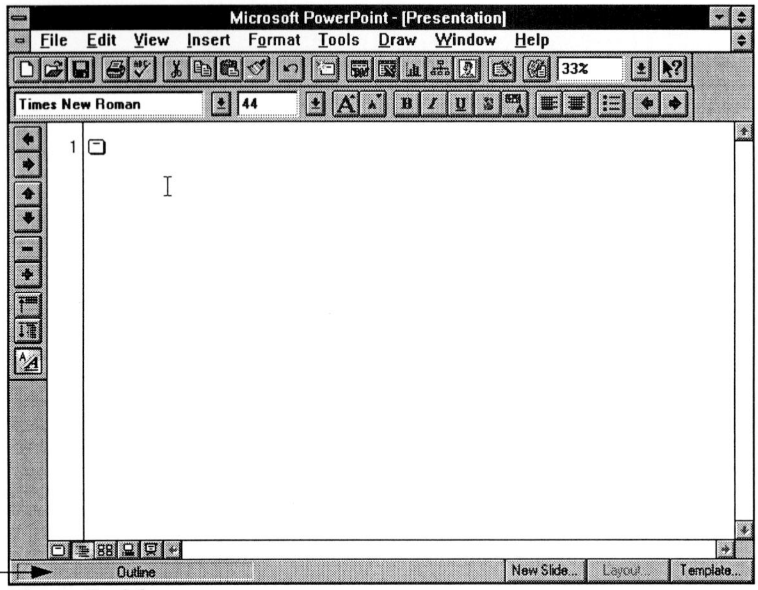

***Outline** label on status bar*

Figure I - 26

14. Choose **VIEW/Slides.**
15. Turn off **Guides** and leave **Ruler** on.

    NOTE: *When the toolbars are turned on, they remain on the screen until you return to the **Toolbars** dialog box to turn them off. They will appear on the screen the next time you enter PowerPoint after having exited the program. The Ruler and Guides, however, remain on the screen only for the current session. The next time you enter PowerPoint, the ruler and guides will not be showing. Therefore, you will need to select them each time you open PowerPoint.*

USING TOOLBAR BUTTONS

Toolbar buttons can be used to perform many of the commands that the menus perform. Though using the toolbars is quicker than using the menus, sometimes your choices are limited or you receive less information about the effects of your command.

One of the improvements *PowerPoint* made in version 4.0 was the inclusion of **ToolTips.** When you point to a toolbar button, the name of the button appears in a colored box next to the button and a description of the button appears on the Status bar. In Activity I.4 you used the **VIEW/Toolbars** command to make sure **Show ToolTips** would be displayed.

To use a toolbar button:

- Move the mouse pointer to the toolbar button and click the left mouse button.

To find out what a specific toolbar button does:

- Move the mouse pointer until it is on the toolbar button.
- Read the name of the button in the **ToolTips** box that appears next to the mouse pointer. Read a description of the button on the Status bar.

GETTING ON-LINE HELP

ToolTips is one of many examples of the help *PowerPoint* provides. Each of the dialog boxes also contains a **Help** button. Choosing that button displays help about the dialog box that you are currently using. The **Help** menu provides three ways of searching for help on a topic: **Table of Contents**, **Search for Help on**, and an **Index**. In addition, **Quick Preview** and **Cue Cards** provide tutorials on performing many tasks in *PowerPoint*. Also **Tip of the Day** can be activated so that every time you start *PowerPoint*, a **Tip of the Day** will appear on the screen. To see a tip any other time while working in *PowerPoint*, select **HELP/Tip of the Day**. Click the **Help** button  and then click on any part of the screen to get help on that part of the screen.

To get Help while working in a dialog box:

- Point to the **Help** command button in the dialog box and click the left mouse button.
- If the Help topic extends beyond the screen, click on the ↓ on the vertical scroll bar to see the rest of the topic.
- Any information on the screen that is green and underlined with a solid line is a *jump term*. If you move the mouse pointer to the jump term, the shape of the mouse changes to a . Click the left mouse button to display the Help topic.
- **Tip** command buttons may appear below a topic. Click on the command button to show the tip.

Activity I.4: Using Help

In this activity you will practice using Help.

1. Open the **Format** menu by pointing to **Format** on the Menu bar and clicking the left mouse button.
2. Point to **Font** and click the left mouse button.
3. Point to the **Help** command button (Figure I - 27) in the **Font** dialog box and click the left mouse button.

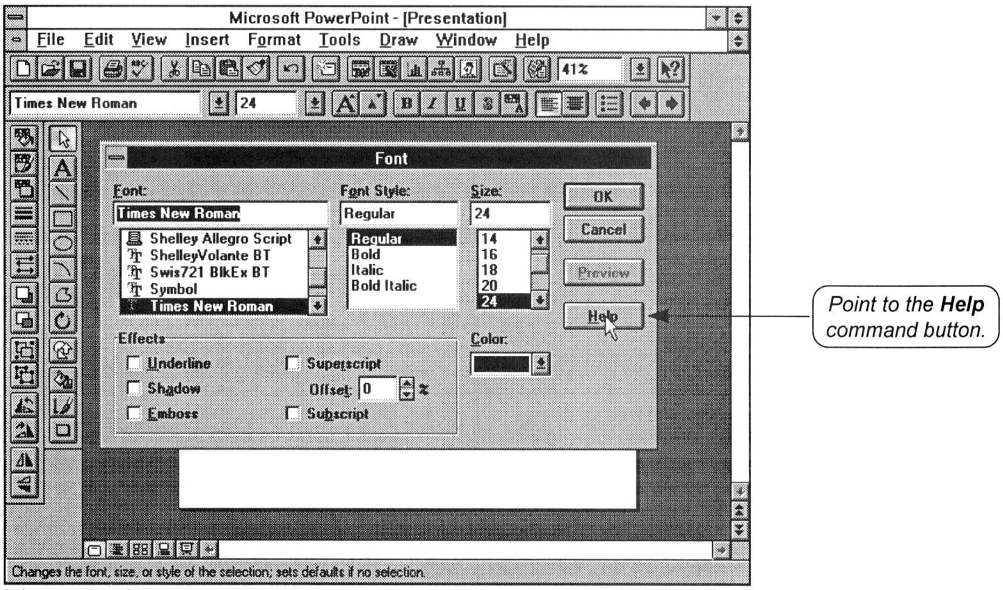

Figure I - 27

*The **Font** Help screen (Figure I - 28) is displayed.*

4. Click on the ↓ on the vertical scroll bar until **About Formatting Text** (in underlined green print) is displayed.

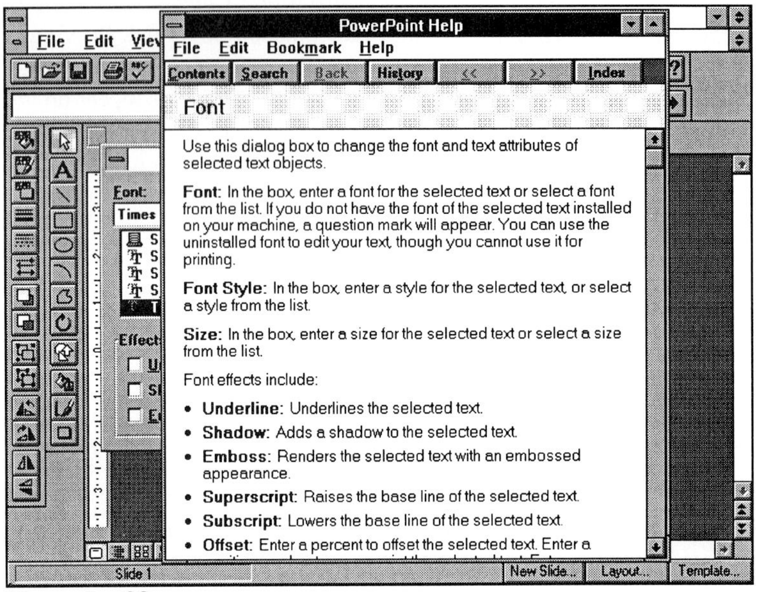

Figure I - 28

5. Since **About Formatting Text** is underlined in a green line, it is a jump term. Move the mouse until it is pointing to **About Formatting Text** and has changed to a hand. Click the left mouse button.
6. Read the help provided for **About Formatting Text**.
7. Point to the jump term, **Changing text attributes**, and click the left mouse button.
8. A **Tip** command button appears in the heading. Click on the command button.

   A Tip appears below the command button (Figure I - 29).

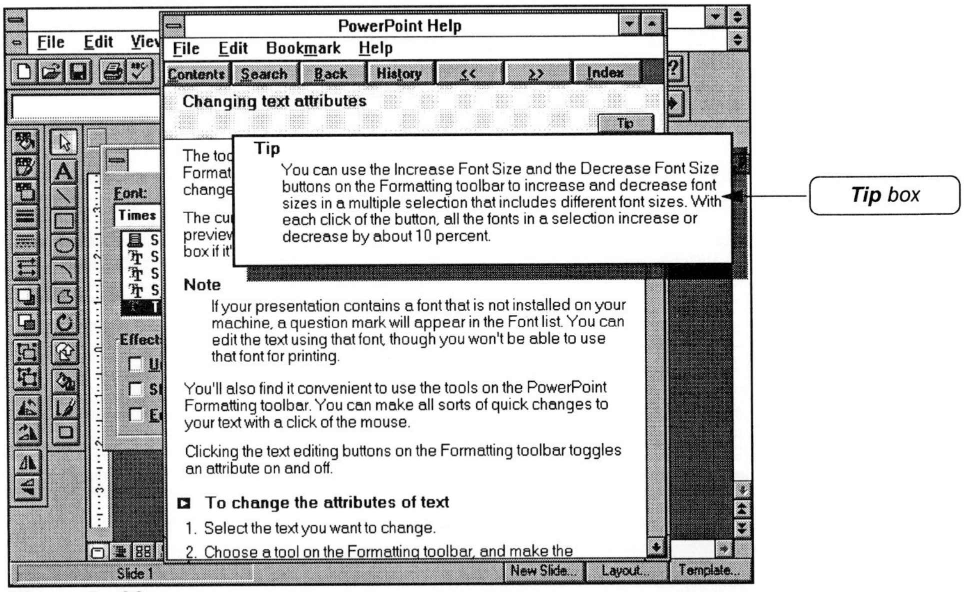

Figure I - 29

9. Clear the Tip from the screen by clicking on a blank area in the **Help** window.
10. To exit from **Help**, click on **File** in the **PowerPoint Help** Menu bar.
11. Click on **Exit** in the **File** menu.
12. Click on the **Cancel** button in the **Font** dialog box to close it.

EXITING FROM *POWERPOINT*

While you are working, *PowerPoint* creates temporary files to help it with its work. Therefore, it is always important to exit correctly from a program, rather than to turn off the computer while in the middle of the program.

To exit from *PowerPoint*:

- Point to **File** on the Menu bar and click the left mouse button.
- Point to **Exit** on the **File** menu and click the left mouse button.
- If you have made any changes to the presentation and not saved your work, an *Alert box* containing three choices, **Yes, No**, and **Cancel**, will appear. To save changes to the file, click on **Yes.** To exit without saving changes to the file, click on **No**. To continue working in *PowerPoint*, choose **Cancel**.
- If you are finished using *Windows*, choose **FILE/Exit** from the Program Manager menu. When the prompt **This will end your Windows session** appears, click on **Yes**.

Activity I.5: Exiting from PowerPoint

1. Point to **File** on the Menu bar and click the left mouse button.
2. Point to **Exit** on the **File** menu and click the left mouse button.
3. If an Alert box asking **Save changes in 'Presentation'?** appears, click on **No** to exit the program *without* saving the presentation.

SUMMARY

In this introduction you have seen the parts of the *PowerPoint* screen that are common to all Windows applications and those that are specific to *PowerPoint* or to presentation graphics software. You have seen how to use the **View** menu to change the appearance of the screen. You have also reviewed the use of menus and dialog boxes and of Help. As you work through this book, if you have trouble with basic presentation terminology or the use of menus and dialog boxes, refer back to this lesson.

KEY TERMS

Check Box
Drawing + Toolbar
Drawing Toolbar
Drop-down List Box
Formatting Toolbar
Guide
Handout
Jump Term
List Box
Maximize Button
Menu Bar
Minimize Button
Notes Pages View
On-screen Presentation
Option Button
Outline
Outline View
Output
Presentation
Restore Button
Ruler
Scroll Bar
Slide
Slide Show
Slide Sorter View
Slide View
Slide Work Area
Speaker's Note
Spinner
Standard Toolbar
Status Bar
Text Box
Title Bar
ToolTip
Transition Effects
View Button

CONVENTIONS FOLLOWED IN THIS BOOK

Table I - 2 shows the way instructions are abbreviated in this book.

Task	Words used in this book	Explanation
Using the mouse	"click on" or "click the mouse button"	Move the mouse pointer to the item to be selected (cell, toolbar button, menu name, command name, etc.) and click the **left** mouse button.
Using the **right** mouse button	"click the right mouse button"	Every time the **right** mouse button is to be used instead of the left mouse button, the instructions will specifically include the word **right**.
Choosing a command from the Menu bar	"Choose **MENU NAME/Command Name, SubMenu Command**" (For example, "Choose **ALIGNMENT/Left**")	• Point to the **menu name** with the mouse and click the left mouse button. • In the menu that is displayed, point to the **Command Name** and click the left mouse button. • If a sub-menu is displayed, point to the **SubMenu Command** and click the left mouse button.
Using two keys together	Press **ALT+letter** (for example, press **ALT+I**)	• Press the **ALT** key (or the **CTRL, SHIFT,** etc. key) and while keeping it depressed, type the letter.

Table I - 2

INDEPENDENT PROJECTS

The two Independent Projects introduce two parts of Help —**Quick Preview** and **Using the Help Icon**—which may be slightly different from **Help** options that you have used in other Windows applications.

Independent Project I.1: Learning More About Help

In this project, you will run the *PowerPoint* **Quick Preview** to learn more about *Microsoft PowerPoint 4.0 for Windows.*

✓ **PROBLEM SOLVER:** ***Quick Preview*** *may have been omitted when PowerPoint was installed on your computer. If an alert box like Figure I - 30 appears on your screen, click on* ***OK****. Skip this project or ask your instructor what you should do.*

Figure I - 30

1. Open *PowerPoint.*
2. Read the **Tip of the Day** if it appears on the screen, and then click on the **OK** command button.
3. Create a blank presentation.
4. Select **Title Slide** as the AutoLayout for Slide 1.
5. Choose **HELP/Quick Preview**.

   *A minimized icon of a film camera will appear in the bottom left corner of the screen, and then the **Quick Preview** screen will be displayed (Figure I - 31).*

Figure I -31

6. To start the Quick Preview, which will take about five minutes to complete, click on the **Click to Start** button.

   This tutorial will describe the PowerPoint program and its capabilities.
7. Read each screen. Click on the **Next>** button at the bottom left of the screen or press the **N** key to display the next screen. Click on the **<Back** button or press the **B** key any time you want to return to the previous screen.
8. When you want to end the tutorial, click on the **Quit** button or press the **Q** key.

   The PowerPoint screen will be displayed.
9. Exit *PowerPoint* without saving the presentation.

Independent Project I.2: Using the Help Button to See Context-Sensitive Help

In this project you will become familiar with the *PowerPoint* screen using the **Help** button on the Standard toolbar.

1. Open *PowerPoint,* if it is not already open.
2. Create a blank presentation with a Title Slide as Slide 1.

3. Click on the **Help** button.

   The mouse pointer appears on the screen with a question mark attached to it (Figure I - 32).

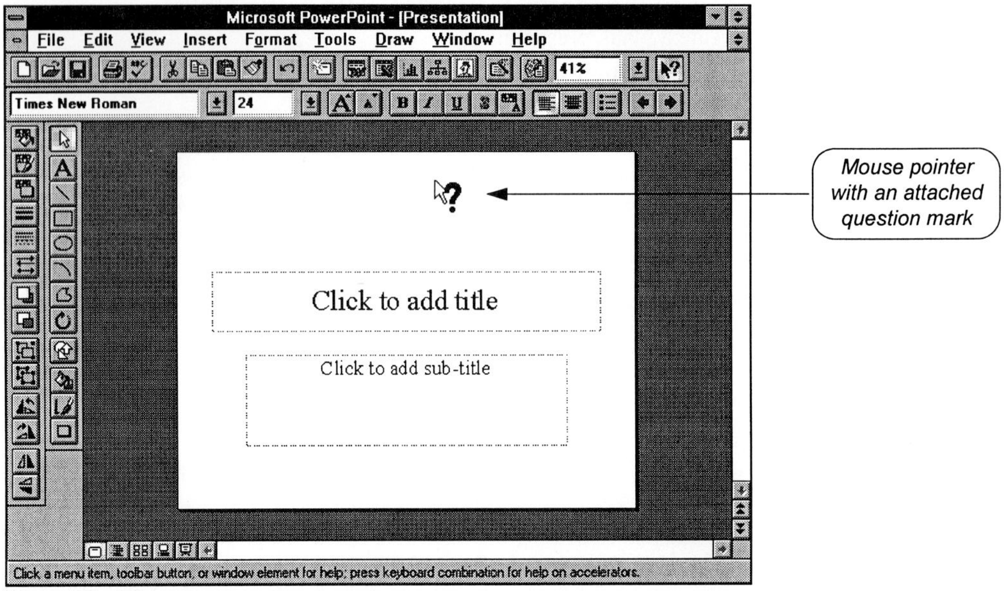

Figure I - 32

4. Click on the **Insert Clip Art** button on the Standard toolbar.

   Help will be displayed for Clip Art (Insert menu).
5. After reading the Help screen, return to the *PowerPoint* screen.
6. Use the **Help** button to see context-sensitive help for the following buttons:
   - **AutoShapes** button on the Drawing toolbar
   - **Free Rotate** button on the Drawing toolbar
   - **Ungroup** button on the Drawing+ toolbar
   - **Send Backward** button on the Drawing+ toolbar
   - **Format Painter** button on the Standard toolbar
   - **Text Color** button on the Formatting toolbar
7. After obtaining help for the items listed above, exit *PowerPoint* without saving any changes.

Lesson 1 Creating a Presentation

Objectives

In this lesson you will learn how to:

- Plan a presentation
- Create a presentation
  - Using a blank presentation
  - Using the AutoContent Wizard
  - Using the Pick a Look Wizard
  - Using a Template
- Add text to a slide
- Save a presentation
  - Using **Save As**
  - Using **Save**
- Switch between two presentations
- Add a new slide to a presentation
- Print a presentation
- Close a presentation

PROJECT DESCRIPTION

In this lesson, you will create your first project. Kaleidoscope Rain is an expanding environmental store. The store manager would like to open a new store in Capital City, but Capital City has already had two environmental stores that have gone out of business. The store manager needs to persuade the owners of Kaleidoscope Rain that the store will prosper in Capital City. In this project you will create two presentations using the available methods for creating a presentation, adding text to a presentation, adding a new slide to a presentation, saving a presentation, and printing a presentation. The presentations that you save in this project will not be complete. You will use them in the next lesson, Editing a Presentation.

PLANNING A PRESENTATION

There are steps that you can take before you even open *PowerPoint* that will help to minimize problems that may occur while in the creation process. Use the following list to help plan your presentation:

- State your objectives (**why** you are creating the presentation). Are you reporting information or trying to persuade someone to agree with you? Are you announcing a new product or trying to sell the product to a customer? Presentations have four basic purposes: to persuade, inform, educate, or motivate.
- Define your audience (**who** will view the presentation). Is your audience a group of co-workers or clients? How much does your audience already know about the subject matter? How large will the audience be?
- Determine the presentation device (**how** you will give the presentation). What kind of equipment is available for your presentation? Does it project well and how far does it project?

- Plan the outline (**what** you want to present). Plan the first level of your presentation first. This will give you the titles of each of the slides in your presentation. The outline is the backbone of your presentation.

Also consider the following questions:

- How **long** do you have to give your presentation? You do not want to run out of information or be cut short without leaving your audience with your bottom line.
- How **much time** do you have to create the presentation? If you do not have much time to create the presentation, you can use *PowerPoint's* timesaving features to create a quick presentation.
- **Where** will you be giving your presentation? This question should be asked along with, "How large is your audience?" How large is the room you will be presenting in? How is the lighting controlled? Where are the electrical outlets? It is a good idea to test the room out before presenting. You want your presentation to go smoothly.

Once you have this information, you can decide how to proceed in *PowerPoint.* You will look at the different paths available when you are first creating your presentation. For example, sometimes you might want to start with a specific look. At other times, one of the AutoContent Wizard presentations may help you organize your presentation. No one method is the "right" method. *PowerPoint* allows for editing and formatting at any point in the creation process. Therefore, you as the user can decide what works best for you and for the specific presentation you are creating.

Planning the Presentation for Kaleidoscope Rain

Table 1-1 outlines a plan for the Kaleidoscope Rain presentation.

State your objectives	The store manager of Kaleidoscope Rain needs to persuade the owners of Kaleidoscope Rain that the store will prosper in Capital City.
Define your audience	The owners of Kaleidoscope Rain
Determine presentation device	Laptop computer hooked up to an LCD panel and an overhead projector
Plan the outline	• Objective • Customer Requirements • Meeting the Needs of the Customers • Survey Results • Best Selling Products • Strengths • Cost Analysis • Benefits
How long do you have to give the presentation?	1/2 hour
How much time do you have to create the presentation?	1 month
Where will you be giving your presentation?	The meeting room at Kaleidoscope Rain's main office: small office, 1 light switch, several well-placed outlets

Table 1 - 1

CREATING A PRESENTATION

When you first enter *PowerPoint* and encounter the **Startup** dialog box, you are given four choices for creating a new presentation: *AutoContent Wizard, Pick a Look Wizard, Template* and *Blank Presentation.* These four choices are also available to you through the Menu bar by selecting **FILE/New**. When **FILE/New** is selected, the **New Presentation** dialog box appears. Steps taken from the **Startup** dialog box and the **New Presentation** dialog box are the same.

ALTERNATE METHOD: *To create a new presentation you can also click on the* ***New*** *button on the Standard toolbar.*

Using a Blank Presentation

The Blank Presentation option gives you the least guidance — or the most freedom (depending on your point of view) — to determine the content and look of your presentation. The color scheme, fonts, and other design features of the presentation are set to the default values.

REMEMBER: Read the bulleted list that follows, but do not actually perform the steps until you read Activity 1.1.

To create a blank presentation:

- From the **Startup** dialog box or the **New Presentation** dialog box, click on the **Blank Presentation** button.
- Click on **OK**. The **New Slide** dialog box appears.
- Click on the AutoLayout desired.
- Click on **OK**. A blank slide with the AutoLayout selected will appear on the screen.

PROBLEM SOLVER: *A blank presentation can be selected only when a new presentation is created.*

Activity 1.1: Creating a Blank Presentation

First, you will create a blank presentation. A blank presentation has no formatting. All formatting and style selection will be made after the presentation has been created.

1. Start *PowerPoint*. Follow the instruction in the Introductory lesson if necessary. Click on **OK** if the **Tip of the Day** dialog box appears. Stop at the **Startup** dialog box.
2. At the **Startup** dialog box, click on the **Blank Presentation** button, then click on **OK**.

   The ***New Slide*** *dialog box appears.*
3. The Title Slide should already be selected. Click on **OK** to accept it.

   A blank title slide appears on the screen (Figure 1-1). In the next activity, you will create another presentation using the AutoContent Wizard. You will come back to this presentation in Activity 1.6, when you switch from one presentation to another.

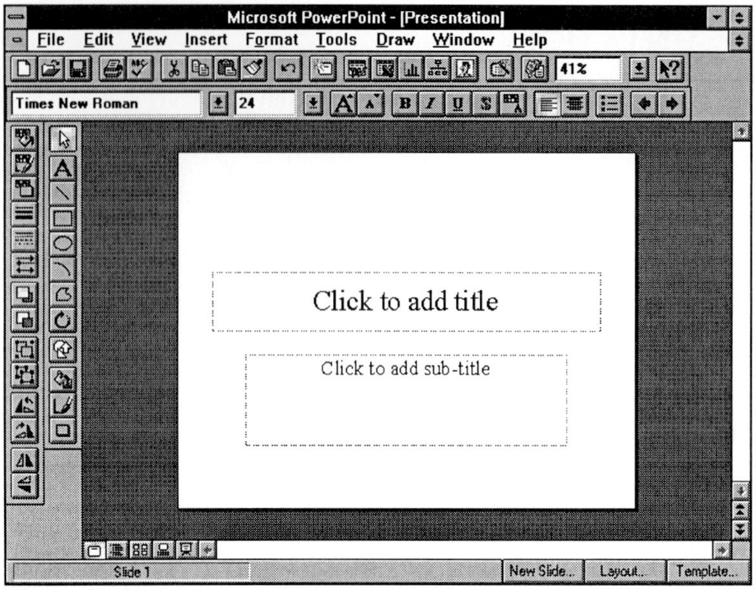

Figure 1 - 1

Using the AutoContent Wizard

If your presentation fits into one of *PowerPoint's* six predefined categories — *Recommending a Strategy, Selling a Product, Service or Idea, Training, Reporting Progress, Communicating Bad News* or *General* — you may want to use the AutoContent Wizard. When the Wizard is finished, you will have an outline that suggests the content and organization that you might want to use in your presentation. This approach helps you get started but doesn't limit your freedom. You can add, delete, or modify the slides.

To create a presentation using the AutoContent Wizard:

- From the **Startup** dialog box or the **New Presentation** dialog box, click on the **AutoContent Wizard** button.
- You will see the first of four steps that will bring you through the Wizard. It describes the AutoContent Wizard. Click on **Next>** to continue with the Wizard.
- In Step 2, tab to each of the text boxes or use the mouse to place the text cursor in the text box to answer the following prompts:
  - What are you going to talk about?
  - What is your name?
  - Other information you'd like to include?
- Click on **Next>** when the information for Step 2 has been inputted.

PROBLEM SOLVER: *At any time during the Wizard you can click on* ***Back>*** *to go to the previous screen.*

- In Step 3, select the type of presentation desired by clicking on the button for the desired choice. The types of presentations available are:
  - Recommending a Strategy
  - Selling a Product, Service or Idea

- Training
- Reporting Progress
- Communicating Bad News
- General

- Click on **Next>** when a presentation choice has been selected.
- The last screen of the AutoContent Wizard appears. Click on **Finish**.

  The presentation is created and appears on the screen in Outline View.

PROBLEM SOLVER: *The AutoContent Wizard can only be selected when creating a new presentation.*

Activity 1.2: Creating a Presentation using the AutoContent Wizard

You now have a blank title slide on your screen. After starting your presentation using the blank presentation approach, you decide you want more guidance. The goal of your presentation, selling your boss on opening a new store, sounds like it fits well into the *Selling a Product, Service or Idea* category. So you decide to create another presentation using the AutoContent Wizard. You will leave the blank presentation on the screen because you will come back to it in a later activity.

1. Select **FILE/New**.

   *The **New Presentation** dialog box appears on the screen (Figure 1 -2). Notice the similarity to the **Startup** dialog box. The only difference is that the **New Presentation** dialog box does not have an option for opening a presentation. Instead, an option is available to keep the current presentation format.*

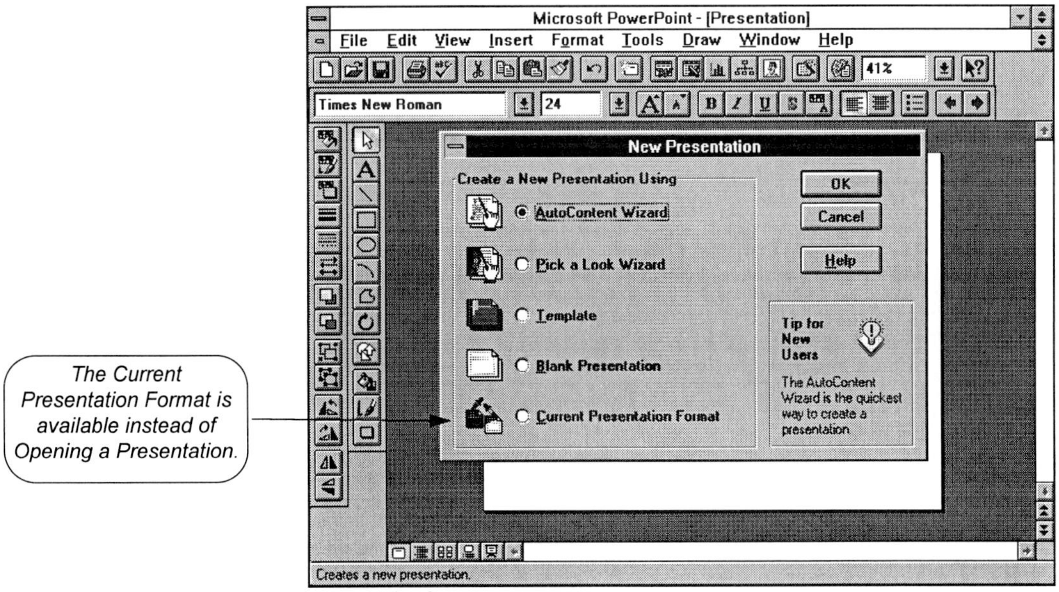

Figure 1 - 2

2. Click on the **AutoContent Wizard** button, and then click on **OK**.

   *Step 1 of 4 of the AutoContent Wizard appears on the screen describing what the Wizard does. Notice the command buttons at the bottom of the dialog box. Clicking on **Next>** will bring you forward. Clicking on **<Back** will bring up the previous step. To cancel the Wizard without creating a presentation, click on **Cancel**. To finish the Wizard and create a presentation, click on **Finish**.*

3. Click on the **Next>** button.

   Step 2 of 4 appears on the screen (Figure 1 - 3).

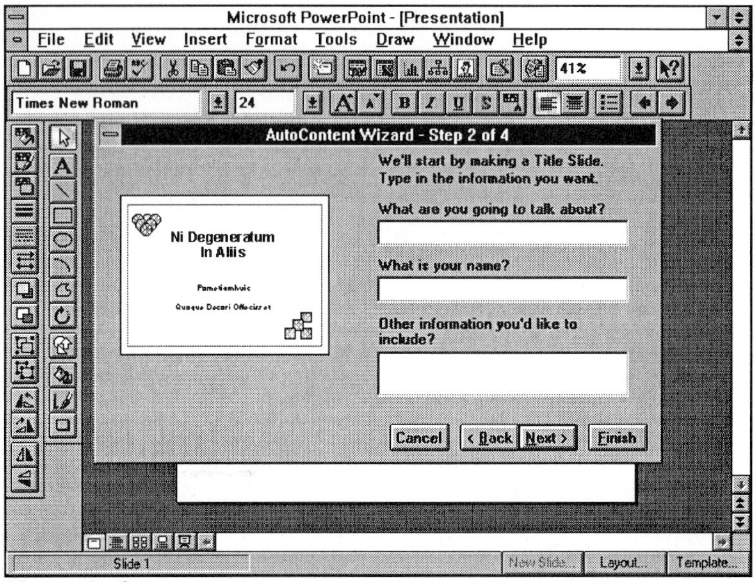

Figure 1 - 3

4. In the **What are you going to talk about?** text box, type: **KALEIDOSCOPE RAIN**
5. Press **TAB** to move to the next text box.
6. In the **What is your name?** text box, type: **MANAGER, STORE 1**
7. Press **TAB** to move to the next text box.
8. In the **Other information you'd like to include?** text box, type: **CAPITAL CITY PROPOSAL** (Figure 1 - 4).

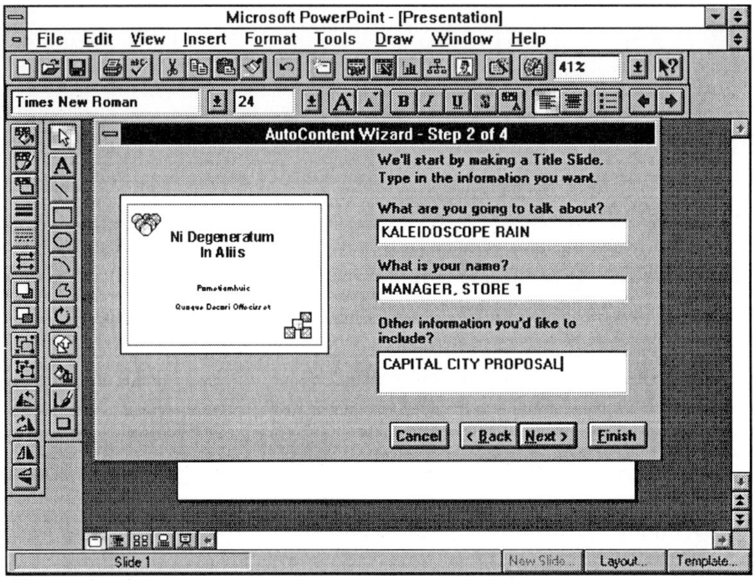

Figure 1 - 4

9. Click on **Next>**.

   Step 3 of 4 appears on the screen. The major points of the presentation selected appear on the left side of the dialog box.

10. Click on each of the option buttons so you can read the major points of each presentation selection.
11. Click on the **Selling a Product, Service or Idea** button (Figure 1 - 5).

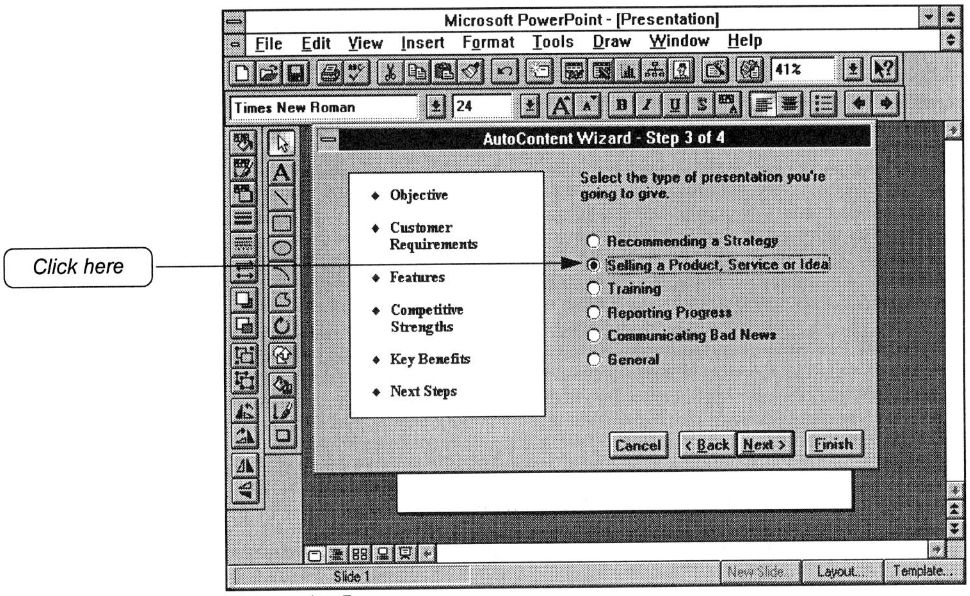

Figure 1 - 5

12. Click on **Next>**.

    Step 4 of 4 appears on the screen. PowerPoint gives several suggestions for editing the presentation once it has been finished.

13. Click on **Finish**.

    PROBLEM SOLVER: *Depending on how PowerPoint was installed on your machine, you may see an error message regarding the installation of Cue Cards. If this happens, click* ***OK*** *to move to the presentation.*

    The presentation appears on the screen in Outline View (Figure 1 - 6).

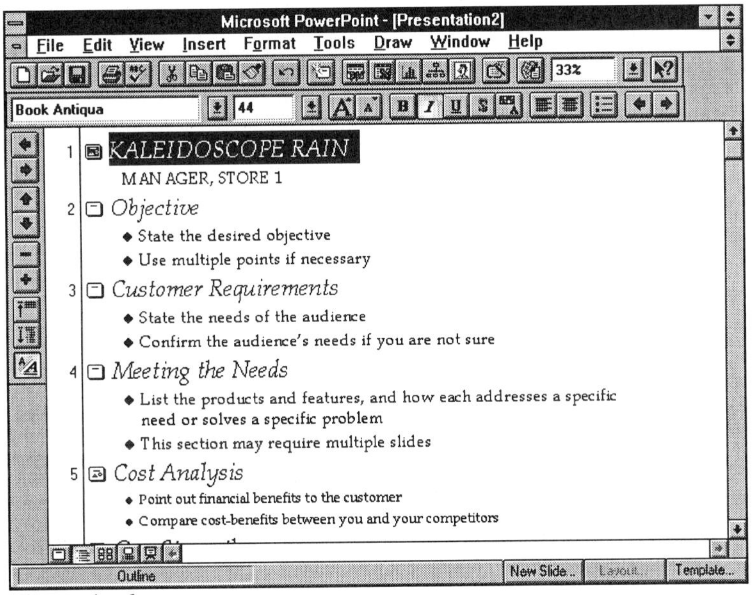

Figure 1 - 6

14. Switch to Slide View by selecting **VIEW/Slides**.

Using the Pick a Look Wizard

The Pick a Look Wizard helps you determine the look and feel of your presentation. You can use this Wizard to create a new presentation or to change the look of an existing presentation. Thus if you use the AutoContent Wizard and then the Pick a Look Wizard, you can let *PowerPoint* help you organize the contents and the look of your presentation.

To create a presentation using the Pick a Look Wizard:

- From the **Startup** dialog box or the **New Presentation** dialog box, click on the **Pick a Look Wizard** button.
- Click on **OK**.
- You will be brought to the first of nine screens of the Pick a Look Wizard. Click on **Next>** to continue with the Wizard.
- In Step 2, select the type of output you will be using (Black and White Overheads, Color Overheads, On-Screen Presentation, 35mm Slides) by clicking on its button.
- Click on **Next>** when the type of output has been selected.

PROBLEM SOLVER: *At any time during the Wizard you can click on* ***Back>*** *to go to the previous screen.*

- In Step 3, select the template design. Select from the choices given (Blue Diagonal, World, Double Line, Multiple Bars) or click on the **More** button to see more choices at the **Presentation Template** dialog box.
    - Click on the template files in the **File Name** list box to see a thumbnail view of the template design in the bottom right corner of the dialog box.
    - When you see a template design that you like, click on the **Apply** button. You will leave the **Presentation Template** dialog box and return to Step 3 of the Wizard.
- Click on **Next>** to move to Step 4.
- In Step 4, select the printing options (Full-Page Slides, Speaker's Notes, Audience Handout Pages, Outline Pages) desired. Initially, all options are selected. If you would like to omit a selection, click in the check box for the option. This will turn off the option by removing the **X** in the check box.

  The next steps include option pages for each of the printing options. If you deselected any of the choices, the corresponding step will be omitted.
- In Steps 5–8 (Slide Options, Notes Options, Handout Options, Outline Options), select what you would like printed on each page (Name, company, or other text, Date, Page Number). Click on **Next>** to proceed to each step.
- Step 9 is the last step in the Wizard. Click on **Finish** to apply the Wizard to the presentation.

To use the Pick a Look Wizard for the current presentation:

- Select **FORMAT/Pick a Look Wizard** or click on the **Pick a Look** button on the Standard toolbar.

- Step 1 of 9 of the Pick a Look Wizard appears on the screen. Follow the steps from Step 1 as listed above.

Activity 1.3: Using the Pick a Look Wizard for the Current Presentation

In Activity 1.2 you created a presentation using the AutoContent Wizard. You do not like the presentation style and are not sure that you've included all the right parts in your presentation. Therefore, you want to use the Pick a Look Wizard to help you change the presentation style.

1. Click on the **Pick a Look** button on the Standard toolbar.

   Step 1 of 9 of the Pick a Look Wizard appears on the screen.

2. Click on **Next>**.

   Step 2 of 9 appears on the screen. In Step 2, you will select the type of output you will be working with.

3. Click on the **On-Screen Presentation** button.
4. Click on **Next>**.

   Step 3 of 9 appears on the screen. In Step 3, you will select the template design that you want to apply to your presentation. If you want to see more template designs, click on the ***More*** *button.*

5. Click on the **Double Lines** button.
6. Click on **Next>**.

   Step 4 of 9 appears on the screen (Figure 1 - 7). In Step 4, you will select options for the output of your presentation. Steps 5–8 are the individual options pages for the selections in Step 4. Only the corresponding steps will appear, and they are labeled according to the output rather than their step number in the Wizard.

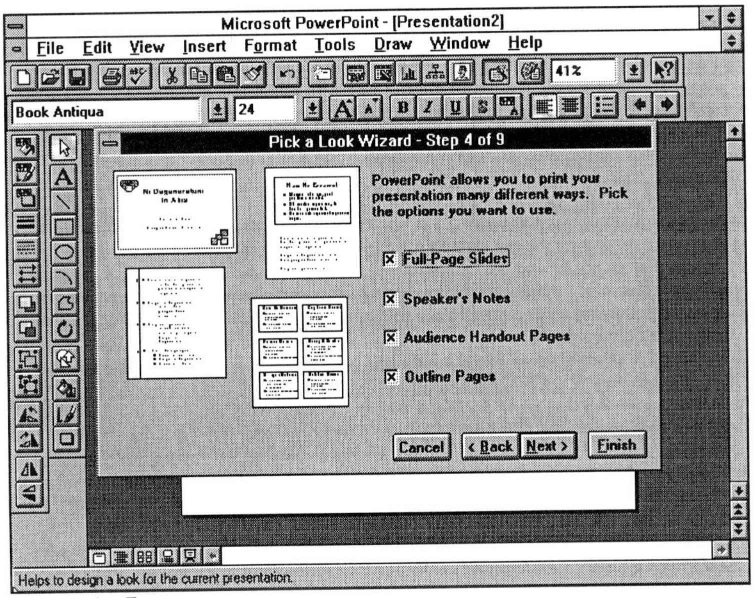

Figure 1 - 7

7. Click in the **Speaker's Notes**, **Audience Handout Pages**, and **Outline Pages** check boxes so that the **X** disappears in each (Figure 1 - 8).

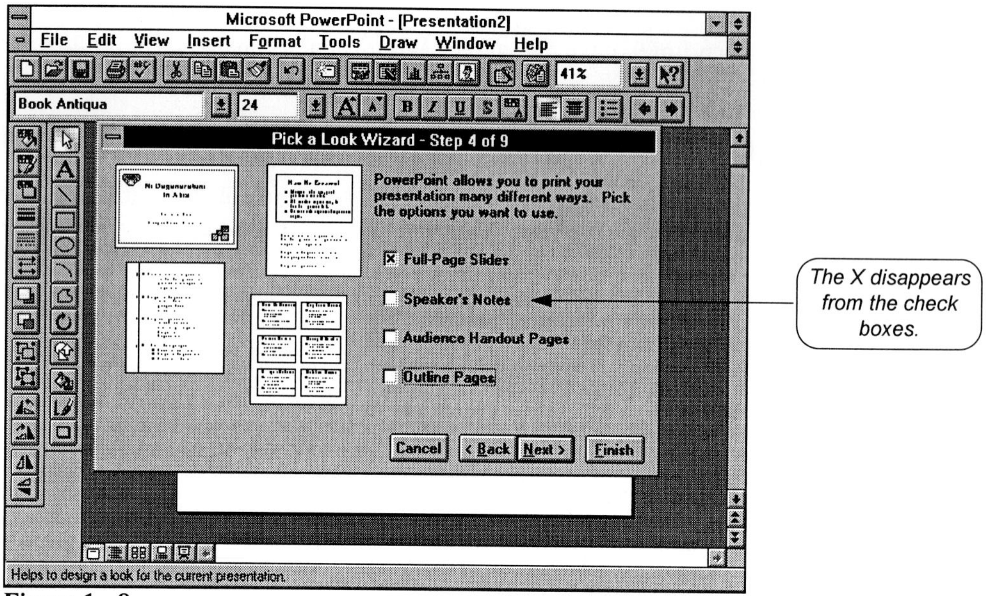

Figure 1 - 8

8. Click on **Next>**.

   *The **Slide Options** dialog box appears on the screen (Figure 1 - 9). The **Options** dialog boxes for Speaker's Notes, Audience Handouts, and Outline are the same as the **Slide Options** dialog box.*

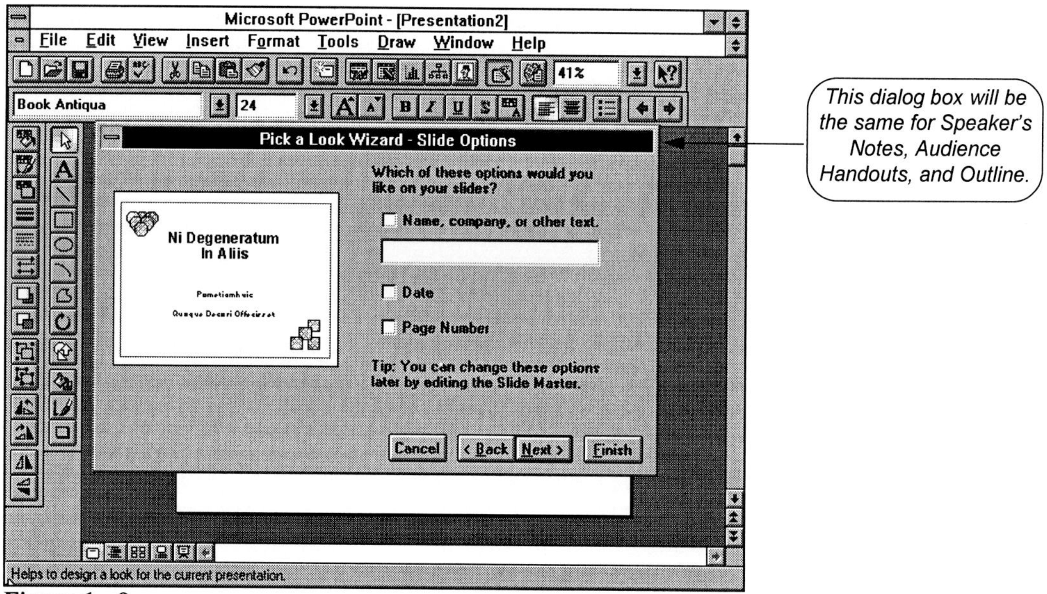

Figure 1 - 9

9. Click in the **Page Number** check box so that an **X** appears in the check box.
10. Click on **Next>**.

    Step 9 of 9 appears on the screen.

11. To finish the Pick a Look Wizard and apply the template design to the presentation, click on **Finish**.

    The slide has a different template design than before you used the Pick a Look Wizard and the page number has been placed in the bottom right corner of the slide (Figure 1 - 10).

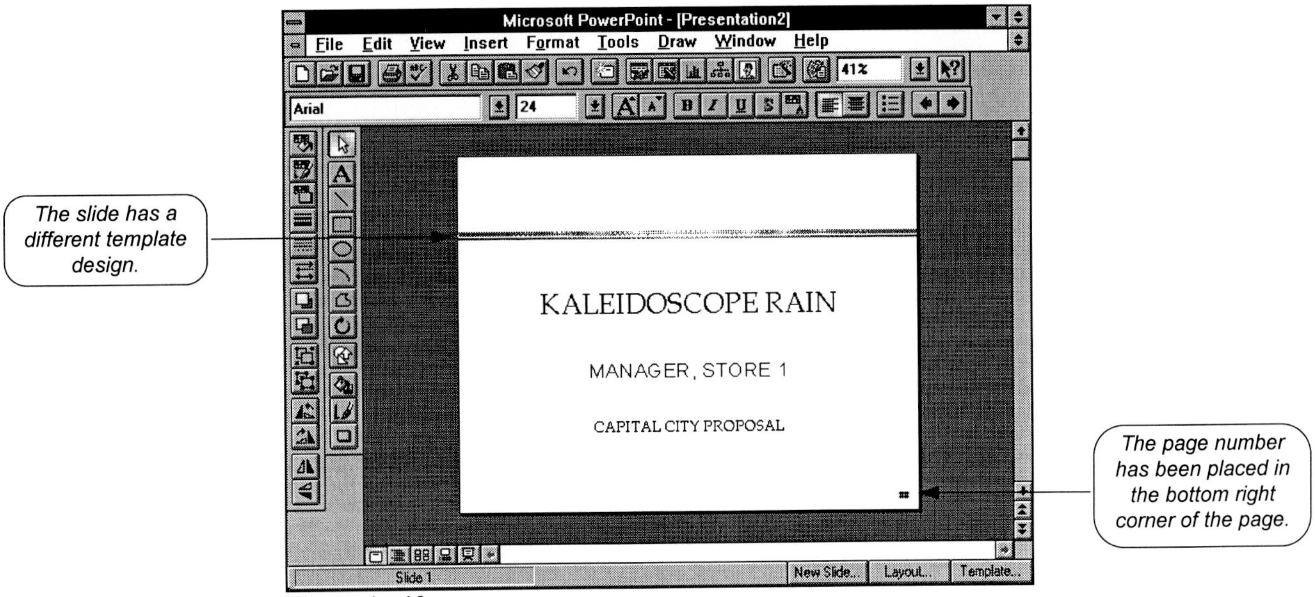

Figure 1 - 10

Using a Template

The Template includes the color scheme, font style, and other design features of the presentation. In Step 3 of the Pick a Look Wizard, four template names appeared in the dialog box. If you had selected the **More** button, you would have seen the same **Presentation Template** dialog box that you see if you pick the **Template** button from the **New Presentation** dialog box. This option gives you less guidance than either the AutoContent or Pick a Look Wizards and is best used by experienced *PowerPoint* users, or to change the template for a presentation that you have already begun.

To create a presentation using Template:

- From the **Startup** dialog box or the **New Presentation** dialog box, click on the **Template** button.
- Click on **OK**.

  *The **Presentation Template** dialog box appears.*

  PROBLEM SOLVER: *You may need to change the drive and directory initially to see the list of template files available. The template files are available in three subdirectories of the **template** directory. There are template files for black and white overheads (**bwovrhd**), color overheads (**clrovrhd**) and on-screen presentations (**sldshow**). Click on the **c:** drive in the **Drives** list box. Then double-click on the **template** directory in the **Directories** list box. This should show the list of subdirectories. Finally, double-click on the **sldshow** subdirectory. The list of template file names should appear in the **File Name** list box.*

- Click on the template files in the **File Name** list box to see a thumbnail view of the template design in the bottom right corner of the dialog box.
- When you see a template design that you like, click on the **Apply** button.

  *The **New Slide** dialog box appears.*

- Click on the desired AutoLayout.

  PROBLEM SOLVER: *Click on the* ↓ *in the vertical scroll bar to see more choices.*

- Click **OK**.

  A slide will appear in Slide View with the selected AutoLayout and Template.

A Template can also be applied to the current presentation.

To apply a template to the current presentation:

- Select **FORMAT/Presentation Template** or click on the **Template** button 

 on the Status bar.

Activity 1.4: Applying a Template to the Current Presentation

In Activity 1.3 you selected the template design as part of the Pick a Look Wizard. After seeing the design in Slide View you decide you want to change the template design. We will use Template this time to change the design.

1. Click on the **Template** button on the Status bar.

   *The **Presentation Template** dialog box appears on the screen (Figure 1 - 11).*

   PROBLEM SOLVER: *If you do not see the **Template** button on the Status bar, move your mouse pointer over to the Slide Work Area. When the mouse pointer is over a button, the description for the button appears on the Status bar, not the **New Slide**, **Layout**, or **Template** buttons.*

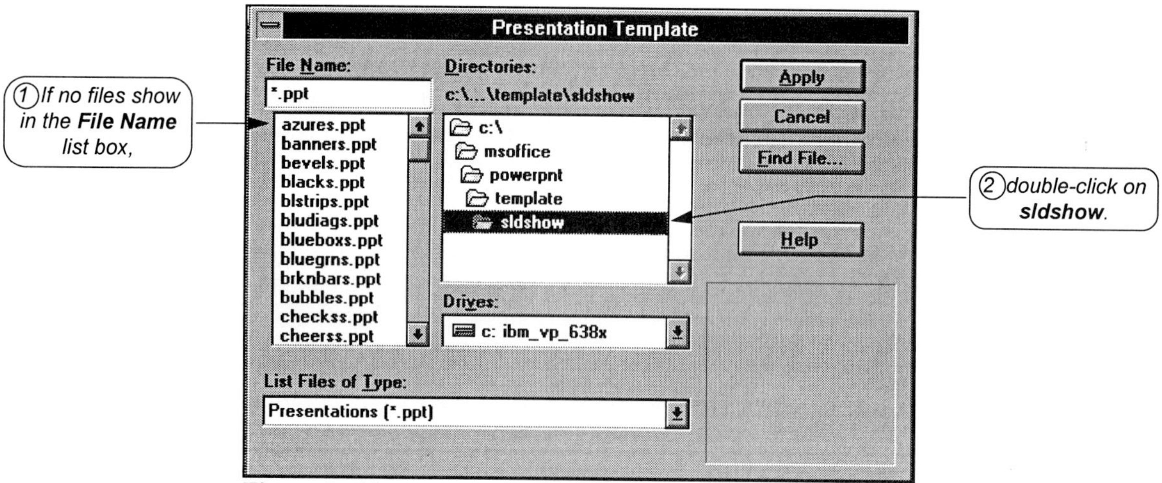

Figure 1 - 11

PROBLEM SOLVER: *If no template files are showing in the **File Name** list box, double-click on **bwovrhd** (Black and White Overheads), **clrovrhd** (Color Overheads), or **sldshow** (On-Screen Presentations) in the **Directories** list box. This will bring up the list of template files in the **File Name** list box. Make sure you select the desired output directory. The template file names are the same in each directory. However, there are differences based on the type of output. For example, Black and White overheads will have the same design as an On-Screen Presentation, only in black, gray, and white. You will select your template from the **sldshow** subdirectory.*

2. Click on the **azures.ppt** file listed in the **File Name** list box.

   *Notice that a thumbnail, a small version of the template, appears in the bottom right corner of the dialog box. You can look at all the templates available in PowerPoint by clicking on the presentation file listed in the **File Name** list box.*

3. Click on the rest of the template files listed in the **File Name** list box. When you are finished looking at the various templates that are available in *PowerPoint*, click on the **forests.ppt** file.

4. Click on **Apply** to apply the template and return to the presentation.

SAVING THE PRESENTATION

While you are working on a presentation, it is held in the *RAM* or *Random Access Memory* of your computer. RAM is the computer work area that stores work in progress until you close the file or the program.

To keep a permanent record of your work, you must save the presentation, as with any other computer task. To save the presentation you must give it a name and tell the computer where to store it. Anything saved on the computer is saved in a file. Once saved, a file can be accessed any time you need it.

It is important to save your work regularly (at least every 15 minutes), so that if you should make a serious mistake, or if the power should fail, you will not lose all your work.

To save a presentation as a file:

- Choose **FILE/Save As**.

  *The **Save As** dialog box appears.*

- Type a name for your file. Your file name must follow the rules in Table 1 -2.

RULES FOR NAMING A FILE
• The file name may have a maximum of 8 characters.
• It may **NOT** include spaces.
• It may **NOT** include any of the following symbols: , . ; : * = [ ] | / \ < > ?
• *PowerPoint* automatically adds the extension ***.ppt*** to the filename, so you should not type an extension of your own.

Table 1 - 2

- If the drive that appears in the **Drives** drop-down list box is not the drive that contains your data disk, click on the arrow to the right of the box and then click on the correct drive.

- If you are saving your file on a network, make sure that the network drive is selected in the previous step. If the directory shown in the **Directories** list box is not the one to which you should store your file, double-click on the name of the correct directory.

- Click on **OK**.

The **Summary Info** dialog box may be displayed. Enter any information that you want then click on **OK**.

Activity 1.5: Saving the Presentation

We have been working with this presentation for a while. You've selected the content and look of the presentation. Now is a good time to save the presentation. Later on in this lesson you will see how to save the presentation with the same name.

1. If you are saving your presentations on a floppy disk, put the disk in the drive.

2. Select **FILE/Save As**.

*The **Save As** dialog box appears on the screen (Figure 1 - 12). Notice the automatic extension of **.ppt** is listed in the **File Name** text box.*

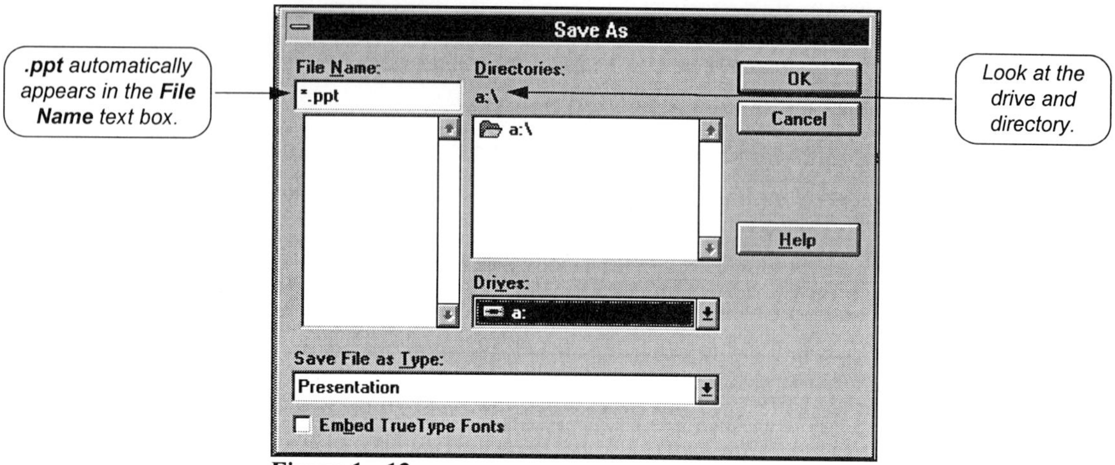

Figure 1 - 12

3. Highlight the text in the **File Name** text box if it is not already highlighted. Type: **rain1** The text will automatically be placed in the **File Name** text box because you highlighted the text. You don't need to put the extension **.ppt** on the filename. *PowerPoint* will do that.
4. Look at the drive and directory listed in the upper middle of the **Save As** dialog box (Figure 1- 12). If the drive listed is not the one to which you are saving your presentation, click the arrow to the right of the **Drives** drop-down list box.
5. Click on the button representing the drive containing your data disk. For floppy disks this will probably be **a:** or **b:**.
6. If you have been instructed to save your files on a network, click on the network drive. Ask your instructor for the name of the directory to which you should save your file. If that directory is not currently listed as the active directory, click on it in the **Directories** list box.

✓ **PROBLEM SOLVER:** *If the directory for which you are looking is not visible, click on the* ↓ *or* ↑ *on the right side of the **Directories** list box. This will scroll the entries. When the directory you want is visible, click on it.*

7. Click on **OK**.
8. The **Summary Info** dialog box may be displayed (Figure 1 - 13). Place the text cursor in the **Keywords** text box by clicking in the text box or by pressing the **TAB** key three times.

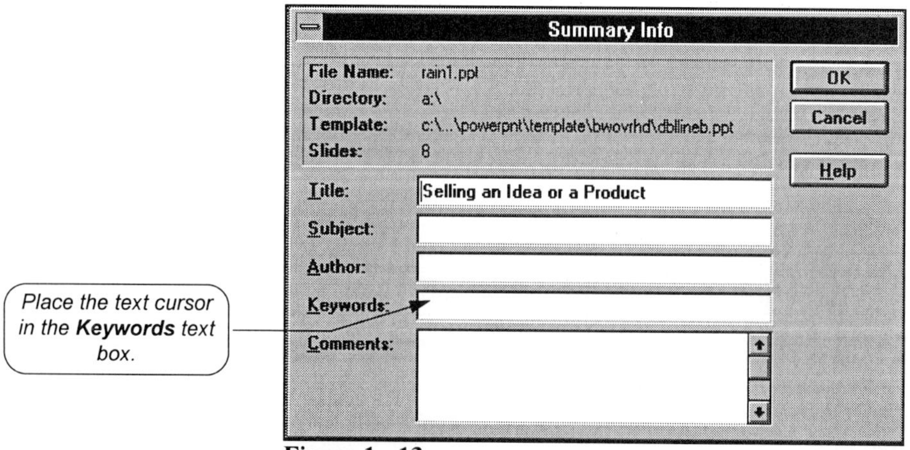

Figure 1 - 13

9. Type: **KALEIDOSCOPE RAIN, CAPITAL CITY**
10. Click on **OK** to save the file.

    *Notice the filename, **RAIN1.PPT** has been added to the Title bar.*

    PROBLEM SOLVER: *If a warning appears on the screen with the message, **Filename is not valid**, click on the **OK** button in the message box. Click in the **File Name** text box and retype or delete characters until only **rain1** appears in the **File Name** text box. Click on **OK** again.*

ADDING TEXT TO A PRESENTATION

Adding text to slides in *PowerPoint* is different from adding text in word processors. In word processors, you place the text cursor on the page where you want to type and then begin typing. *PowerPoint* uses placeholders for all the objects placed on the slide, including text. These placeholders include directions for adding text. For example, the title placeholder reads, **Click to add title**. This text disappears once you begin typing.

To add text to a slide:

- Click on the text placeholder (either title, sub-title, or bullet).

  A vertical line text cursor will appear in the placeholder.

- Begin typing text.

SWITCHING TO ANOTHER PRESENTATION

You can have as many presentations open at the same time as your machine's memory can handle. You can create several versions of a presentation depending on the audience and use elements from each of these presentations when creating new presentations. The **Window** menu manages the switching capability. In Lesson 2, you will see how to copy slides from one presentation to another using switching.

To switch to another presentation:

- Click on the **Window** menu.

  The menu opens. The open presentations are listed at the bottom of the menu.

- Click on the name of the presentation you wish to switch to.

  *If the presentation hasn't been saved yet, the listed file will be **Presentation, Presentation2**, etc., depending on the order in which you created the presentations.*

Activity 1.6: Adding Text to a Slide

You will switch back to the blank presentation and add text to it. In Lesson 2, this presentation will be used to copy a slide from one presentation to another.

1. Click on **Window** on the Menu bar.

   *All open presentations will be listed at the end of the **Window** menu in the order that they were opened. In this case, **Presentation** is listed first and **RAIN1.PPT** is listed second.*

2. Click on **1 Presentation** to switch to the blank presentation.

   *There are two text placeholders on the Title slide. Notice the directions for adding text (**Click to add title** and **Click to add sub-title**).*

3. Click anywhere inside the Title placeholder.

   A text cursor appears centered inside the Title placeholder. Notice the mouse pointer. If it is placed over the Title placeholder (or any text area) it appears as an ***I-beam*** *(Figure 1 - 14).*

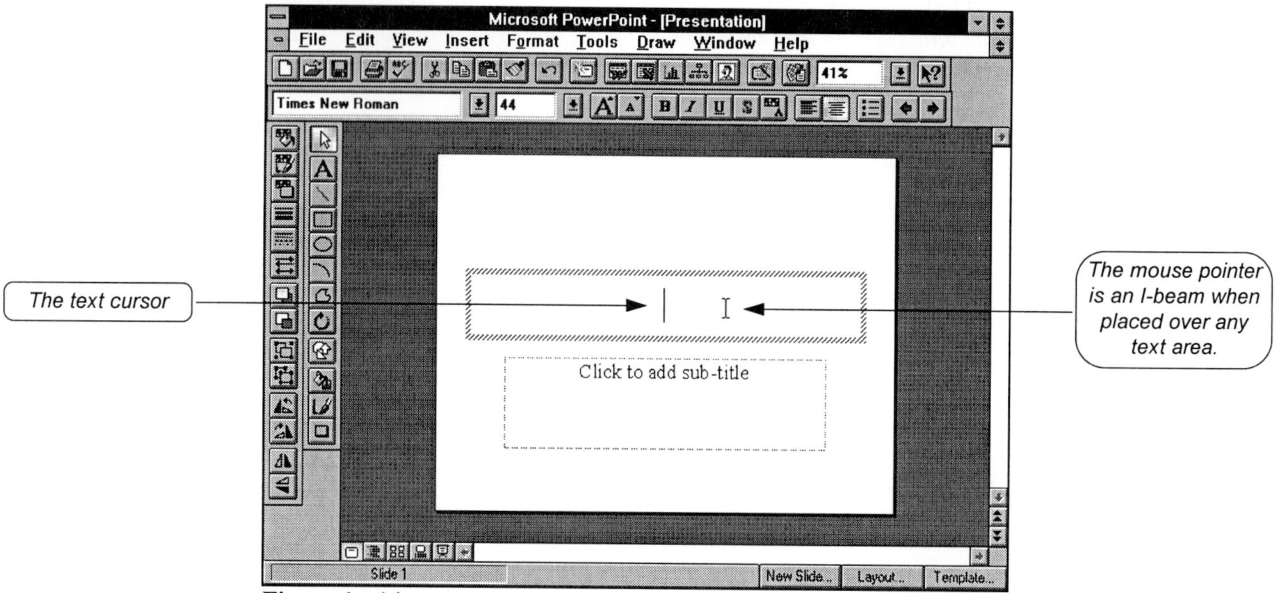

Figure 1 - 14

4. Type: **KALEIDOSCOPE RAIN**
5. Click anywhere in the Sub-title placeholder.
6. Type: **PROPOSED STORE EXPANSION TO CAPITAL CITY LOCATION**

   Text will automatically wordwrap according to the size of the text block. The subtitle text should wordwrap after ***EXPANSION****. It is possible to change the size of the text block, thus changing the way the text wordwraps. You will see how to do that in Lesson 3. It is also possible to change the font and size of the text, possibly changing the way the text will wordwrap. You will see how to do this in Lesson 3.*
7. Save the presentation as **rain2**.

ADDING A NEW SLIDE TO A PRESENTATION

When you create any presentation, you have selected the style of the presentation and the layout of the first slide. In the case of the AutoContent Wizard, you will have several sample slides that will be edited with your information. In all cases you will need to add slides to your presentation.

To add a slide to a presentation:

- Click on the **New Slide** button on the right side of the Status bar.

  ALTERNATIVE METHODS: *Select* ***INSERT/New Slide*** *from the Menu bar or click on the* ***Insert New Slide*** *button on the Standard toolbar.*

  The ***New Slide*** *dialog box appears on the screen.*
- Click on the desired AutoLayout.

  PROBLEM SOLVER: *Click on the* ↓ *in the vertical scroll bar to see more choices.*

- Click **OK**.

  A slide will appear in Slide View with the selected AutoLayout. It will be placed after the slide you were on when you selected the New Slide option.

Activity 1.7: Adding a Slide to a Presentation

You will add a bullet slide to the **rain2.ppt** presentation, and then you will add text to the slide using the placeholders.

1. Make sure that the **rain2.ppt** presentation is the current presentation. If not, switch to it using the **Window** menu.
2. Click on the **New Slide** button on the Status bar.

   *The **New Slide** dialog box appears on the screen.*
3. Click on the **Bulleted List** AutoLayout. It is the middle slide in the top row (Figure 1 - 15). The name of the AutoLayout will appear in the bottom right corner of the dialog box as you select different layouts.

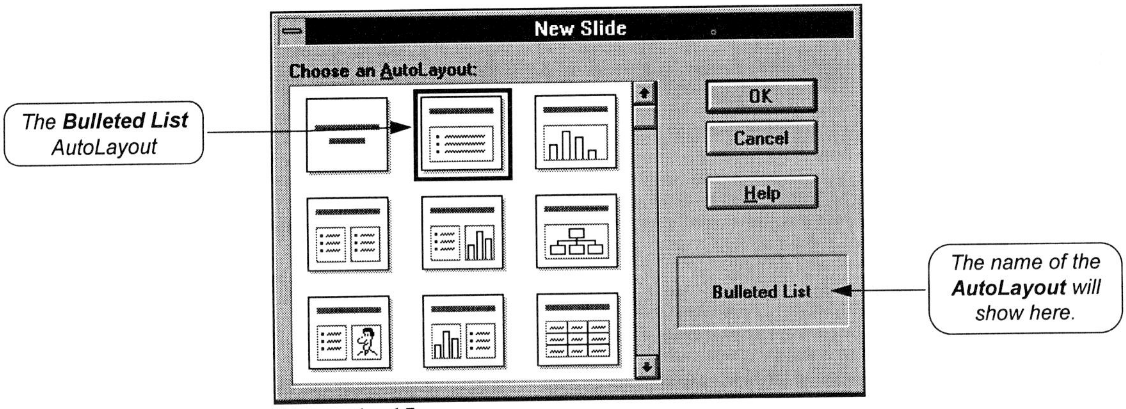

Figure 1 - 15

4. Click on **OK**.

   A Bulleted List slide appears on the screen. Placeholders are available for the Title and the Bulleted text. Notice the difference between the Title layout and the Bulleted List layout.
5. Click anywhere in the **Title** placeholder.
6. Type: **Best Selling Products**
7. Click anywhere in the **Bulleted text** placeholder.

   *A bullet is already in place for the first line of bulleted text and the text cursor appears next to this bullet. Every time you press **ENTER**, another bullet will appear.*
8. Type the following lines. Press **ENTER** after each line.

   Jazz Wolf CD

   Wilderness Thunderstorm CD

   Topo Map Stationary Set

   Forest Essentials Jasmine Gift Set

   Terrapax Clutch Briefcase

   Circuit Board Products

When completed your slide should look like Figure 1 - 16.

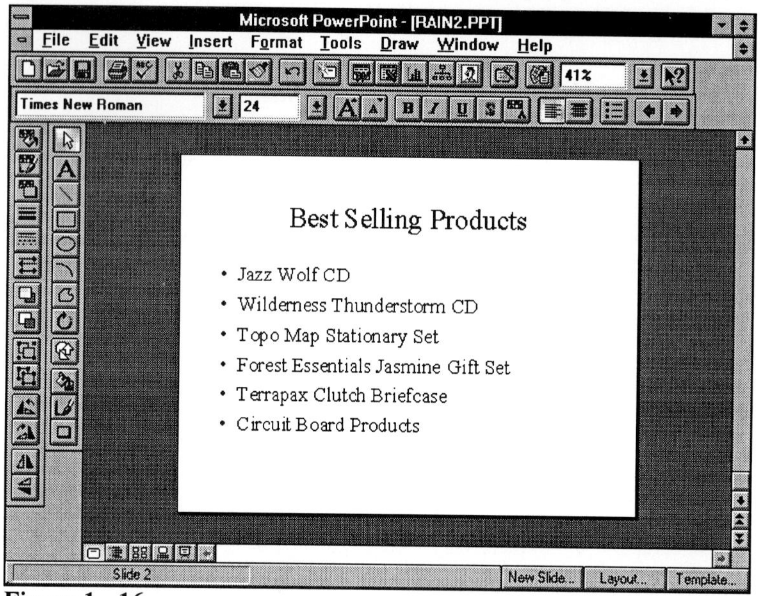

Figure 1 - 16

SAVING A PRESENTATION WITH THE SAME NAME

Every time you make changes to the file, you must save the file again or the changes will be lost when you close the presentation or exit from *PowerPoint*. When you save the file using the same name, the current version of the presentation replaces the previously saved version.

To save the file using the same name:

- Choose **FILE/Save** or click the **Save** button  on the Standard toolbar.

Activity 1.8: Saving the Presentation with the Same Name

You will now save the **rain2.ppt** presentation using the same name.

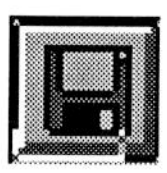

1. Select **FILE/Save** or click on the **Save** button on the Standard toolbar.

   The mouse pointer will change to an hourglass indicating that an operation is being performed. In this case, the presentation is being saved.

   *For future exercises, if you are saving a presentation for the first time or you want to have two different copies of the presentation on the disk, use **FILE/Save As**. If you are saving the presentation again with the same name, use **FILE/Save** or the **Save** button on the Standard toolbar. Make sure you want to overwrite the file on the disk before using either of these last two options!*

PRINTING A PRESENTATION

There are several options involved in printing a presentation. Because you may not always want to print the whole presentation, or even the current slide, you have options that allow you to print one page or several. Options are also available for printing Notes Pages, Handouts, and Outlines for your presentation.

To print a presentation:

- Make sure that the printer is turned on.
- Select **FILE/Print** or click on the **Print** button on the Standard toolbar.
- Select what you would like to print from the **Print What** drop-down list box (Slides, Notes Pages, Handouts (2, 3, or 6 slides per page), Outline).
- Select the number of copies you would like to print using the **Copies** spinner.
- Select the **Slide Range** (All, Current Slide, Slide range).
- Select any miscellaneous options (Print to File, Print Hidden Slides, Black & White, Collate Copies, Scale to Fit Paper, Pure Black & White).
- Click on **OK**.

PROBLEM SOLVER: *You may have printing problems if your printer does not have enough memory to print graphics images. If you have a problem printing the whole presentation, try printing one slide at a time. If you have a problem printing* ***Handouts (6 per page)****, try printing* ***Handouts (2 per page)****. For example, you might encounter problems with the HP Laserjet 4. The HP Laserjet 4 is shipped with 2 megabytes of memory. You can add extra memory. 2 megabytes of memory is not enough to print many of the graphics that are available in PowerPoint. Try the solutions listed above, if they do not work, ask your instructor or lab assistant what to do.*

Activity 1.9: Printing a Presentation

You want to get samples of the printed documents you can make from your presentation before you have entered too many slides. In this activity, you will print the **rain2.ppt** presentation using several of the Print options.

1. Make sure **rain2.ppt** is the current presentation.
2. Select **FILE/Print** from the Menu bar.

   The Print dialog box appears on the screen (Figure 1-17).

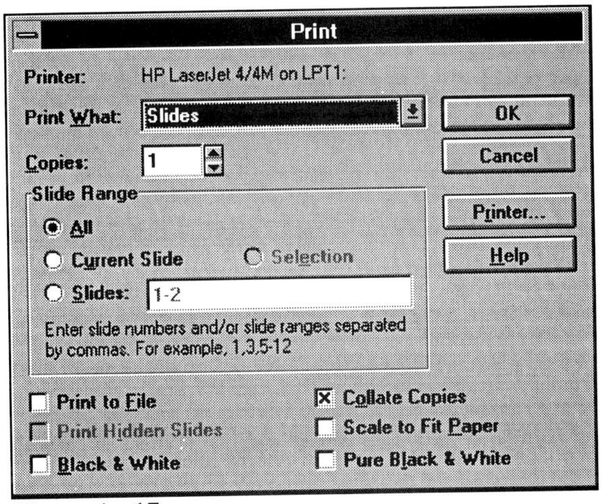

Figure 1 - 17

3. Keep the default settings. Click on **OK** to print the two-slide presentation.

A message appears on the screen announcing the progress of the printing (Figure 1 - 18). Your computer processes it, and then sends it to the printer. Each of the two slides will be printed on separate pieces of paper taking up the full sheet of paper.

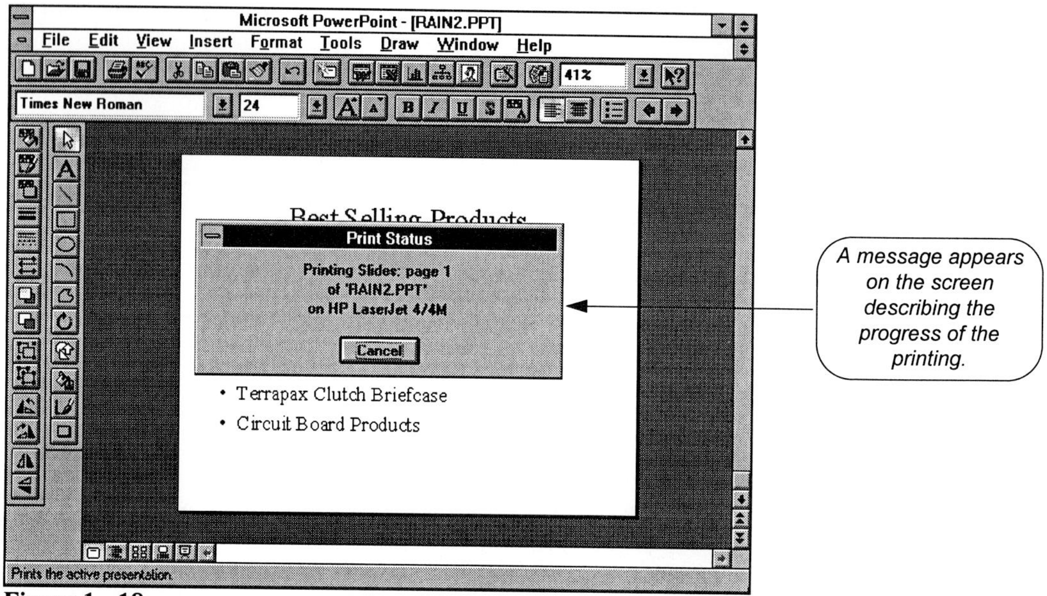

Figure 1 - 18

4. Select **FILE/Print** again.
5. Select **Notes Pages** from the **Print What** drop-down list box.
6. Click on the **Current Slide** button in the Slide Range section.
7. Click on **OK** to print the Notes Page for Slide 2.

   The progress message indicates that PowerPoint printed the Notes Page for Slide 2. The printout will have the slide at the top of the page with space at the bottom for notes. If you had entered text in Notes Pages View, it would have shown up in the bottom section. You will add a note in Notes Pages View in Lesson 2.

   *The **Print** button on the Standard toolbar will print what was last sent to the printer.*

8. Click on the **Print** button on the Standard toolbar.

   *Notice the progress message indicates that PowerPoint printed the Notes Page for Slide 2. When you click on the **Print** button on the Standard toolbar, the last print job selected is repeated. If a print job has not been selected yet, the default (Slides, print all slides) selection is sent to the printer.*

9. Select **FILE/Print.**
10. Select **Handouts (2 slides per page)** from the **Print What** drop-down list box.
11. Click on the **All** button in the Slide Range section.
12. Click on **OK** to send the job to the printer.

   Look at your printout. Now both slides are placed on one page, either side by side (landscape) or top to bottom (portrait) depending on the default setting. You will see how to change this option in Lesson 2.

PROBLEM SOLVER: *Printing worked well because we used a blank presentation. You didn't have to worry about the background color for an on-screen presentation. If you want to print an on-screen presentation to a black and white printer, you will need to use the* ***Black & White*** *and* ***Pure Black & White*** *options at the bottom of the* ***Print*** *dialog box.*

CLOSING A PRESENTATION

You can have several presentations open on the desktop at the same time. After working with a presentation and saving it, you will want to close it.

To close a presentation:

- Select **FILE/Close**.

Activity 1.10: Closing a Presentation

Now, you will close both the **rain1.ppt** and **rain2.ppt** presentations.

1. Both presentations have been saved and you have not made any changes or additions since you saved last.
2. **Rain2.ppt** should be on the screen. Select **FILE/Close**.

   PROBLEM SOLVER: *If you did happen to make a change or pressed some extra keys and a prompt appears on the screen asking you to save changes to the presentation, click on* ***No****.*

3. **Rain1.ppt** appears on the screen. Select **FILE/Close**.

   Now both presentations have been closed. No presentation is open on the screen. Notice the Slide Work Area is empty.

4. Open several of the menus.

   Most of the commands are gray, also referred to as ghost print because you cannot use them. These commands need to have a presentation open on the screen to be active.

5. Exit from *PowerPoint*.

SUMMARY

In this lesson you completed the basic tasks of creating a presentation using different methods. You added text to a slide, added a slide to a presentation, saved a presentation, printed a presentation, and closed a presentation. In Lesson 2, you will learn how to edit the presentations you created in this lesson.

KEY TERMS

Audience Handout Pages
AutoContent Wizard
Blank Presentation
Closing
Edit Mode
Full-Page Slides
New Slide
Outline Pages
Pick a Look Wizard
Placeholder
Planning
Printing
RAM
Saving
Slide Range
Speaker's Notes
Template
Template Design
Text Cursor
Thumbnail

INDEPENDENT PROJECTS

The four independent projects allow you to practice the basic skills involved in creating presentations: creating the presentation using the various methods, adding text to a slide, adding a slide to the presentation, saving and printing the presentation. The first two projects indicate all the tasks that you need to complete the project. The directions for Independent Project 1.3 will tell you what operation to perform, but may not tell you which keys to press or buttons to click. In Independent Project 1.4, you will be asked to create a presentation and the design choices will be left up to you.

Independent Project 1.1: Creating a Presentation for History Class

You are taking an American History class at the local University. One of the assignments is to give a speech to the class on a topic of your choice. You choose to do your report on Ellis Island. You are allowed to use any equipment from the Audio-Visual department. You check with A.V. They have a computer and an LCD panel that can be placed on an overhead projector to project your presentation.

You decide to use the AutoContent Wizard and the Pick a Look Wizard to make the creation process faster and easier. When you have completed this exercise, the presentation will not be complete. You will create the presentation using the AutoContent Wizard, but the text will be edited in an Independent Project at the end of Lesson 2 and formatted in an Independent Project at the end of Lesson 3. A plan for the presentation follows (Table 1 - 3):

State your objectives	Report information about Ellis Island and immigration
Define your audience	American History class
Determine presentation device	Computer hooked up to an LCD panel and an overhead projector
Plan the outline	• Objectives • Topics • History of Ellis Island • Definition of Immigration • Causes of Immigration
How long do you have to give the presentation?	15 minutes
How much time to you have to create the presentation?	1 month
Where will you be giving your presentation?	American History classroom, 1 light switch and 1 outlet in the front of the room

Table 1 - 3

1. Open the *PowerPoint* program, if it is not already open.
2. Click on **OK** in the **Tip of the Day** dialog box if it appears.
3. At the **Startup** dialog box, click on the **AutoContent Wizard** button then click on **OK**.

   NOTE: *If you are already in PowerPoint, select **FILE/New**, then follow Step 3.*

4. Click on **Next>** when Step 1 of 4 of the AutoContent Wizard appears on the screen.
5. Type the following text in Step 2 of 4:

What are you going to talk about?	**ELLIS ISLAND**
What is your name?	***Your name***
Other information you'd like to include?	**HIS 105, Spring Semester**

6. Click on **Next>** to go to Step 3 of 4.
7. Select **General** as the type of presentation you are going to give.
8. Click on **Next>** to go to Step 4 of 4.
9. Click on **Finish** to end the Wizard. Remember that the presentation appears in Outline View when you use the AutoContent Wizard. Your screen should resemble Figure 1 - 19.

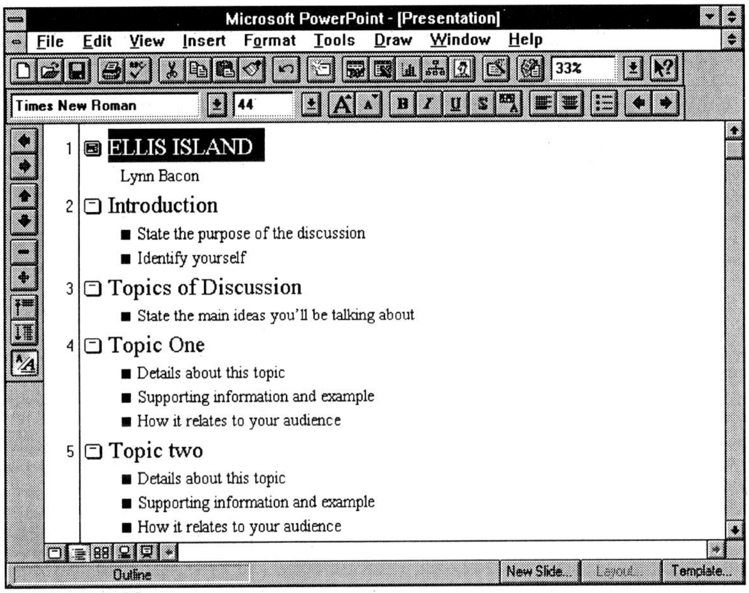

Figure 1 - 19

10. Switch to Slide View by selecting **VIEW/Slides**.

11. Click on the **Pick a Look** button on the Standard toolbar.
12. At Step 1 of 9 click on **Next>**.
13. Select the **On-Screen Presentation** button at Step 2 of 9, and then click on **Next>**.
14. Select **World** as the template design in Step 3 of 9, and then click on **Next>**.
15. Click off **Speaker's Notes**, **Audience Handout Pages**, and **Outline Pages** so that an **X** appears in the **Full-Page Slides** check box only, and then click on **Next>**.
16. Click in the **Name, company, or other** text check box so that an **X** appears.
17. Select the text in the text block, if there is text, and replace it with your name.
18. Click in both the **Date** and the **Page Number** check boxes so an **X** appears in both, then click on **Next>**.
19. At Step 9 of 9 click on **Finish**.
20. Select **FILE/Save As**.
21. In the **File Name** text box, type: **ellis1**

22. Change the drive to the data disk, if necessary, by selecting the correct drive from the **Drives** drop-down list box and click on **OK**.
23. If the **Summary Info** dialog box appears, click on **OK**.
24. Choose **FILE/Print**.
25. Select **Handout (2 slides per page)** from the **Print What** drop-down list box.
26. Click on the **Pure Black & White** print option so that an **X** appears in the check box.
27. Click on **OK** to send the job to the printer.
28. Exit *PowerPoint* or continue with the next project.

Independent Project 1.2: Creating a Presentation for the Browning Museum

You work for the Browning Museum. William Jack, the Executive Director, has asked you to create a presentation describing the programs at the museum. The presentation will run on a computer in the main hall. The director gives you the first pages of information. More information will need to be added to the presentation.

You decide to use the Blank Presentation and the Template option. When you have completed this exercise, the presentation will not be complete. Text will be edited in an Independent Project at the end of Lesson 2 and formatted in an Independent Project at the end of Lesson 3.

1. Open the *PowerPoint* program, if it is not already open.
2. Click on **OK** in the **Tip of the Day** dialog box if it appears.
3. At the **Startup** dialog box, click on the **Blank Presentation** button then click on **OK**.

   NOTE: *If are already in PowerPoint, select **FILE/New**, then follow Step 3.*

4. At the **New Slide** dialog box, select the **Title Slide** and click on **OK**.
5. Click in the Title placeholder and type: **The Browning Museum**
6. Click in the Sub-title placeholder and type: **Programs, 1995-1996**
7. Click on the **New Slide** button on the Status bar.
8. The selected AutoLayout should be **Bulleted List**. Click on **OK** to accept it.
9. Click in the Title placeholder and type: **The Browning Museum Staff**
10. Click in the Bulleted Text placeholder and type the following text:

    William Jack, Executive Director

    Nancy James-Hall, Curator of Art

    Mary Mulligan, Curator of Natural Sciences

    Robert Billings, Curator of Education

    Bonnie Peters, Director of Public Affairs

    Susan Whitney, Director of Development

11. Follow Steps 7 and 8 to add a new Bulleted Text slide to the presentation.
12. Click in the Title placeholder and type: **Statement of Purpose**
13. Click in the Bulleted Text placeholder and type the following text:

    The Browning Museum is a teaching museum of the arts and natural sciences.

14. Add a new Bulleted Text slide to the presentation.

15. Add the following title: **Events and Exhibits**
16. Type the following text in the Bulleted text placeholder:

    Annual Strawberry Craft Festival (Spring)

    Annual Patio Arts Festival (Summer)

    Museum Gift Shop International Bazaar (Fall)

    Natural History Galleries (Hands-on Activities)
17. Deselect the text by clicking on a blank area of the slide.
18. Click on the **Template** button on the Status bar.
19. Select the **twinkles.ppt** file in the **File Name** list box.
20. Click on **Apply**.
21. Select **VIEW/Slide Sorter** to switch to Slide Sorter View.
22. Your presentation should resemble Figure 1 - 20.

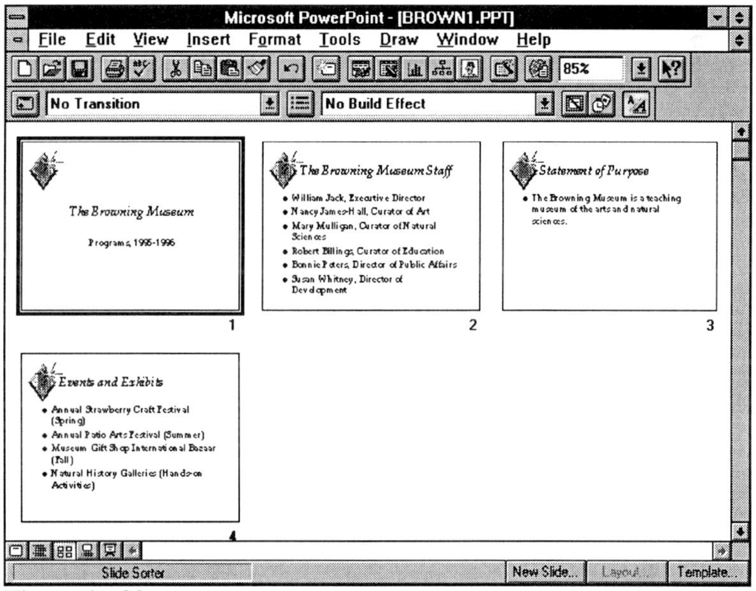

Figure 1 - 20

23. Save the presentation as **brown1**.
24. Print **Handout (2 slides per page)** using the **Pure Black & White** print option.
25. Close the presentation.
26. Exit *PowerPoint* or continue with the next project.

Independent Project 1.3: Creating a Presentation for Julie's Travel Agency

You work for Julie's Travel Agency. Julie Morgan is the owner of Julie's Travel Agency. Business at Julie's has been very good. So good that customers have walked out because an agent wasn't available. Julie wants you to create a presentation introducing customers to the services at the agency. Her plan is to have the screenshow set up so that a waiting customer can watch the presentation. By the time the presentation is completed, an agent will be available. She gives you her draft copy.

You decide to create the presentation using the Template option. When you have completed this exercise, the presentation will not be complete. Text will be edited in an Independent Project at the end of Lesson 2 and formatted in an Independent Project at the end of Lesson 3.

1. Open the *PowerPoint* program, if it is not already open.
2. Click on **OK** in the **Tip of the Day** dialog box if it appears.
3. At the **Startup** dialog box, select **Template**.

NOTE: *If are already in PowerPoint, select **FILE/New**, then follow Step 3.*

4. At the **Presentation Template** dialog box, select the **travels.ppt** template.
5. At the **New Slide** dialog box, select the **Title Slide** AutoLayout.
6. In the Title placeholder, type: **Julie's Travel Agency**
7. In the Sub-title placeholder, type: **County Shopping Center**
8. Press **ENTER** after typing the first line and type: **Pinebrook, NY**
9. Add a Bulleted Text slide to the presentation with the following information:

Title:	**Available Services**
Bulleted Text:	**Airline Ticket Information**
	Hotel Reservation Information
	Car Rental Information
	Travel Books & Magazine Travel Articles
	Bed & Breakfast Inns and Hostels

10. Add a second Bulleted Text slide to the presentation with the following information:

Title:	**Available International Services**
Bulleted Text:	**Airline Ticket and Hotel Reservation Information**
	Car Rental Information
	Cruise Information
	Railway and International Subway Information
	World Cities Sightseeing Guide
	International Currency Converter
	Tourist Offices
	Tour Information
	Hostel Information

NOTE: *The text will extend past the bottom of the slide. Do not worry about it for now. You will format the text in an Independent Project at the end of Lesson 3.*

11. Save the presentation as **travel1**.
12. Print the presentation using the **Pure Black & White** print option.
13. Change to Slide Sorter View. Your presentation should resemble Figure 1 - 21.

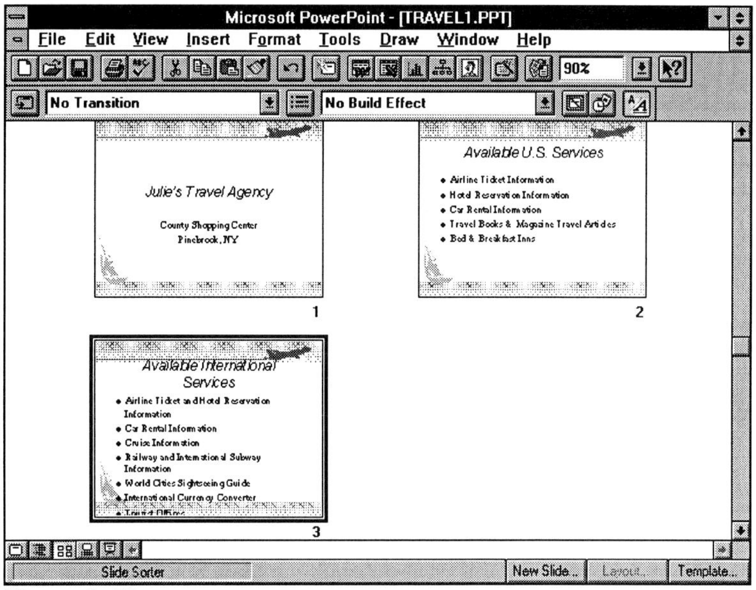

Figure 1- 21

14. Exit *PowerPoint* or continue with the next project.

Independent Project 1.4: Creating a Presentation for a Training Program

You are a trainer at a popular computer store. You like to begin your training classes with a short presentation showing your clients an overview of the software package you are working with for the day and the format of the class. You want to create a presentation in *PowerPoint* for the **PowerPoint class**. You decide to use the AutoContent Wizard because there is a **Training** selection in the Wizard.

1. Think of a name for your popular computer store. The example used in this project is **Computers R Us**.
2. Create a presentation using the AutoContent Wizard. Use the following information.

   Step 2 of 2:

What are you going to talk about?	**PowerPoint 4.0 for Windows**
What is your name?	***name of your computer store***
Other information you'd like to include?	**1 day training class**

   Step 3 of 3:

Type of presentation:	**Training**

3. Save the presentation as **train1**. Your presentation should resemble Figure 1 - 22.

   NOTE: *The presentation is not complete. You will edit the presentation in an Independent Project at the end of Lesson 2 and format the presentation at the end of Lesson 3.*

4. Print an **Outline View** of the presentation.
5. Close **train1.ppt** and exit *PowerPoint*.

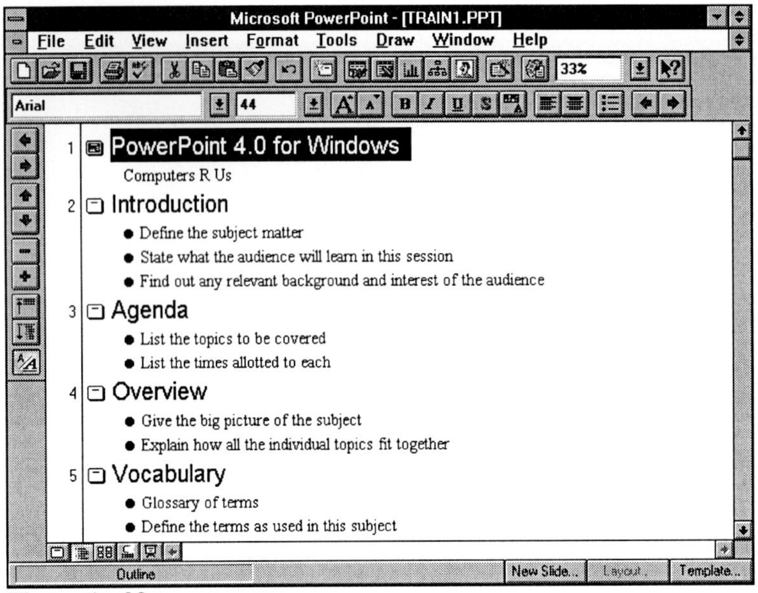
Microsoft PowerPoint - [TRAIN1.PPT]
File Edit View Insert Format Tools Draw Window Help
33%
Arial
44
1 PowerPoint 4.0 for Windows
Computers R Us
2 Introduction
Define the subject matter
State what the audience will learn in this session
Find out any relevant background and interest of the audience
3 Agenda
List the topics to be covered
List the times allotted to each
4 Overview
Give the big picture of the subject
Explain how all the individual topics fit together
5 Vocabulary
Glossary of terms
Define the terms as used in this subject
Outline
New Slide...
Layout...
Template...

Figure 1 - 22

Lesson

2 Editing a Presentation

Objectives

In this lesson you will learn how to:

- Open a presentation
- Move around a presentation
- Insert and delete text
- Move text
- Copy text
- Spell check the presentation
- Edit in Slide Sorter View, Outline View and Notes Pages View
- Edit the Slide Setup
- Change the Zoom Control

PROJECT DESCRIPTION

In Lesson 2, you will continue to work with **rain1.ppt** and **rain2.ppt** to develop your presentation to the owners of Kaleidoscope Rain. In Lesson 1, you started adding text to **rain2.ppt**. You decide that it would be easier to use the **rain1.ppt** presentation created using the AutoContent Wizard to help you organize your presentation. Since the **rain1.ppt** presentation contains the outline text, you will need to learn how to edit text in order to replace the general concepts with words appropriate to your presentation. To make the creation of your presentation easier, you will learn to copy text. No one creates a presentation perfectly the first time, so you will move, copy, and delete slides to improve your presentation. You'll even copy one of the slides from **rain2.ppt**. The presentation that you save in this lesson will not be complete. You will format the presentation in Lesson 3. When you are finished with this lesson, your presentation will resemble Figure 2 - 1a and Figure 2 -1b.

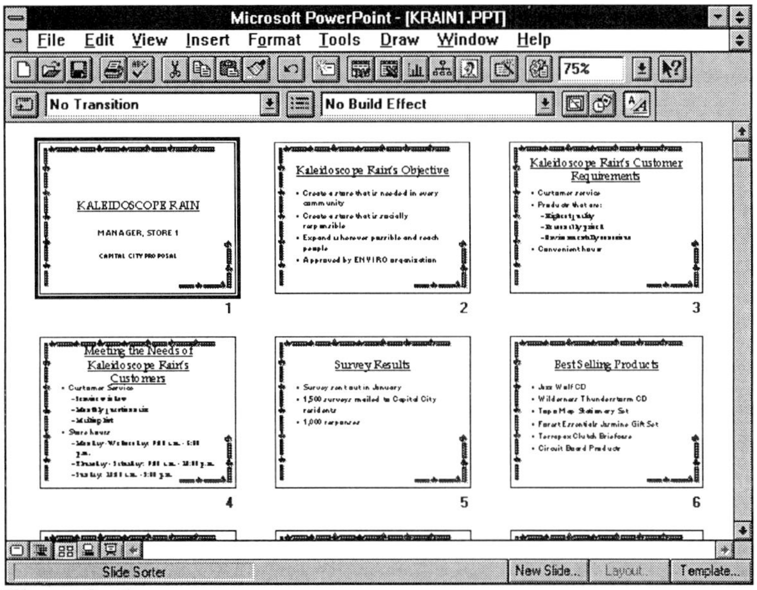

Figure 2 - 1a

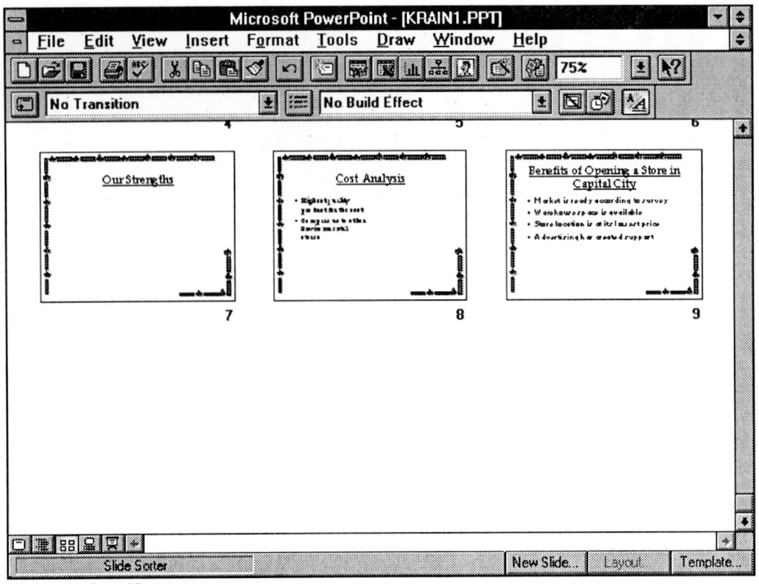

Figure 2 - 1b

CAUTION: *PowerPoint may be installed differently on each machine. Because of this, presentation features may be different. For example, the text for a presentation in color may be in italics on one machine, but regular text on another machine. This particular difference may also cause text to wordwrap differently. If this difference occurs for you, your screen may differ slightly from the figures.*

OPENING A PRESENTATION

You will continue to change the **rain1.ppt** and **rain2.ppt** presentations throughout this book. As you are working through the activities, you may decide to stop in the middle of the lesson. Once the presentation has been saved to a data disk, you can take a break, and if you close the presentation, you can open it up again at any time.

To open a presentation:

- If you are starting *PowerPoint* for the first time, click on the **Open an Existing Presentation** button in the **Startup** dialog box.
- If you are opening a presentation and you are already in *PowerPoint*, select **FILE/Open** or click on the **Open** button on the Standard toolbar.

  *The **Open** dialog box will appear on the screen.*
- The current drive appears in the **Drives** list box. If your file has been saved to a different drive, click on the ↓ at the right of the list box and click on the name of the drive that contains your data.
- The current directory is highlighted in the **Directories** list box. If your file has been saved in a different directory, double-click on the name of the directory containing your data.
- The file names are listed in alphabetical order in the **File Name** list box. Click on the name of the file you want to open. If the file name is not visible, click on the ↓ on the vertical scroll bar until the file name is visible and then click on it.
- Click on **OK**.

Activity 2.1: Opening the rain1.ppt Presentation

At the end of Lesson 1, you closed and exited *PowerPoint*. Now you want to open the **rain1.ppt** presentation and continue working where you left off.

1. Open *PowerPoint* if it is not already open.

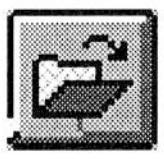

2. At the **Startup** dialog box, click on the **Open an Existing Presentation** button, and then click on **OK**. If you are already in *PowerPoint*, select **FILE/Open** or click on the **Open** button on the Standard toolbar.

   *The **Open** dialog box will appear on the screen (Figure 2 - 2).*

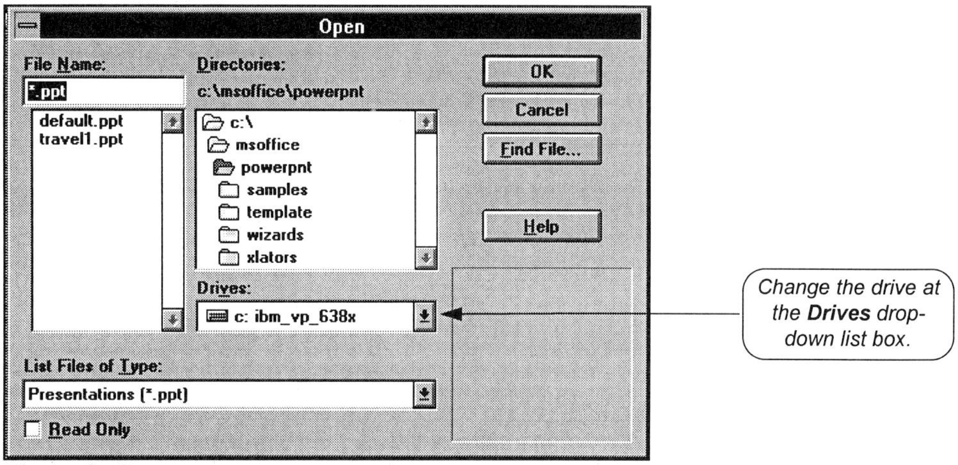

Figure 2 - 2

3. The first time you enter the **Open** dialog box the drive listing will be of the **c:** drive. Change the drive location to your data disk. To change the drive, click on the correct drive listed in the **Drives** list box.
4. Check to see that the correct directory is listed above the **Directories** list box. If not, double-click on the correct subdirectory.

   *The list of files on your data disk should appear in the **File Name** list box.*

5. Click on **rain1.ppt**.
6. Click on **OK**.

   *The **rain1.ppt** presentation should appear on the screen on Slide 1 in Slide View.*

MOVING AROUND THE PRESENTATION

Once you have more than one slide in your presentation, you will need to know how to move around in the presentation. There are two ways to move around in the presentation. One way is to use the **Previous** and **Next Slide** buttons located at the end of the vertical scroll bar. Another way is to use the scroll box in the vertical scroll bar.

To move to the previous slide:

- Click on the **Previous** button  located at the bottom of the vertical scroll bar.

To move to the next slide:

- Click on the **Next** button 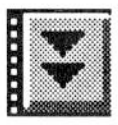 located at the bottom of the vertical scroll bar.

To move around the presentation using the vertical scroll bar:

- When you point to the scroll box and click and hold the left mouse button down, a tab will appear with a slide number. Drag the scroll box until you see the slide number you want; then release the left mouse button.

Activity 2.2: Moving Around the rain1.ppt Presentation

So far you have only seen Slide 1 of the **rain1.ppt** presentation in Slide View. In this activity, you will use the movement methods to move around the **rain1.ppt** presentation.

1. After opening the **rain1.ppt** presentation, you should be on Slide 1 as indicated on the left side of the Status bar.

2. Click on the **Next Slide** button at the bottom of the vertical scroll bar.

   You will move to Slide 2. The title of Slide 2 is Objective. Later on in the activities, when you move to a particular slide, you will probably edit the slide in some way or need to see information on that slide. For this activity only, you will move to the slide so you become familiar with the movement methods available in PowerPoint.

3. Click on the **Next Slide** button two more times to move to Slide 3, then Slide 4.

   Slide 3's title is Customer Requirements and Slide 4's title is Meeting the Needs.

4. Click on the **Previous Slide** button at the bottom of the vertical scroll bar.

   You will move back to Slide 3 (Customer Requirements).

5. Click the **Previous Slide** button two more times until you return to Slide 1.

6. The other method of movement involves using the scroll box in the vertical scroll bar. Point to the scroll box, and then click and hold the left mouse button down. A tab with the slide number will appear to the left of the vertical scroll bar (Figure 2 - 3). Drag the scroll box to Slide 6.

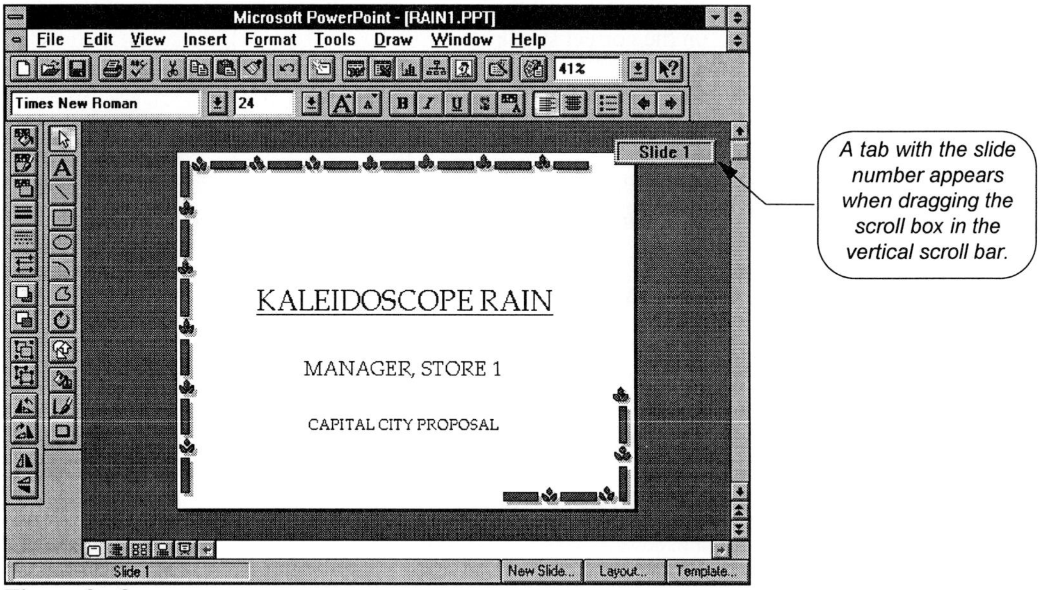

Figure 2 - 3

   Slide 6's title is Our Strengths.

7. Use the drag method to move to Slide 8, the last slide in the presentation.

   Slide 8's title is Next Steps.

8. Use the drag method to return to Slide 1.

EDITING TEXT

As mentioned in Lesson 1, in *PowerPoint* text is entered using placeholders. There are two types of placeholders. You have already seen preset placeholders. These placeholders are placed on a slide automatically when a particular AutoLayout is selected. When text has not yet been entered in a preset placeholder, a prompt will appear such as **Click to add text**.

The other type of placeholder is created using the Text Tool on the Drawing toolbar. You will use the Text Tool in Lesson 5. You will use the Text Tool when you want to add text that cannot be added using the preset placeholders (i.e., labels in a diagram).

Text entered using a preset placeholder can be edited in Slide View or Outline View. Text entered using the Text Tool can be edited in Slide View only.

Editing Text

When the mouse pointer appears over a text block, it will appear as an I-beam as in *Word* or *Excel.* This is true for text blocks as well as text boxes, such as the **Font** text box or the **Size** text box on the Formatting toolbar. Operations for editing text include inserting, deleting, copying, and moving text.

To insert text:

- Place the insertion point where you want to insert text, by moving the I-beam over the area and clicking once.
- Type the text to be inserted.

To delete text:

- One character at a time:
    - Press the **DELETE** key to delete text to the right of the cursor.
    - Press the **BACKSPACE** key to delete text to the left of the cursor.
- A block of text:
    - Point to the beginning of the text block.
    - Click once so that the text cursor is placed at the beginning of the text block.
    - Highlight the text block by dragging the mouse over the text.
    - Press the **DELETE** key.

Activity 2.3: Inserting and Deleting Text in the rain1.ppt Presentation

In this activity, you will edit the text of the **rain1.ppt** presentation by deleting the text created using the AutoContent Wizard and inserting the information about Kaleidoscope Rain.

1. After Activity 2.2 you should be on Slide 1 of the **rain1.ppt** presentation.

   *The text you will be entering will have some spelling errors. Type the words exactly as you see them. They are necessary for Activity 2.5: Spell Checking the **krain1.ppt** presentation.*

2. Use the **Next Slide** button to move to Slide 2.
3. Point to the Title (Objective).

   The I-beam appears when the mouse pointer is over text.

4. Click before the **O** in **Objective** so that the text cursor is placed before the **O** and the border appears around the text block (Figure 2 - 4).

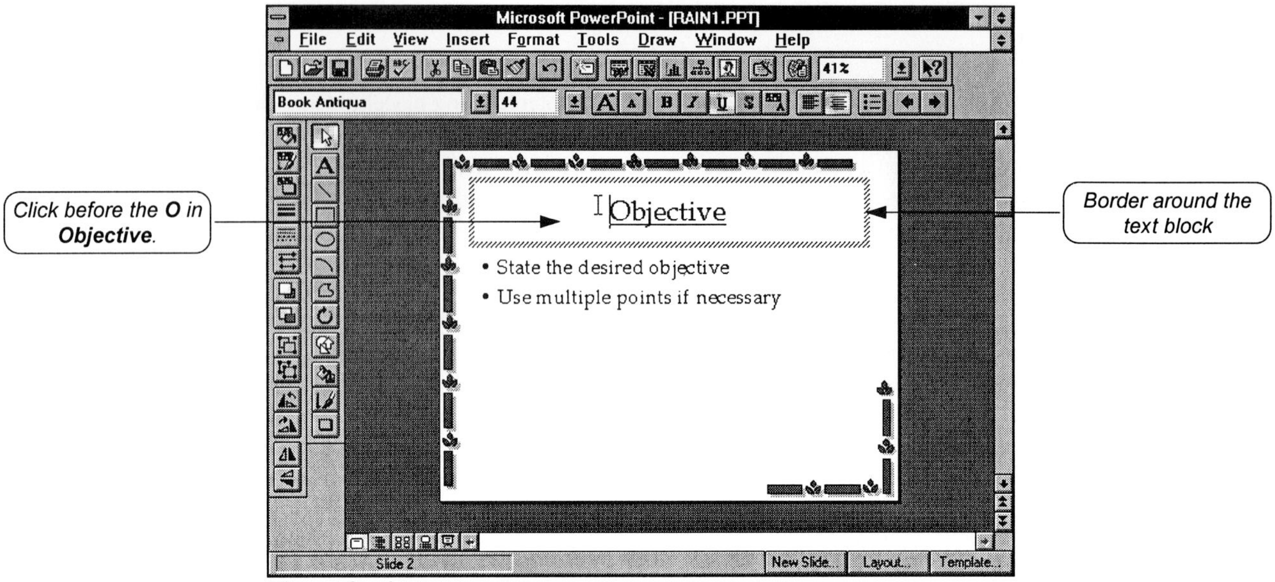

Figure 2 - 4

5. Type: **Kaleidoscope Rain's**
6. Press the **SPACEBAR** once.
7. Point before the **S** of **State** in the first bullet. The I-beam will appear. Click so that the text cursor appears before the **S** and the border around the bulleted text appears (Figure 2 - 5).

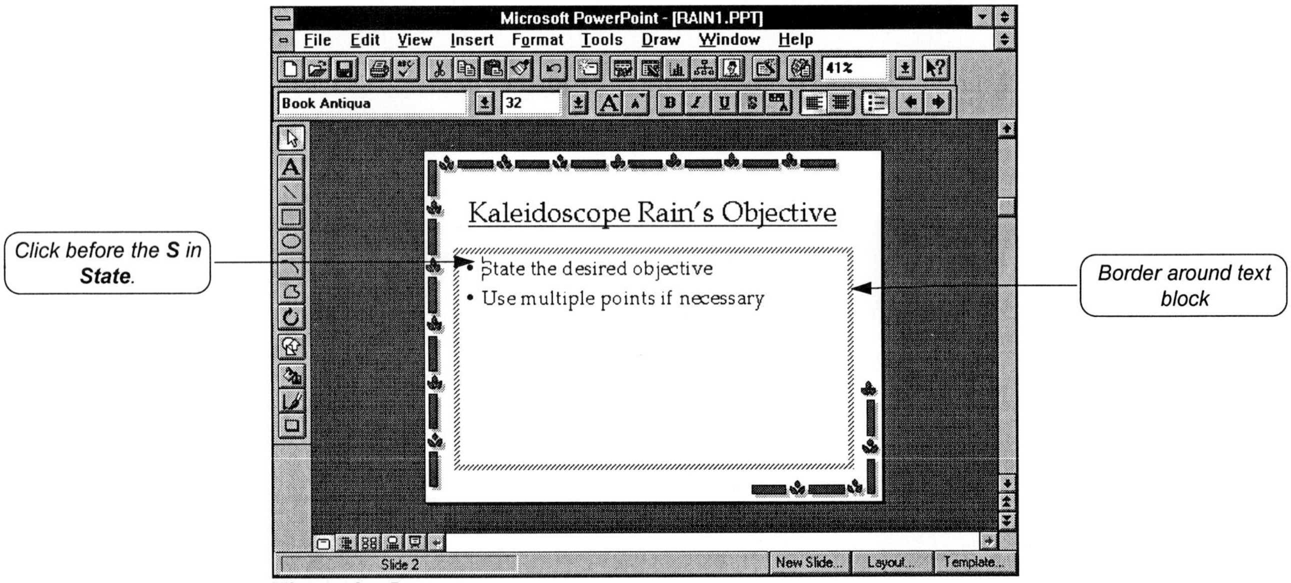

Figure 2 - 5

8. Press the **DELETE** key until the text for the first bullet has been deleted.
9. Type: **Create a store that is needed in every community**
10. Delete the text in the second bullet.
11. Type: **Create a store that is socially responsible**
12. Press **ENTER** to create another bullet.
13. Type: **Expand whereever possible and reach people**

    Slide 2 should resemble Figure 2 - 6.

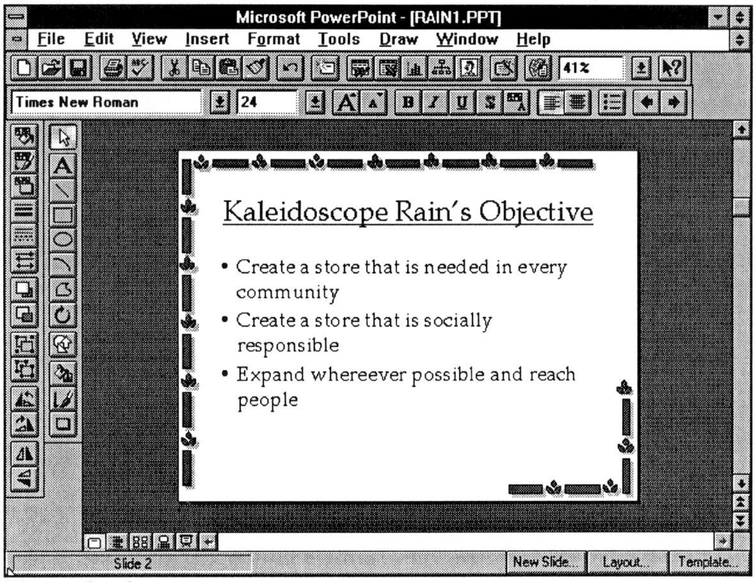

Figure 2 - 6

14. Use the **Next Slide** button to move to Slide 3.
15. Delete the text in bullet 1 and type: **Customer service**
16. Delete the text in bullet 2 and type: **Productts that are:**

    REMEMBER: *Enter bullet 2 with the typing error shown above.*

17. Press **ENTER**.
18. Press **TAB** and type: **Enveronmentally conscience**
19. Press **ENTER** and type: **Highest qualitie**
20. Press **ENTER** and type: **Resonalably prieced**
21. Press **ENTER**, and then press **SHIFT+TAB** to move back to Level 1 (Figure 2 - 7).

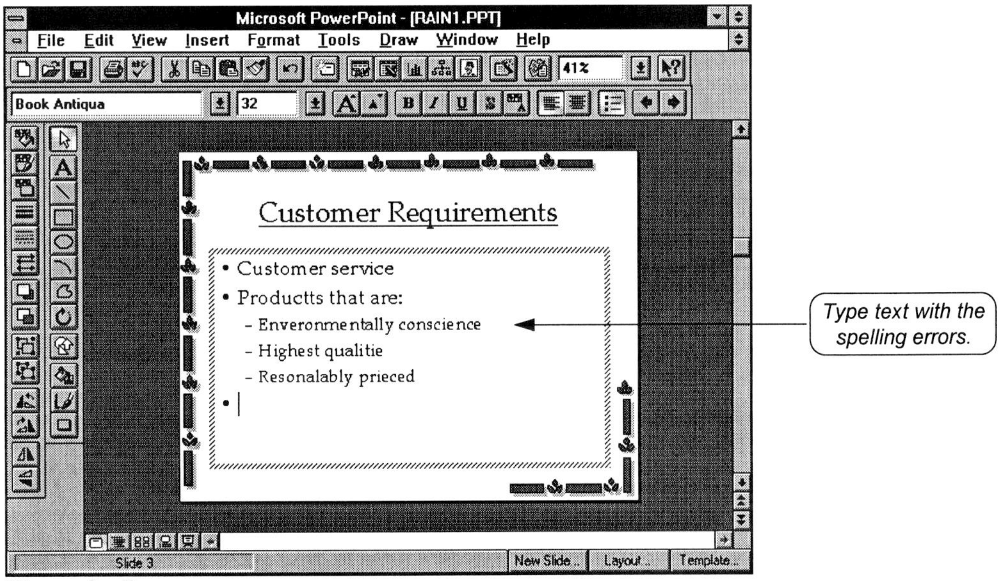

Figure 2 - 7

22. Type: **Conveenient ours**

23. Deselect the text block by clicking on a blank area of the slide.

    Slide 3 should resemble Figure 2 - 8.

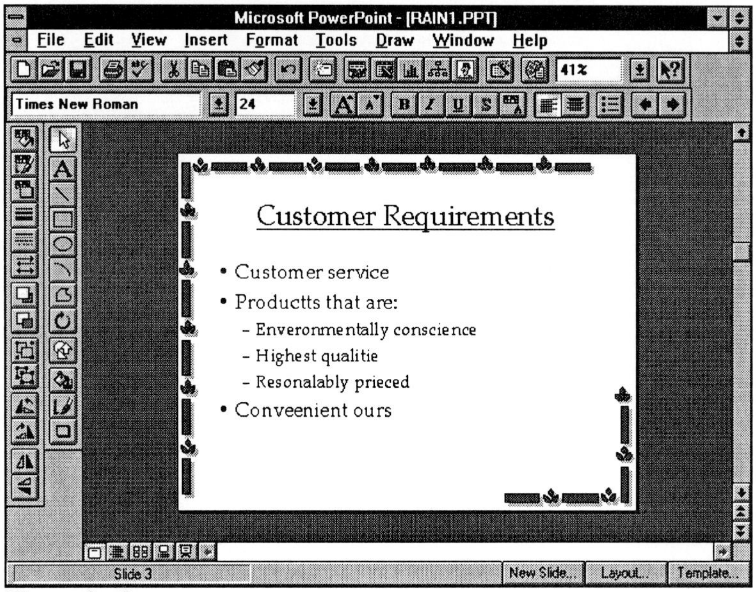

Figure 2 - 8

24. Save the presentation with the new name of **krain1.ppt**.

To move text:

- Point to the text block. Highlight the text you wish to move.
- Select **EDIT/Cut** or click on the **Cut** button on the Standard toolbar.
- Move the text insertion point to where you want to move the text.

  NOTE: *Text can be moved anywhere in the presentation. You can move text in the same text block, on the same page, or on a different page. Just move to the place where you want to insert the text before selecting **Paste**.*

- Select **EDIT/Paste** or click on the **Paste** button on the Standard toolbar.

  The highlighted text will be moved from the first location to the second location.

To copy text:

- Point to the text block. Highlight the text you wish to copy.
- Select **EDIT/Copy** or click on the **Copy** button on the Standard toolbar.
- Move the text insertion point to where you want to move the text.
- Select **EDIT/Paste** or click on the **Paste** button on the Standard toolbar.

  A copy of the highlighted text will be placed in the second location.

Activity 2.4: Moving and Copying Text in the krain1.ppt Presentation

In Activity 2.3, you started editing text in the **rain1.ppt**. In this activity, you will continue to edit text by moving and copying text.

1. After Activity 2.3 you should be on Slide 3 of the **krain1.ppt** presentation.
2. Use the **Previous Slide** button to move to Slide 2.
3. Highlight the text, **Kaleidoscope Rain's**, from the title.

4. Choose **EDIT/Copy** or click on the **Copy** button on the Standard toolbar.
5. Use the **Next Slide** button to move to Slide 3.
6. Place the text cursor before the **C** in **Customer Requirements** (Title).

7. Choose **EDIT/Paste** or click on the **Paste** button on the Standard toolbar.
8. Add a space between **Rain's** and **Customer** if necessary.

   Slide 3 should resemble Figure 2 - 9. Next, you will move the subbullet, ***Enveronmentally conscience****, below the subbullet,* ***Resonalably prieced****.*

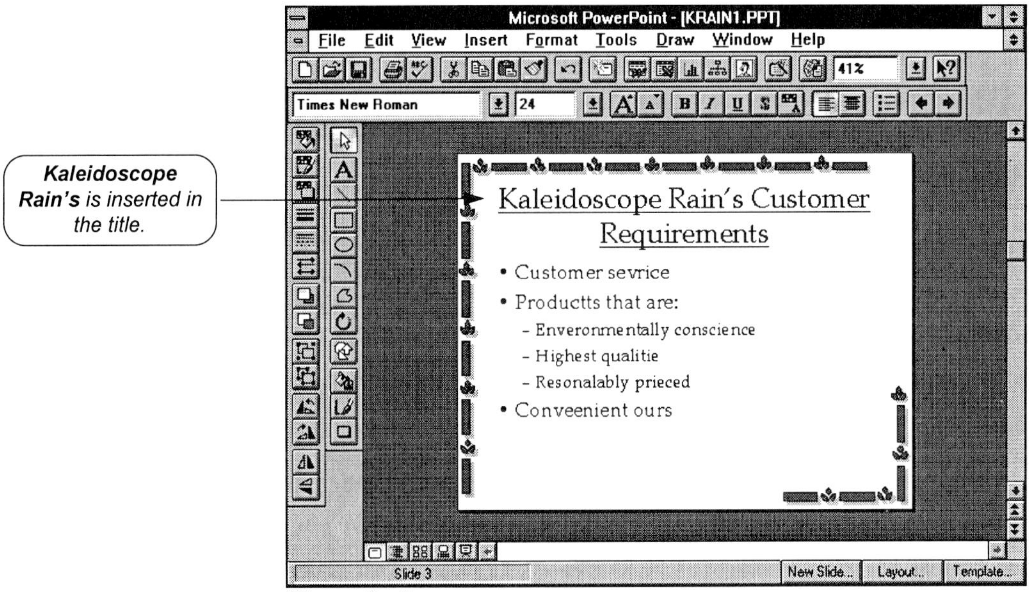

Figure 2 - 9

9. Highlight the subbullet, ***Enveronmentally conscience.***

10. Select **EDIT/Cut** or click on the **Cut** button on the Standard toolbar.

    Enveronmentally conscience *will be removed from the screen.*

11. Press the **BACKSPACE** key to delete the bullet shape.
12. Click at the end of the *Resonalably prieced* bullet so the text cursor appears.
13. Press **ENTER** so that a bullet shape appears. It should be on Level 2.
14. Select **EDIT/Paste** or click on the **Paste** button on the Standard toolbar.

    The ***Enveronmentally conscience*** *bullet will be placed next to the bullet shape. When you are finished Slide 3 will resemble Figure 2 - 10.*

15. Save the presentation using the same name.

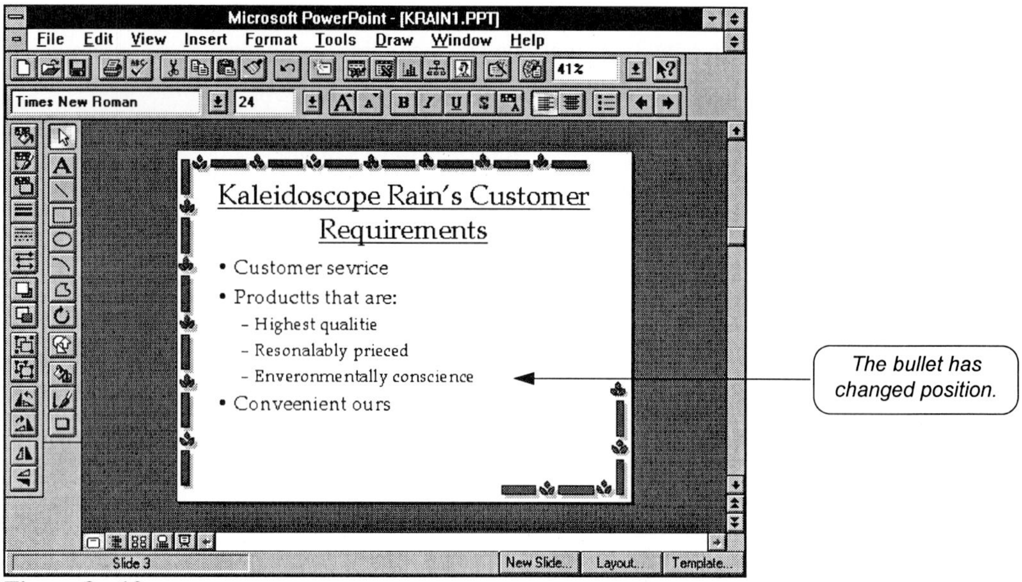

Figure 2 - 10

SPELL CHECKING THE PRESENTATION

After entering text in a presentation you will want to use the Spell Checker to correct any misspellings. After using a spell checker it is still important to proofread the presentation because the spell checker will not pick up words that have been spelled correctly but used incorrectly (i.e., *too* when *two* should be used).

To spell check the presentation using the Standard toolbar:

- Click on the **Spell Check** button.

  *PowerPoint begins the spell check process and will stop at the first potential error. The **Spelling** dialog box will appear in the bottom right corner of the screen.*

- A suggested spelling will appear in the **Change To** text box. A list of other suggestions may appear in the **Suggestions** list box below the **Change To** text box. You can continue the spell check process with the following actions:

  - Click on the **Ignore** button if you want to continue checking without changing the word.
  - Click on the **Ignore All** button if you want to ignore the current and all following examples of the current "misspelling."
  - To correct the word, place the correct spelling of the word in the **Change To** text box either by clicking on one of the listed suggestions or typing the correction in the **Change To** text box. Once the correct spelling appears in the **Change To** text box, click on the **Change** button to correct this occurrence of the misspelling.
  - To correct the word and all further occurrences of the word, place the correct spelling of the word in the **Change To** text box as listed above, then click on the **Change All** button.
  - There may be words that do not appear in the dictionary, such as proper names or acronyms. You may want to add these words to your dictionary so that the next time you spell check the words will not be flagged. To add the word to the dictionary, click on the **Add** button.

!

CAUTION: ***DO NOT** use the **Add** button for doing any of the activities in this book. If the **Add** button shows up in light print, it has been disabled on your computer.*

- If the Always Suggest feature allowing for the list of suggestions to appear has been disabled and you want to see a list of suggestions, click on the **Suggest** button.

- Once you have taken one of the above actions, the Spell Check process will continue to the next possible error. Continue to make selections for each of the flagged words. When Spell Check is complete, a prompt will appear on the screen stating, **Finished spell checking entire presentation**. Click on **OK**.

To spell check using the Menu bar:

- Select **TOOLS/Spelling**.
- The **Spelling** dialog box will appear on the screen and the process for spell checking at this point will be the same as using the Standard toolbar.

Activity 2.5: Spell Checking the krain1.ppt Presentation

Since you have entered text into your presentation, you will spell check the presentation. You purposely made some typing errors so that you will practice using the different Spell Checking features, but this will also help you find unintentional errors in your presentation.

1. After Activity 2.4 you should be on Slide 3 of the **krain1.ppt** presentation. Move to Slide 2.
2. Add the following bullet to Slide 2:

   Approved by ENVIRO organization

3. Click on the **Spelling** button on the Standard toolbar.

   *The **Spelling** dialog box appears in the bottom right corner of the screen (Figure 2 - 11).*

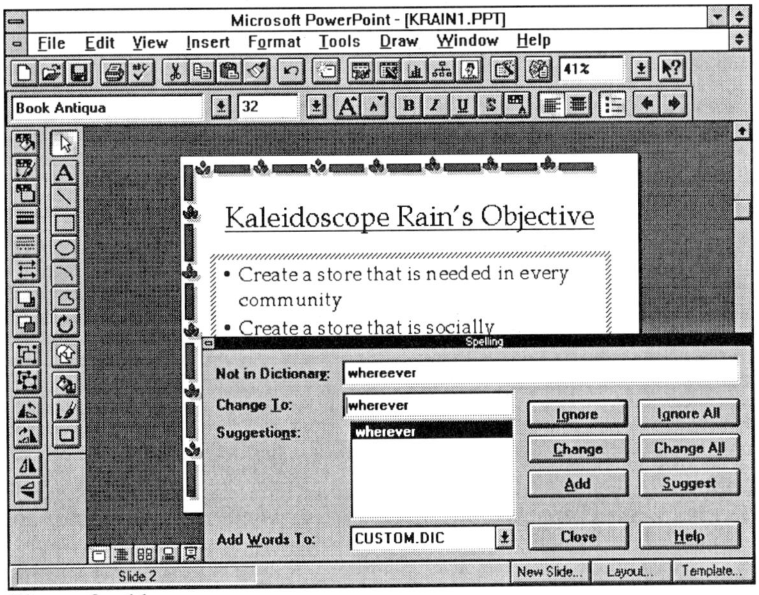

Figure 2 - 11

4. Unless you have made other typing errors, the first word to be flagged is **whereever** on Slide 2. The correct spelling is listed in the **Suggestions** list box and also placed in the **Change To** text box. Click on the **Change** button to change the spelling and move on to the next word.

   PROBLEM SOLVER: *If there are no suggestions listed in the **Suggestions** list box, click on the **Suggest** button.*

5. Continue correcting errors until **ENVIRO** on Slide 2 is flagged. **ENVIRO** is a proper noun that does not appear in the *PowerPoint* dictionary. Click on the **Ignore** button to continue spell checking.

6. Continue correcting errors until **Resonalably** on Slide 3 is flagged. There are no suggestions available for this misspelling. Highlight the text in the **Change To** text box and type: **Reasonably**. Then click on the **Change** button.

7. Continue spell checking until **Conveenient** or the last word misspelled in your presentation is flagged. A prompt should appear on the screen telling you that *PowerPoint* is finished spell checking the entire presentation.

   PROBLEM SOLVER: ***ENVIRO** may be flagged one more time. If this happens, click on the **Ignore** button.*

8. Click on **OK** to return to the presentation.

9. Proofread Slides 1, 2, and 3 to make sure there were no errors that were spelled correctly, but used incorrectly and change them.

   *There are two errors on Slide 3 that spell checking did not flag. Change **conscience** to **conscious** and **ours** to **hours**.*

10. Save the presentation using the same name.

USING VIEWS TO EDIT THE PRESENTATION

PowerPoint has four different Views or areas to work in (Slide View, Outline View, Slide Sorter View, and Notes Pages View), each one with its own editing focus. While working in *PowerPoint* you will probably spend most of your time in Slide View, because most of the editing you do will be applied to the one slide you are working on. However, the other Views are important for specific editing procedures.

Editing in Slide Sorter View

In Slide Sorter View you work with the whole presentation at once. In this View you will see miniature or thumbnail prints of each of the slides. This is where you will change the order of the presentation. You can copy, move, and delete slides in this View.

To copy a slide:

- Select Slide Sorter View, if necessary.
- Select a slide by clicking on it.

  A border will appear around the selected slide.
- Select **EDIT/Copy** or click on the **Copy** button  on the Standard toolbar.

  The slide will remain on the screen. No apparent change occurs. However, a copy of the selected slide has been place on the Windows clipboard.
- Select the slide *before* the intended insertion point or click in between slides so that a vertical line the length of a slide will appear between the two slides.
- Select **EDIT/Paste** or click on the **Paste** button  on the Standard toolbar.

  A copy of the initially selected slide will appear after the currently selected slide or at the point of the vertical line depending on the method of placement used.

To move a slide:

- Select Slide Sorter View, if necessary.
- Select a slide by clicking on it.

  A border will appear around the selected slide.
- Select **EDIT/Cut** or click on the **Cut** button on the Standard toolbar.

  The selected slide will disappear. It has been placed in the Windows clipboard.
- Select the previous slide before the intended insertion point or click in between slides so that a vertical line the length of a slide will appear between the two slides.
- Select **EDIT/Paste** or click on the **Paste** button on the Standard toolbar.

  The initially selected slide will appear after the currently selected slide or at the point of the vertical line depending on the method of placement used.

ALTERNATE METHOD: *If the presentation is not too long and all the slides involved are showing on the screen, you can also click on the slide to be moved, keep the mouse button depressed, and drag the slide to a new location.*

TIMESAVER: *Copying and moving can also be done between presentations. For example, if you have presentation 1 and presentation 2 open, you can copy or move slides from presentation 1 to presentation 2. The process is the same as copying or moving within the presentation. Just switch to the second presentation using the* ***Window*** *menu, as described and used in Lesson 1, before pasting the copied or moved slide.*

To delete a slide:

- Select Slide Sorter View, if necessary.
- Select a slide by clicking on it.

  A border will appear around the selected slide.
- Select **EDIT/Cut** or press the **DEL** key.

  The selected slide will be removed from the presentation.

TIMESAVER: *To select multiple slides, press the* ***SHIFT*** *key down before selecting additional slides after the first slide selection. A border will appear around each slide that you select. You can perform all the operations listed above with multiple slides as well as single slides. You can select random slides or a range of slides.*

Activity 2.6: Editing in Slide Sorter View

In Lesson 1, you created two presentations: **rain1.ppt** using the AutoContent Wizard and **rain2.ppt** using a blank presentation. You want to use a slide from the **rain2.ppt** presentation in the current presentation, **krain1.ppt**. You will copy the slide from the **rain2.ppt** presentation right into the **krain1.ppt** presentation. You will also change the order of the presentation by moving a slide and deleting an unwanted slide.

1. After Activity 2.5 you should be on Slide 3 of the **krain1.ppt** presentation. Switch to Slide Sorter View by clicking on the **Slide Sorter View** button at the bottom of the Slide Work Area. Your screen should be similar to Figure 2 - 12.

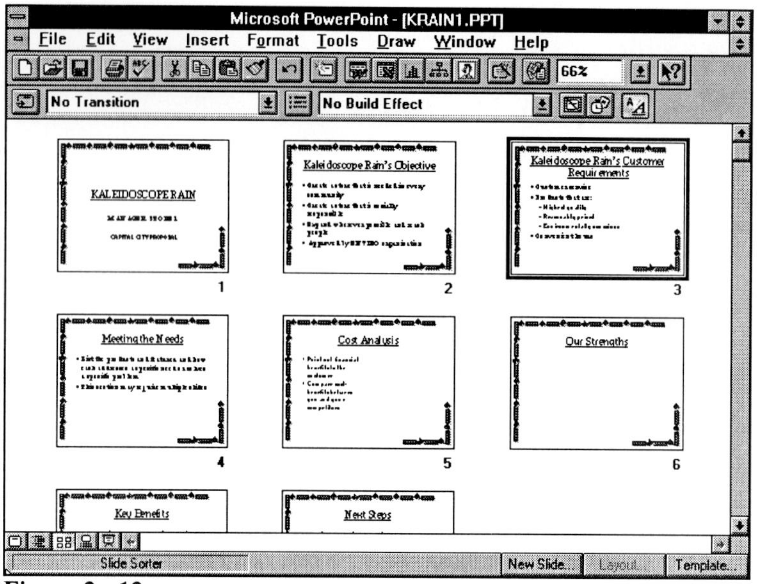

Figure 2 - 12

2. Open the **rain2.ppt** presentation by selecting **FILE/Open** from the Menu bar.

   *The **Open** dialog box will appear.*

3. Change the drive selection in the **Drives** list box if the drive with the data disk is not listed and double-click on the correct subdirectory in the **Directories** list box if you used a subdirectory.

   *A list of saved presentations should appear in the **File Name** list box.*

4. Click on the **rain2.ppt** presentation, and then click on **OK**.

   *The **rain2.ppt** presentation will appear on the screen on Slide 1 in Slide View.*

5. Click on the **Slide Sorter View** button.

6. Select Slide 2 by clicking on it.

   A border should appear around Slide 2.

7. Select **EDIT/Copy**.

8. Switch to the **krain1.ppt** presentation by clicking on the **Window** menu, then click on **1 KRAIN1.PPT**.

   You want the copied slide to appear after Slide 4.

9. Click on Slide 4 (Meeting the Needs).

10. Select **EDIT/Paste**.

    *Slide 2 from the **rain2.ppt** presentation (Best Selling Products) has been copied to the **krain1.ppt** presentation and is now Slide 5. Notice that the slide was automatically updated with the presentation style (Figure 2 - 13).*

11. Click on Slide 7 (Our Strengths). Keep the mouse button depressed and drag Slide 7 before Slide 6 (Cost Analysis). A gray vertical line will appear indicating placement for the slide (Figure 2 - 14).

    Slide 6 is now Our Strengths and Slide 7 is Cost Analysis.

12. Select Slide 9 (Next Steps).

13. Select **EDIT/Cut** or press the **DELETE** key.

    Slide 9 (Next Steps) will be deleted.

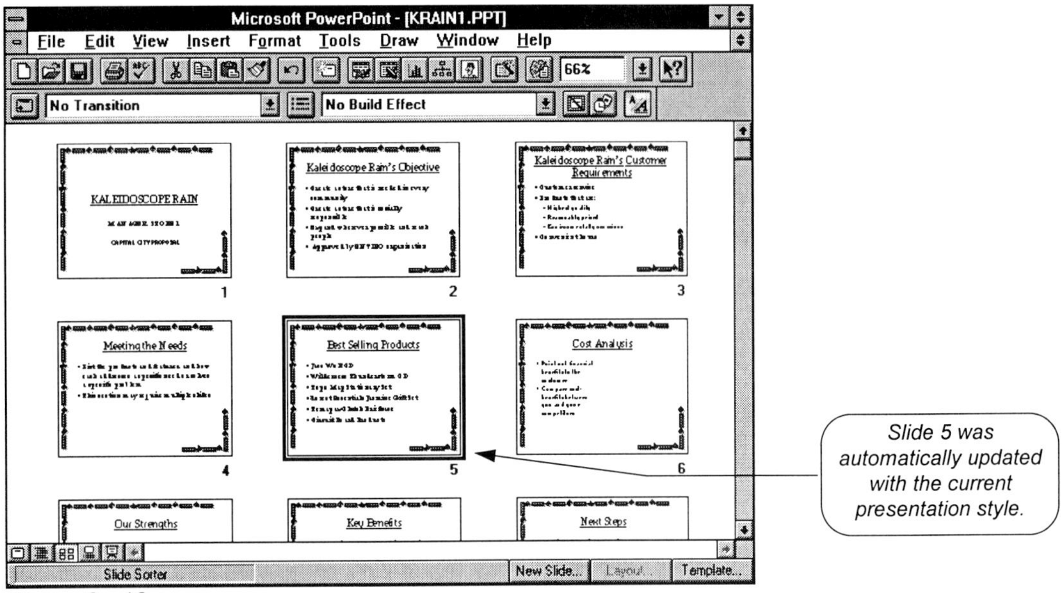

Figure 2 - 13

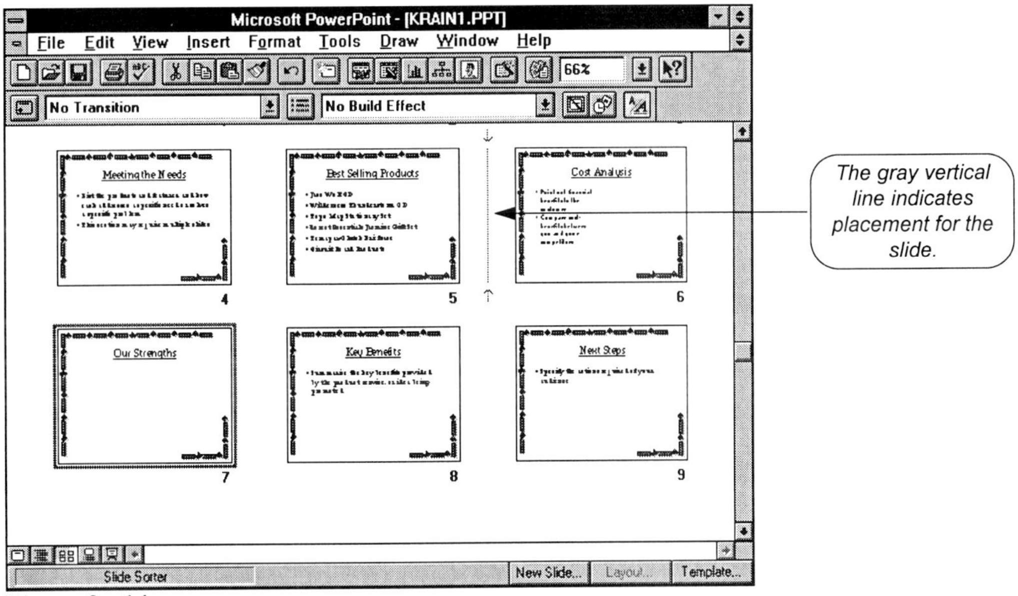

Figure 2 - 14

14. Save the presentation using the same name.
15. Switch to the **rain2.ppt** presentation using the **Window** menu.
16. Close the presentation without saving it.

Editing in Outline View

In Outline View, you work with all the text of your presentation at once in outline form. Because you see all your text on one screen, it becomes very easy to edit your text. For example, it is much easier to move a bullet from Slide 1 to Slide 5 in Outline View than it is to do it in Slide View. The basic operation is the same except in Slide View you have to add the step of moving to the correct slide, whereas in Outline View, you already have the text in front of you on the screen.

To create a new slide in Outline View:

- Select Outline View, if necessary.
- Place the text cursor on the first level of a slide below where you want to insert a slide. For example, if you want to create a new slide before Slide 2, place your cursor on the Title level of Slide 2.
- Press **ENTER**.

  A new number and slide icon will appear in the outline above the slide with the text cursor.
- Place the text cursor on the Title line of the new slide.
- Type the new text.

PROBLEM SOLVER: *If your cursor is on a level other than Level 1 or the Title Level, when you press **ENTER**, a new line will appear on the current level. To move up a level, click on the **Promote (Indent less)** button located on the Outlining toolbar to the left of the Slide Work Area.*

To move a slide in Outline View:

- Select Outline View, if necessary.
- Point to the Slide icon for the slide you want to move. It is located between the Slide number and the Slide Title on Level 1.

  A four-tipped arrow will appear indicating that you can move the text.
- Drag the slide to the desired location.

  Notice that the Title and all the subbullets move together. The Title and its subbullets is often called a family. Each family of text appears on one slide.

PROBLEM SOLVER: *Moving subbullets works the same way as moving slides. Instead of initially pointing to the Slide icon, point to the particular bullet. A four-tipped arrow will also appear indicating movement.*

To add a bullet to a slide:

- Select Outline View, if necessary.
- Place the text cursor at the end of the bulleted text preceding where you want to insert the new bullet.
- Press **ENTER**.

  A bullet symbol will appear with the text cursor blinking next to it.
- Enter text.

To promote or demote bullets:

In an outline, promoting a bullet means moving the bullet up a level or to the left one level. Demoting a bullet means moving the bullet down a level or to the right one level.

- Select Outline View, if necessary.
- Place the text cursor in the line you want to demote or promote.
- To promote a bullet, press the **SHIFT+TAB** keys or click on the **Promote (Indent less)** button on the Formatting toolbar or the Outlining toolbar.

The bullet will move to the left one tab stop or if the bullet is a second level bullet, it will become a new slide title (Level 1).

- To demote a bullet, press the **TAB** key or click on the **Demote (Indent more)** button on the Formatting or the Outlining toolbar.

  The bullet will move to the right one tab stop.

Activity 2.7: Editing in Outline View

You will switch to Outline View to edit the rest of the text in the presentation. In Outline View you will see all the text for the presentation. This will make it easier to edit the text and check the flow of the presentation.

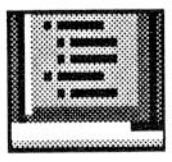

1. After Activity 2.6 you should be in Slide Sorter View. Switch to Outline View by clicking on the **Outline View** button at the bottom of the Slide Work Area.

   Outline View appears on the screen.

2. Use the vertical scroll bar to move up until you see Slide 4 (Meeting the Needs) on the screen.
3. Place the text cursor at the end of **Meeting the Needs**.
4. Press the **SPACEBAR** and type: **of Kaleidoscope Rain's Customers**
5. Highlight the text for Bullet 1 on Slide 4 and press the **DELETE** key.
6. Type: **Customer Service**
7. Press **ENTER**, and then **TAB**.
8. Type the following subbullets. Press **ENTER** after the first two lines.

   Service window

   Monthly questionnaire

   Mailing list

   *After pressing **ENTER**, the insertion point remains at the same level as the last bullet. After typing in the subbullets, your outline should resemble Figure 2 - 15.*

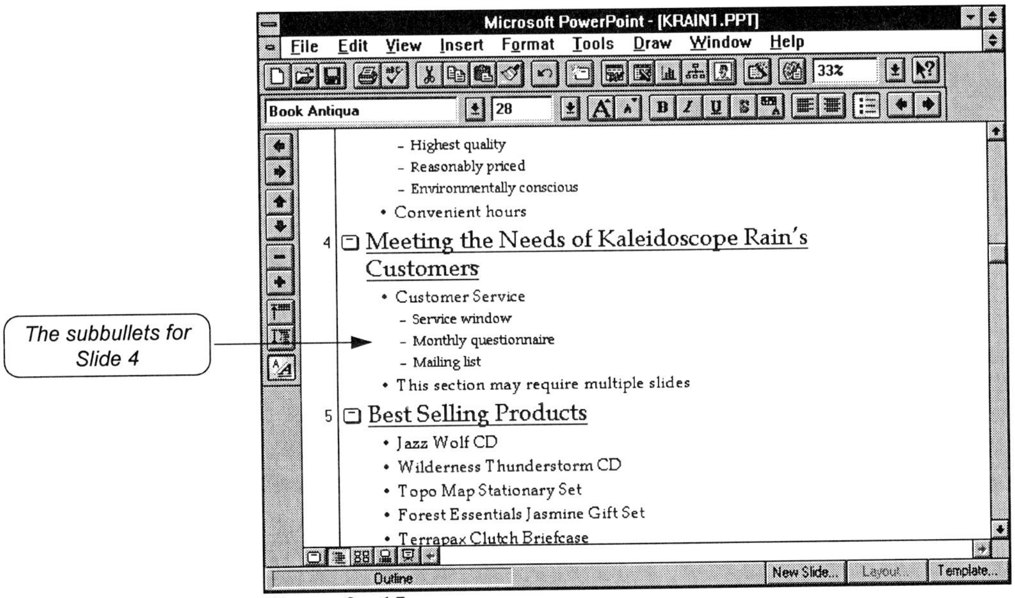

Figure 2 - 15

9. Highlight and delete the text for Bullet 2 of Slide 4.
10. Type: **Store hours**
11. Press **ENTER**, and then **TAB**.
12. Type the following subbullets. Press **ENTER** after the first two lines.

    Monday - Wednesday: 9:00 a.m. - 8:00 p.m.

    Thursday - Saturday: 9:00 a.m. - 10:00 p.m.

    Sunday: 10:00 a.m. - 5:00 p.m.

    After typing the subbullets, your outline will resemble Figure 2 - 16.

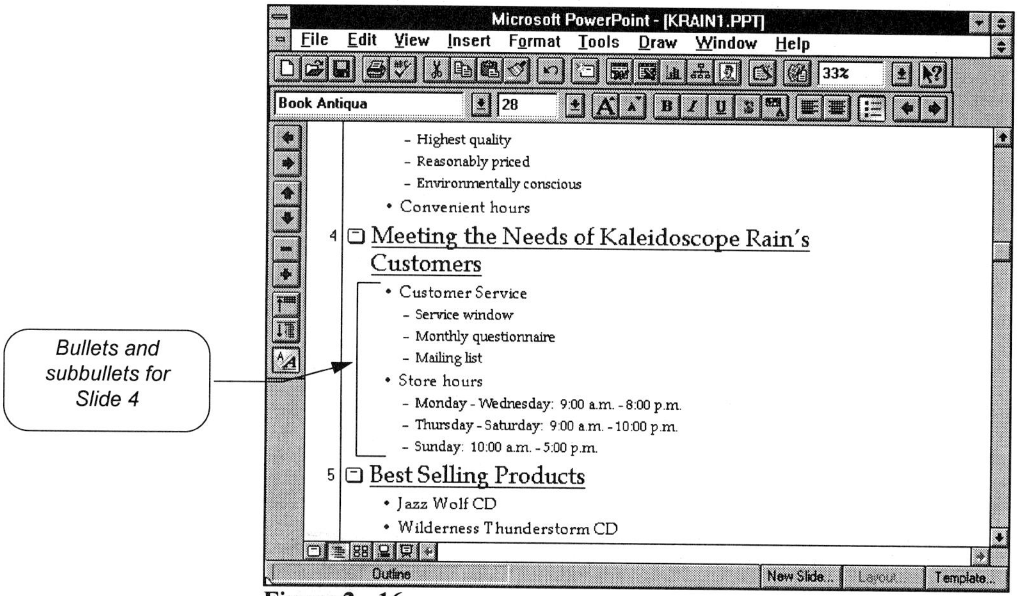

Figure 2 - 16

13. Delete the text on Slide 7 (Cost Analysis) and type the following text:

    Bullet 1: **Highest quality product for the cost**

    Bullet 2: **Compare us to other Environmental stores**

    ✓ **PROBLEM SOLVER:** *If you delete the bullets as well as the text, the text cursor will appear at the beginning of the next slide. If this happens, place the text cursor at the end of the title of Slide 7 (Cost Analysis) and press* ***ENTER****. Then press the* ***TAB*** *key and begin typing the bulleted text. If you delete the text and the bullets remain, you can place the text cursor on one of the bulleted text lines and begin typing.*

14. Edit the title of Slide 8 (Key Benefits) so that it reads, **Benefits of Opening a Store in Capital City**.
15. Delete the bullet on Slide 8 and type the following text:

    Bullet 1: **Market is ready according to survey**

    Bullet 2: **Warehouse space is available**

    Bullet 3: **Store location is at its lowest price**

    Bullet 4: **Advertising has created support**

Your outline should resemble Figure 2 - 17. Notice that on Slide 8 a survey is mentioned. The presentation hasn't mentioned this survey yet. You are going to add the slide that addresses the survey now.

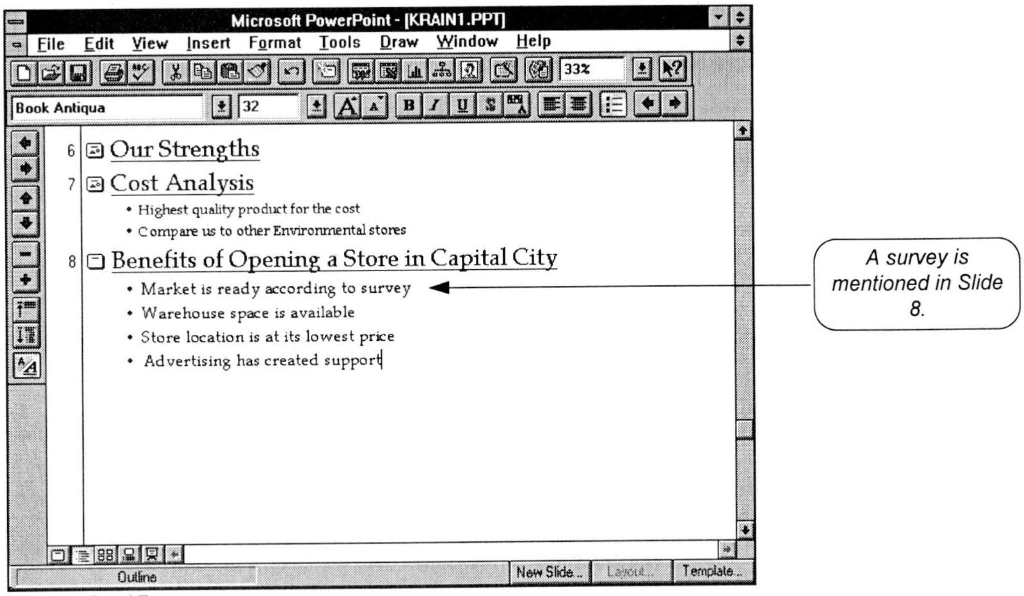

Figure 2 - 17

16. After typing the bullets for Slide 8, place the text cursor at the end of the bulleted text and press **ENTER**.

    Another bullet appears on the same level as the previous bullet.

17. Click on the **Promote (Indent less)** button on the Outlining toolbar.

    Slide 9's slide icon appears on the screen.

18. Type the following text for the slide:

Title:	**Survey Results**
Bulleted text:	**Survey sent out in January**
	1,500 surveys mailed to Capital City residents
	1,000 responses

    This slide is not complete yet. However, this is all the editing you can do in Outline View. In Lesson 4 you will add a graph to this slide. After entering Slide 9 you realize you really want it to appear above Slide 5. You will move Slide 9 (<u>Survey Results</u>) above Slide 5 (<u>Best Selling Products</u>).

19. Point to the slide icon for Slide 9 so that the four-tipped arrow appears (Figure 2 - 18).

20. Drag Slide 9 above Slide 5. When you click and hold the left mouse button down, the entire Slide 9 will become selected. As you drag up to Slide 5 a horizontal line will appear to guide the placement of the new text (Figure 2 - 19).

    <u>Survey Results</u> is now Slide 5 and <u>Best Selling Products</u> is now Slide 6.

21. Save the presentation using the same name.

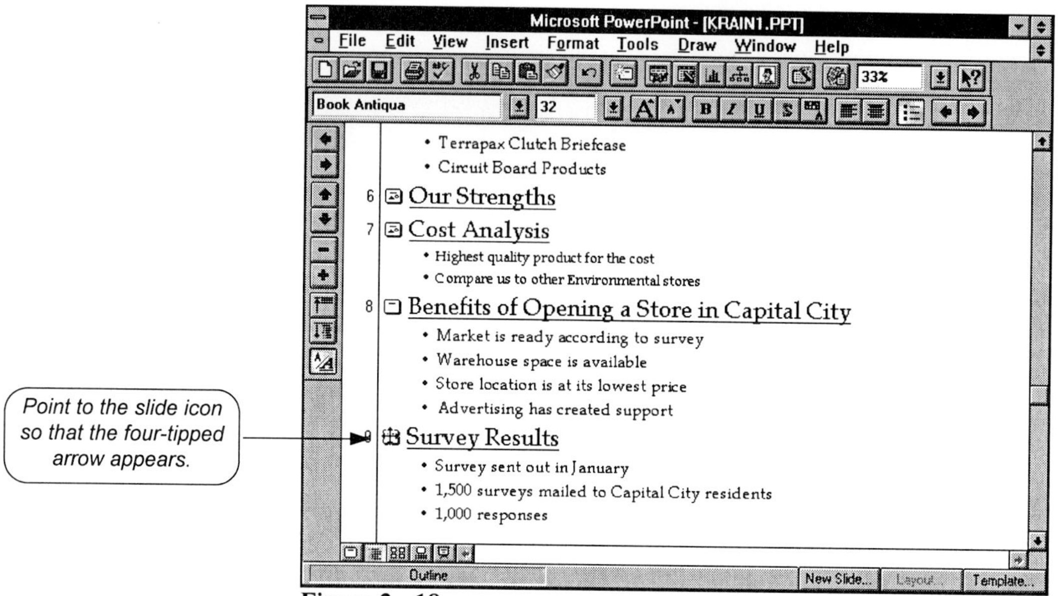

Figure 2 - 18

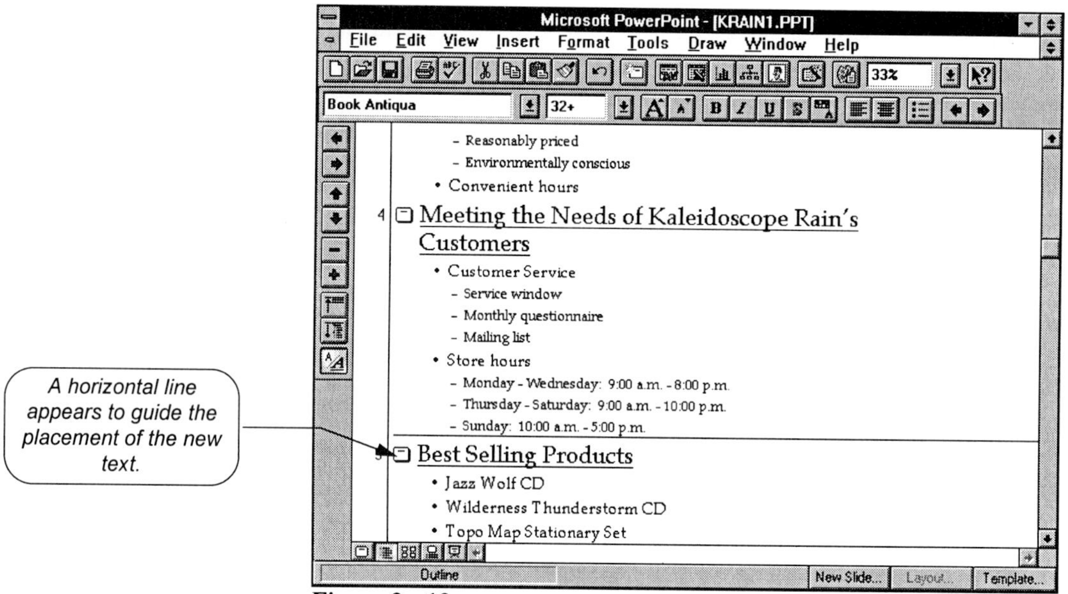

Figure 2 - 19

Adding Notes in Notes Pages View

You may want to create Speaker's note pages to go along with the presentation. You can use these notes to help you guide the presentation. Another possible purpose for creating notes on the bottom of the page is to create a handout for your audience that can be handed out along with the presentation. This might be a good place to define terms that are used in the slides or adding details, thus allowing for the use of as few words as possible on the actual slides.

To insert text in Notes Pages View:

- Click on the text placeholder at the bottom of the page.

  A text cursor appears in the text block.

- Type the desired text.

When you enter text in Notes Pages View, you will want to change the Zoom Control of the text so that you can read it.

To change the Zoom Control:

- Click on the ↓ located to the right of the **Zoom Control** list box on the Standard toolbar.

  A list of magnification percentages will appear.

- Click on the desired magnification.

Depending on how you created your presentation, your notes pages may be in either landscape or portrait orientation. Landscape is a page that measures 11 by 8 ½ and portrait is a page that measures 8 ½ by 11. In most cases you will want your notes pages to have a portrait orientation.

To change the orientation of notes pages:

- Choose **FILE/Slide Setup** from the Menu bar.

  *The **Slide Setup** dialog box will appear on the screen.*

- Click on the desired orientation under the **Notes, Handouts, Outline** section.
- Click on **OK**.

Activity 2.8: Adding Notes in Notes Pages View

You want to add notes at the bottom of the page that can be handed out to the owners of Kaleidoscope Rain.

1. After Activity 2.7 you should be in Outline View. Switch to Notes Pages View by clicking on the **Notes Pages View** button at the bottom of the Slide Work Area.

   The Notes page for the Slide the text cursor was on appears on the screen. The orientation of the Notes page should be portrait. You will change it to landscape so that you can see the difference between the two orientations; then you will change the orientation back to portrait.

2. Choose **FILE/Slide Setup**.

   *The **Slide Setup** dialog box appears on the screen (Figure 2 - 20).*

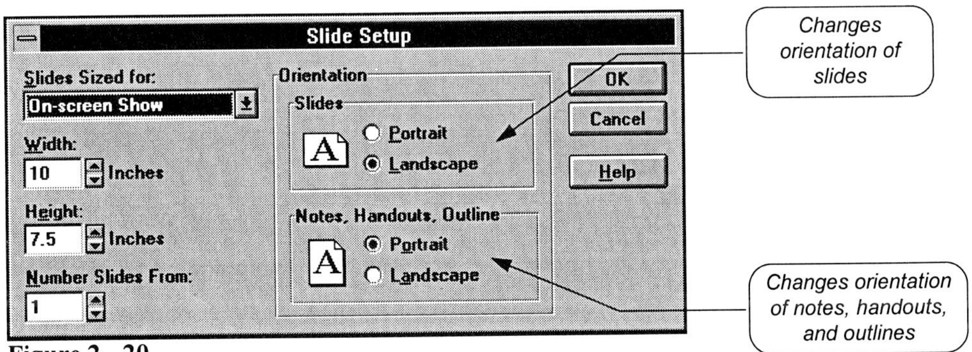

Figure 2 - 20

3. Click on the **Landscape** button in the **Notes, Handouts, Outline** section, and then click on **OK**.

The orientation of the page changes to landscape. The slide is still on the top of the page with the notes section on the bottom of the page. However, it is proportioned differently because of the orientation (Figure 2 - 21).

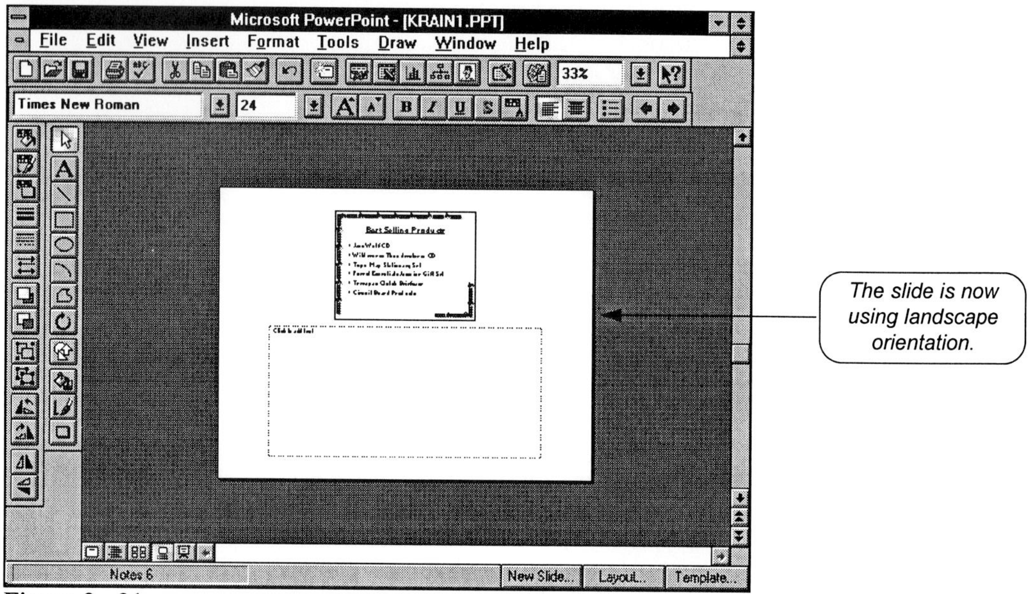

Figure 2 - 21

4. Change the orientation of the Notes page back to Portrait by following steps 2 and 3.
5. Move to Notes 6, if necessary, using the **Previous** or **Next Slide** buttons.
6. Click on the text placeholder at the bottom of the page.

   The text cursor begins to blink in the top left corner of the text block. However, it is very small. You will change the magnification of the page using the Zoom Control on the Standard toolbar.
7. Click on the ↓ next to the **Zoom Control** list box on the Standard toolbar.

   A list of the available magnifications will drop down (Figure 2 - 22).

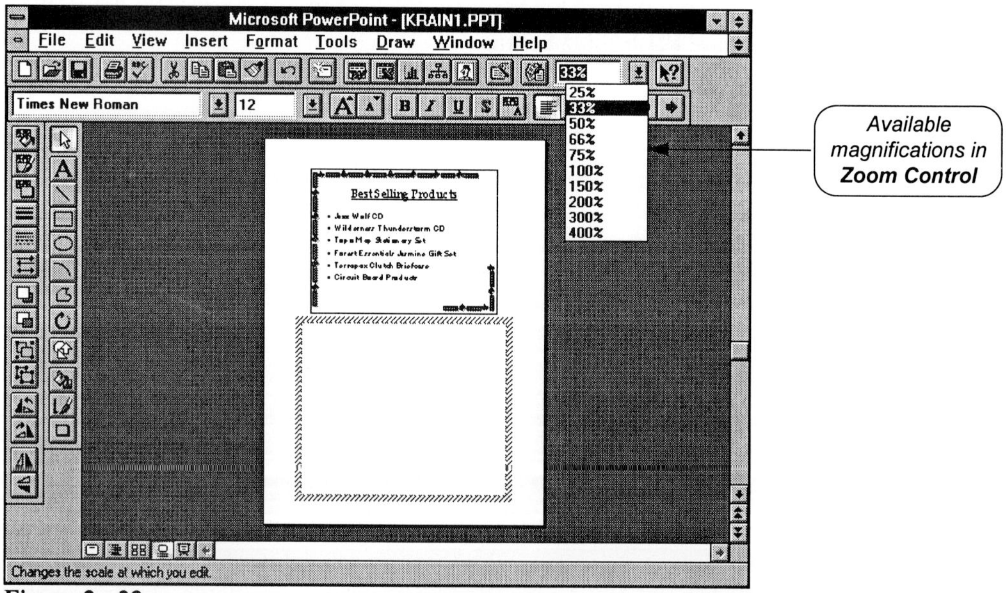

Figure 2 - 22

8. Click on **100%**.

   The magnification of the page will change to 100% and it will be much easier to read the text.

9. Type the following notes pressing **ENTER** at the end of each line, including the last line:

   Jazz Wolf CD: $15.98, 500 sold since January

   Wilderness Thunderstorm CD: $15.98, 345 sold since January

   Topo Map Stationary Set: $7.95, 700 sold since January

   Forest Essentials Jasmine Gift Set: $24.95, 300 sold since January

   Terrapax Clutch Briefcase: $130.00, 150 sold since January

   Circuit Board Products:

10. Type the following subitems for *Circuit Board Products*. Press **TAB** to move one tab stop, and press **ENTER** at the end of each line.

    Chess Set, $170.00

    Wall Clock, $31.95

    Desk Clock, $25.95

    Clipboard, $7.95

    3-Ring Binder, $10.50

    Money Clip, $19.95

    Earrings, $15.95

    After the notes have been typed, your screen should be similar to Figure 2 - 23.

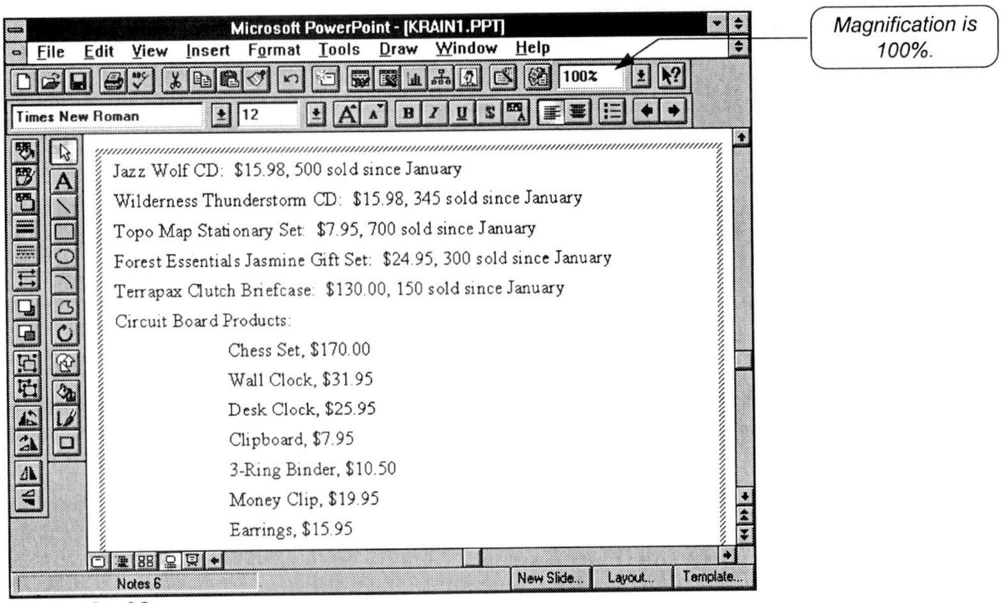

Figure 2 - 23

11. Use the **Zoom Control** list box on the Standard toolbar to change the magnification to **33%**.
12. Deselect the text by clicking on a blank area of the note page.
13. Change to Slide View.

14. Save the presentation using the same name.
15. Close the presentation.
16. Exit from *PowerPoint*.

SUMMARY

In this lesson you have completed the basic tasks of editing a presentation. After saving the **rain1.ppt** presentation in Lesson 1, you learned how to open the presentation in this lesson. You saw how to move around the presentation using the **Previous** and **Next** buttons and the vertical scroll bar. You edited text and learned how to spell check your presentation. Finally, you learned how to edit your presentation using the different views that are available in *PowerPoint*. In Lesson 3 you will open the **krain1.ppt** presentation and continue working with the presentation to format it.

KEY TERMS

Copy
Cut
Delete
Demote (Indent more)
Insert
Landscape
Move
Next Slide
Opening
Paste
Portrait
Previous Slide
Promote (Indent less)
Slide Setup
Spell Check
Zoom

INDEPENDENT PROJECTS

The four independent projects allow you to practice the basic skills involved in editing presentations: opening a presentation, moving around a presentation, editing text, spell checking a presentation, and editing a presentation in Outline View, Slide Sorter View, and Notes Pages View. The independent projects are continuations of those started in Lesson 1. You will open those presentations saved at the end of Lesson 1 and edit them using the topics covered in this lesson.

Independent Project 2.1: Editing a Presentation for History Class

In Independent Project 1.1 you created a presentation using the AutoContent and Pick a Look Wizards that when completed will be used to give a presentation to an American History class on Ellis Island. In Independent Project 1.1, just the layout of the presentation was created. The AutoContent Wizard created slides with text that act as placeholders and also prompt you for information, which can be a great timesaver. You selected the design for the presentation using the Pick a Look Wizard.

In this Independent Project you will edit the text of the **ellis1.ppt** presentation so that the information of the presentation will be about Ellis Island. Refer back to Independent Project 1.1 to review the plan for this presentation.

1. Open the *PowerPoint* program, if it is not already open.
2. Click on **OK** in the **Tip of the Day** dialog box if it appears.
3. At the **Startup** dialog box, choose **Open an Existing Presentation**, then click on **OK**, and open the **ellis1.ppt** presentation.

   NOTE: *If you are already in PowerPoint, select **FILE/Open**, and then follow Step 3.*

4. Switch to Outline View.
5. Delete the title for Slide 2 (<u>Introduction</u>) and type: **Objectives of Presentation**

6. Delete the bullets on Slide 2. Type the following text:

   To discuss the importance of Ellis Island in American History

   To discuss the process of immigration

7. Delete the bullet on Slide 3. Type the following text:

   History of Ellis Island

   Definition of Immigration

   Causes of Immigration to the U.S.

8. Delete the title of Slide 4 (<u>Topic One</u>) and type: **History of Ellis Island**

9. Delete the bullets on Slide 4 and type the following text:

   One natural and two artificial islands, joined by causeways in New York Bay

   Originally called Oyster Island by the early Dutch colonists

   Later called Gibbet Island after a pirate was hanged there in 1765

   Sam Ellis bought the island during 18th century and gave it his name

10. Place the text cursor at the end of the last bullet in Slide 4 and press **ENTER**.

11. Click on the **Promote (Indent less)** button on the Outlining toolbar.

12. Type: **History of Ellis Island (Continued)**

13. Press **ENTER** then click on the **Demote (Indent more)** button on the Outlining toolbar. Type the following text:

    New York State bought it from Ellis

    The Federal government bought it in 1808 and used it as a federal arsenal

    Became a headquarters for immigration in 1892

    Two additional islands were created in 1898 and 1905

14. Repeat the process listed in steps 11 and 12 to create a continuation slide for the *History of Ellis Island*. Use the same title as Slide 5 and the following text:

    By 1947 approximately 20 million immigrants had passed through Ellis Island

    Closed in 1954 due to decline in immigration

    In 1990 became a museum

15. Delete the text from Slide 7 (<u>Topic two</u>) and type the following text:

Title:	**Definition of Immigration**
Bulleted text:	**Transfer of residence from one country to another, regarded from the standpoint of the country in which the new residence is taken**

16. Delete the text from Slide 8 (<u>Topic Three</u>) and type the following text:

Title:	**Causes of Immigration to the U.S.**
Bulleted text:	**Transformation of industry by the factory system**
	Shift from small-scale to large-scale farming
	Wars
	Political oppression
	Religious persecution

17. Click on the **Slide Sorter View** button at the bottom of the Slide Work Area.

18. Select Slide 9 (Real Life), Slide 10 (What This Means), and Slide 11 (Next Steps) by selecting Slide 9, then pressing the **SHIFT** key down before clicking on Slide 10 and Slide 11.
19. Press the **DELETE** key.
20. Click on the **Notes Pages View** button at the bottom of the Slide Work Area.
21. Use the scroll box in the vertical scroll bar to move to *Notes 4.*
22. Click on the ↓ to the right of the **Zoom Control** list box on the Standard toolbar to see a list of magnifications, and then click on **100%**.
23. Click in the notes placeholder and type: **"Ellis Island," Microsoft (R) Encarta. Copyright (c) 1993 Microsoft Corporation. Copyright (c) 1993 Funk & Wagnall's Corporation.**
24. Highlight the following text from the note: **Microsoft (R) Encarta. Copyright (c) 1993 Microsoft Corporation. Copyright (c) 1993 Funk & Wagnall's Corporation.**
25. Click on the **Copy** button on the Standard toolbar.
26. Use the **Next Slide** button at the bottom of the vertical scroll bar to move to *Notes 7.*
27. Click in the notes placeholder and type: **"Immigration,"**
28. Press the **SPACE BAR** once.
29. Click on the **Paste** button on the Standard toolbar.
30. Change the magnification back to **33%** using the **Zoom Control** list box on the Standard toolbar.
31. Click on the **Spelling** button on the Standard toolbar and follow the prompts to spell check the presentation.
32. Click on the **Slide Sorter View** button at the bottom of the Slide Work Area.
33. Save the presentation as **ellis2.ppt**. Your presentation should resemble Figure 2 - 24.

NOTE: *The Zoom Control in Figure 2 - 24 was changed to 65% so that all the slides in the presentation could fit on the screen. Your screen may be slightly different because of the magnification.*

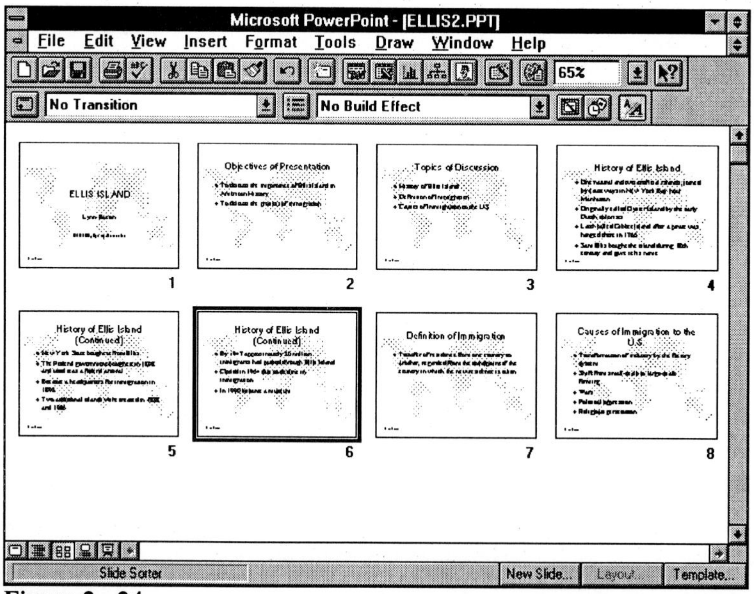

Figure 2 - 24

34. Print the presentation as **Handouts (2 slides per page)** using the **Black & White** print option.
35. Close the presentation and exit *PowerPoint* or continue with the next project.

Independent Project 2.2: Editing a Presentation for the Browning Museum

You have saved the presentation created in Independent Project 1.2 as **brown1.ppt**. You will open the **brown1.ppt** presentation and add additional slides for the presentation that you have just received from Susan Whitney, the Director of Development. You are going to add the slides in Outline View because you know this is the best view for editing text. After adding the slides, you will spell check the presentation and print it out so that Susan Whitney can make changes to the presentation. You will then add her editing changes to the presentation, save, and then print the presentation again so that the rest of the museum staff can read the presentation and add their comments.

1. Open the *PowerPoint* program, if it is not already open and open **brown1.ppt**.
2. Switch to Outline View by clicking on the **Outline View** button at the bottom of the Slide Work Area.
3. Place the cursor at the end of the last bullet of Slide 4 and press **ENTER**.
4. Click on the **Promote (Indent less)** button on the Outlining toolbar.

NOTE: *Use the* ***Promote (indent less)*** *button and the* ***Demote (indent more)*** *button on the Outlining toolbar as needed while adding the following slides.*

KEYBOARD ALTERNATIVE: *To indent more using the keyboard, press the* ***TAB*** *key. To indent less using the keyboard, press the* ***SHIFT+TAB*** *keys.*

5. Type the following text for Slide 5:

Title:	**Annual Strawberry Craft Festival**
Bulleted text:	**Held at Williams Park**
	Craft vendors come from all over the tri-state area
	Hours: 9:00 - 7:00, rain or shine (tents are set up)
	Saturday and Sunday before Memorial Day
	Over 700 craft enthusiasts attended last year
	For information contact: Nancy Hall-Duncan at (214) 454-8998

6. Follow steps 3 and 4 to add Slide 6 to the presentation.
7. Type the following text for Slide 6:

Title:	**Annual Patio Arts Festival**
Bulleted text:	**Held at Browning Museum on the Patio**
	Artists come from all over the country
	Hours: 10:00 - 5:00, rain or shine (use Museum if it rains)
	Saturday and Sunday of Independence Weekend
	Over 500 art enthusiasts attended last year
	For information contact: Nancy Hall-Duncan at (214) 454-8998

8. Follow steps 3 and 4 to add Slide 7 to the presentation.

9. Type the following text for Slide 7:

Title:	**Museum Gift Shop International Bazaar**
Bulleted text:	**Held at the Museum Store**
	Spectacular gifts from all over the world are showcased
	Different countries every year
	Bazaar held during November
	For information contact: Elizabeth Kelly at (214) 454-8980

10. Follow steps 3 and 4 to add Slide 8 to the presentation.
11. Type the following text for Slide 8:

Title:	**Natural History Galleries**
Bulleted text:	**Hands-on activities**
	Mounted specimens
	Mammals in Diorama
	Minerals and Fossils
	Wigwam Model
	National Children's Museum Award last year
	For information contact: Mary Mulligan at (214) 454-8981

12. Click on the **Spelling** button on the Standard toolbar to spell check the presentation. Follow the prompts for each flagged word.
13. Save the presentation as **brown2.ppt**. Your presentation should resemble Figure 2 - 25.
14. Print the presentation as **Handouts (2 slides per page)**. Use the **Black & White** option to print.

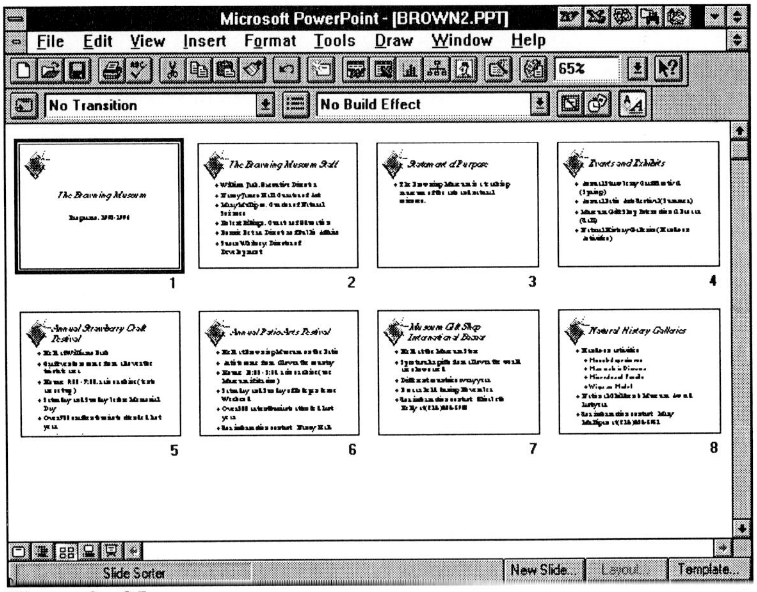

Figure 2 - 25

15. Print the presentation again using **Handout (3 slides per page)**.
16. Close the presentation and exit *PowerPoint* or continue with the next project.

Independent Project 2.3: Editing a Presentation for Julie's Travel Agency

Julie has had a chance to read through the copy of the presentation that you printed out in Independent Project 1.3. She has some changes for you to make, as well as some additional slides to add to the presentation. In this project you will add the additional charts in Outline View, make text changes in Slide View, and change the order of the presentation in Slide Sorter View. The presentation will not be complete at the end of this project. Formatting will be done in Independent Project 3.3.

1. Open the *PowerPoint* program, if it is not already open, and open **travel1.ppt**.
2. Change to Outline View.
3. Add a slide after Slide 3 and type the following text:

   Title: **Airline Ticket Information**

   Bulleted text: **Lowest consolidator**

   Cheapest ticket quotations

   - **Tourist**
   - **Discount**
   - **Domestic**

4. Add a slide after Slide 4 and type the following text:

   Title: **Railway Information**

   Bulleted text: **Quick quotes and agent assistance**

   - **Amtrak**
   - **Eurail**
   - **Britrail**

   English Channel crossings from Dover to Calais

   - **Ferry**
   - **Hovercraft**

   London to Paris and Brussels Chunnel rates on Eurostar

5. Add a slide after Slide 5 and type the following text:

   Title: **Tour Information**

   Bulleted text: **Current tours**

   - **Alpine Europe**
   - **South America**
   - **Galapagos Islands**
   - **Kenya**

6. Add a slide after Slide 6 and type the following title: **Most Popular Travel Places**
7. For the bullets, type four destinations you would like to visit.
8. Switch to Slide View.
9. Edit the text in the title of Slide 3 to read: **Additional International Services**.
10. Delete the subbullet, **Amtrak**, from the bulleted text on Slide 5.
11. Switch to Slide Sorter View.

12. Move Slide 4 (Airline Ticket Information) after Slide 2 (Available Services).
13. Spell check the presentation.
14. Save the presentation as **travel2.ppt**. Your presentation should resemble Figure 2 - 26.

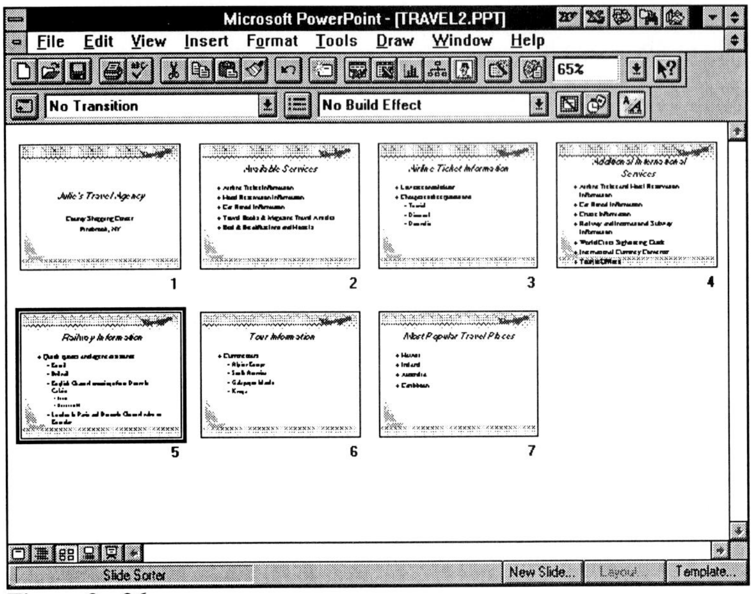

Figure 2 - 26

15. Print the **Outline View** of the presentation.
16. Close the presentation and exit *PowerPoint* or continue with the next project.

Independent Project 2.4: Editing a Presentation for a Training Program

The **train1.ppt** presentation was created in Independent Project 1.4. You created the presentation using the Training selection of the AutoContent Wizard. In this Independent Project, you will edit the text of the AutoContent Wizard. You will use the Introduction section of this book and On-line help to get the information that you need. You will edit the text in Outline View, and edit the flow of the presentation in Slide Sorter View.

1. Edit the titles of the following slides as indicated:

   Slide 2: **Starting PowerPoint**

   Slide 3: **Parts of the PowerPoint Screen**

   Slide 4: **Views in PowerPoint**

   Slide 5: **Getting On-line Help**

2. Use the Introduction of this book and On-line help to create the bullets that you will type on each of these slides. You will need to replace the text that is there with your text.
3. Switch to Slide Sorter View and delete Slides 6, 7, 8, and 9.
4. Change the presentation style using the Template option.
5. Spell check the presentation.
6. Save the presentation as **train2.ppt**. The structure of your presentation will be similar to Figure 2 - 27.

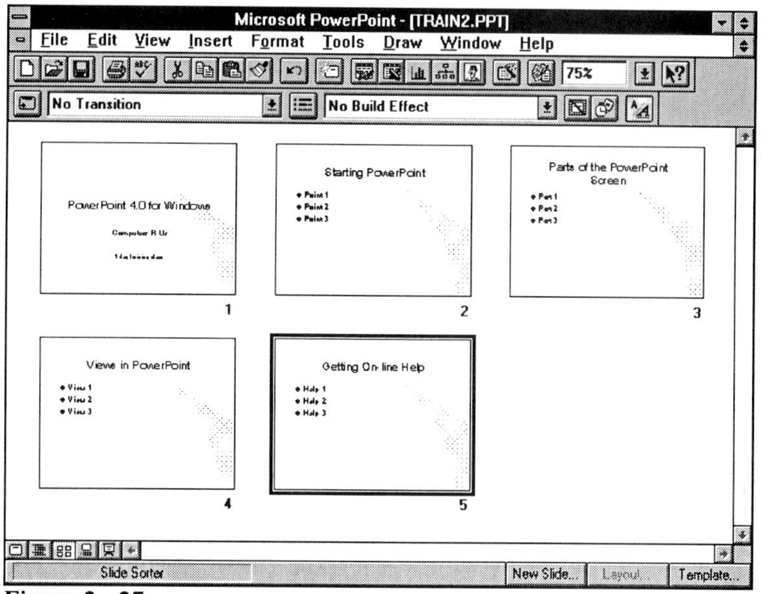

Figure 2 - 27

7. Print the presentation using the **Handouts (2 slides per page)** option. Use the **Black & White** print option.

Lesson 3 Formatting a Presentation

Objectives

In this lesson you will learn how to:

- Edit text attributes
- Align text
- Change line spacing of text
- Change the case of text
- Turn bullets on and off
- Edit the bullet symbol
- Change the size of a text block
- Change the layout of a slide
- Add the date, time, or page number to a Master
- Change a Slide Master
- Create a slide that is different from the Slide Master
- Hide objects that appear on the Slide Master

PROJECT DESCRIPTION

In Lesson 2, you edited the **rain1.ppt** presentation. The text has been added to the presentation. All the ideas for the presentation that can be expressed using text only have been added. The real impact of the presentation, however, is the actual style and delivery of the presentation. A presentation may have a message or an idea, but it can get lost if the style of the presentation is not effective. In this project, you will format the **krain1.ppt** presentation using the following features of *PowerPoint*: formatting the text, changing the layout of the slide, and using master pages. The presentation that you save in this project will not be complete. In the next two lessons, you will add additional elements (objects). You will add two different types of objects to your presentation. In Lesson 4 you will work with application objects — objects that are created using different applications, such as *Word* or *Excel*. In Lesson 5 you will work with drawing objects. These are shapes, lines, or arcs that are created using tools in *PowerPoint*. However, the text will be completely formatted. When you are finished with this lesson, your presentation will resemble Figure 3 - 1 and Figure 3 - 2.

TEXT FORMATTING

Once text is entered into your presentation, you will want to accentuate or highlight specific words or you may decide that you want to change the font, font style, or size of the text. There are two ways to edit text attributes: using the Formatting toolbar and using the Menu bar. In this lesson you will look at the basic text attribute features of bold, italic, underline, shadow, font, and text size.

Also in this lesson, you will look at other formatting features that are available for text, which include changing the alignment of text, changing the line spacing of text, changing the case of text, and formatting the bullet style that appears with text.

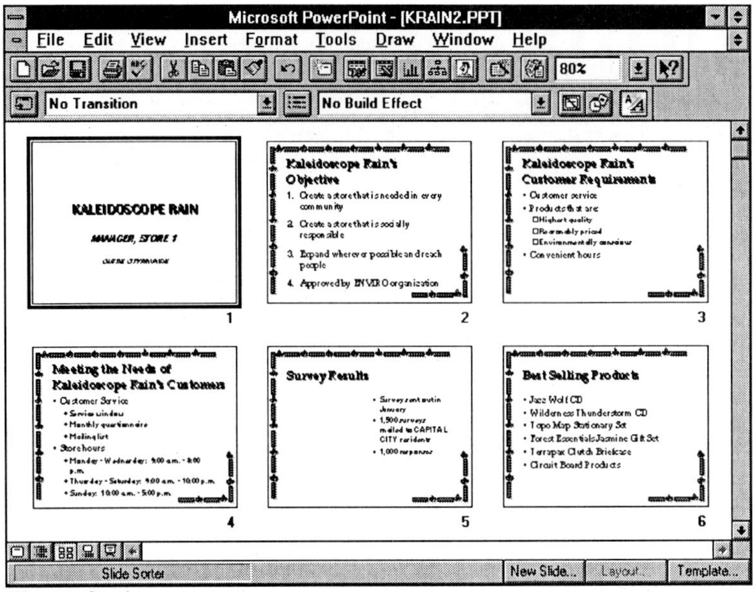

Figure 3 - 1

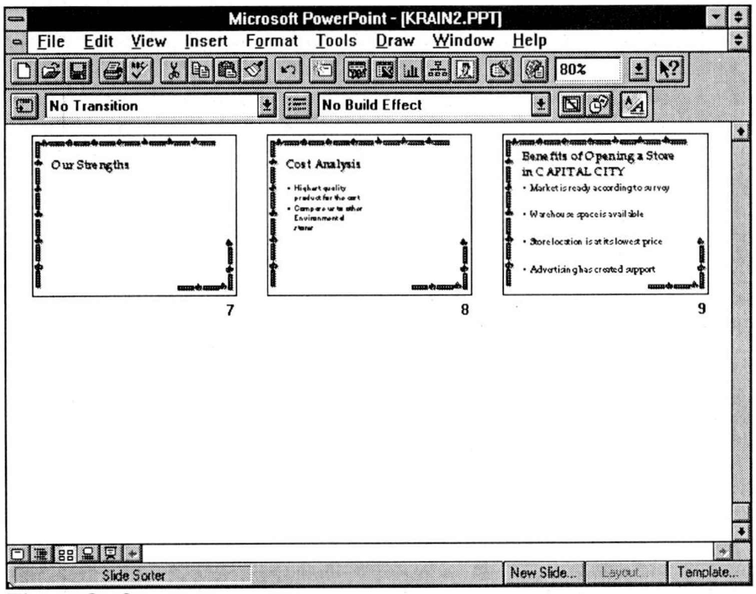

Figure 3 - 2

To edit text attributes using the Formatting toolbar:

- If you want to edit the attributes of a portion of a text block, you must first highlight the text you wish to format. If you want to edit the attributes of the whole text block, select the text block by first clicking in the text block so that the text cursor and the border of the text block appear; then click on the border so that eight handles (or squares) appear around the border.
- Click on the option on the Formatting toolbar that you desire.
  - To select *bold*, *italic*, *underline* or *shadow*, click on the corresponding button.
  - To select a font or text size, click on the ↓ to unfold the appropriate list; then click on the desired font or text size.
  - To increase text size automatically to the preset sizes as listed in the **Size** list box, click on the **Increase Font Size** button.

- To decrease text size automatically to the preset sizes as listed in the **Size** list box, click on the **Decrease Font Size** button.

The selected attribute will be applied to either the highlighted text or the selected text block.

To edit text attributes using the Menu bar:

- Highlight the text you wish to change.
- Choose **FORMAT/Font**.

  *The **Font** dialog box appears with selections for font, font style, size, effects, and color.*
- Make the desired attribute selection.
  - To select a new font attribute, click on the desired font in the **Font** list box. Use the ↑ and ↓ to see the entire list. Fonts are listed alphabetically.
  - To select a new font style, click on the desired style in the **Font Style** list box.
  - To select a new text size, click on the desired text size in the **Size** list box. Use the ↑ and ↓ to see the entire list. Sizes are listed in ascending order.
  - To select the Underline font style, click in the **Underline** check box in the **Effects** section.
- Click on **OK** to return to the presentation and apply the selected text attribute(s).

  TIME SAVER: *Using the Menu bar is the easiest way to add multiple text attributes. You can make as many changes as you want in the **Font** dialog box before clicking on **OK** and returning to the presentation.*

Activity 3.1: Editing Text Attributes in the krain1.ppt Presentation

In this activity you will accentuate text of the **krain1.ppt** presentation so that it stands out. With a presentation you want to get a point across to the audience. Editing text attributes is one way of highlighting text so that it is brought to your audience's attention.

1. Open the **krain1.ppt** presentation. You should be on Slide 1.
2. Select the Title text block (Kaleidoscope Rain) by first placing the text cursor in the text block, and then clicking on the border of the text block so that handles appear around the text border (Figure 3 - 3).

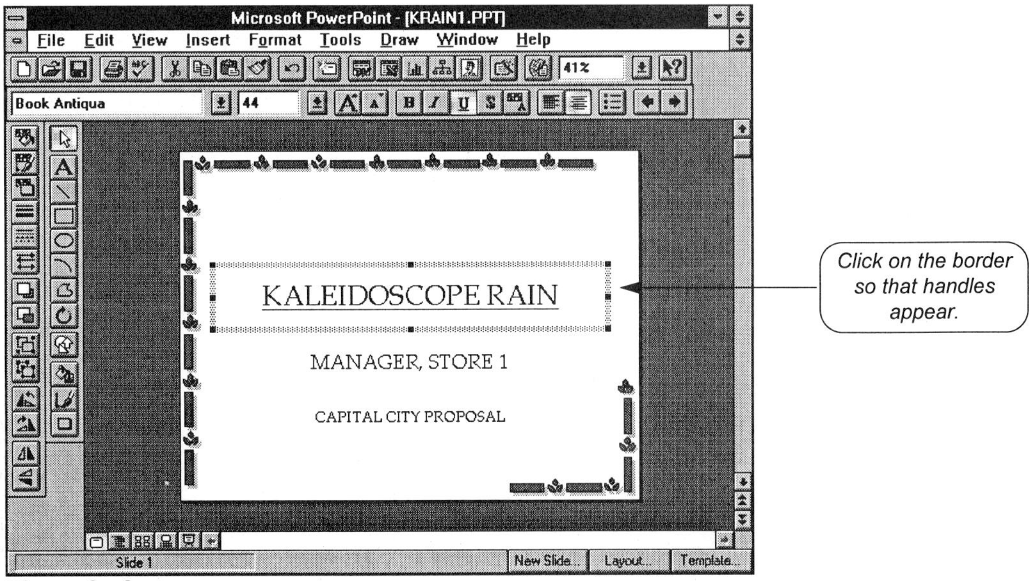

Figure 3 - 3

3. The current text size of the title is **44 pt.**, according to the **Size** list box. Click on the **Increase Font Size** button twice to increase the text size to **54 pt**.
4. The size looks a little too big, so you will decrease the font size to **50 pt**. Since 50 pt. is not listed in the **Size** list box, click on **54**, which is showing in the **Size** text box on the Formatting toolbar. **54** should be highlighted. Type: **50** and press **ENTER.**
5. Make sure the title is still selected. You want to take the underlining off of the title. Click on the **Underline** button of the Formatting toolbar.

   It is currently depressed. When you click on it, it will no longer be depressed and the underlining will be removed from the title.
6. Select **Bold** and **Shadow** by clicking on both of the buttons on the Formatting toolbar so that they are depressed. **Shadow** may already be depressed.
7. Select the **Britannic Bold** font by clicking on the ↓ next to the **Font** text box to unfold the **Font** list, and then clicking on the font name.

   PROBLEM SOLVER: *If the **Britannic Bold** font is not available on your machine, select a different font.*
8. Select the subtitle so that handles appear around the text block.

   PROBLEM SOLVER: *It may appear that the last line of text, **Capital City Proposal**, is part of the subtitle text block. It is not. You will need to select the third line separately to apply text attributes.*
9. Choose **FORMAT/Font.**

   *The **Font** dialog box appears on the screen (Figure 3 - 4). You will use the dialog box to change the font, font style, and font size.*

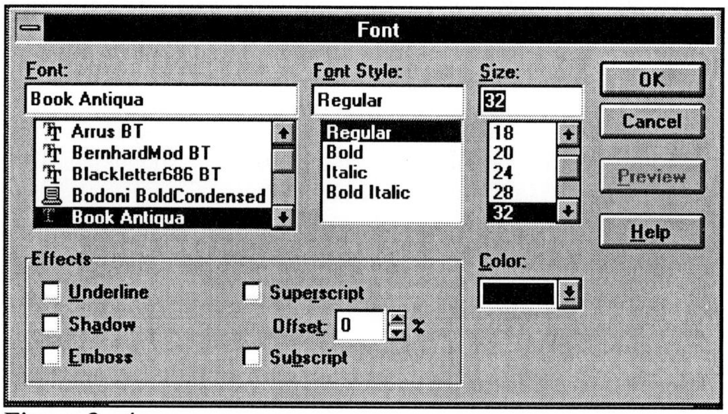

Figure 3 - 4

10. Select the **Britannic Bold** font from the **Font** list box or the font you selected in step 7.
11. Select **Bold Italic** in the **Font Style** list box.
12. Select a size of **36 pt.** from the **Size** list box.
13. Click on **OK** to return to Slide 1.

    The Britannic Bold font, Bold Italic font style, and 36 point size should be applied to the subtitle.
14. Select the third line of text, **Capital City Proposal**, so that handles appear around the text border.

15. Click on the **Decrease Font Size** button to decrease the text size from **24 pt.** to **20 pt.**

16. Click on the **Italic** button on the Formatting toolbar.
17. Deselect the text by clicking in a blank area of the slide.

    When you are finished making these text attribute changes, Slide 1 should resemble Figure 3 - 5.

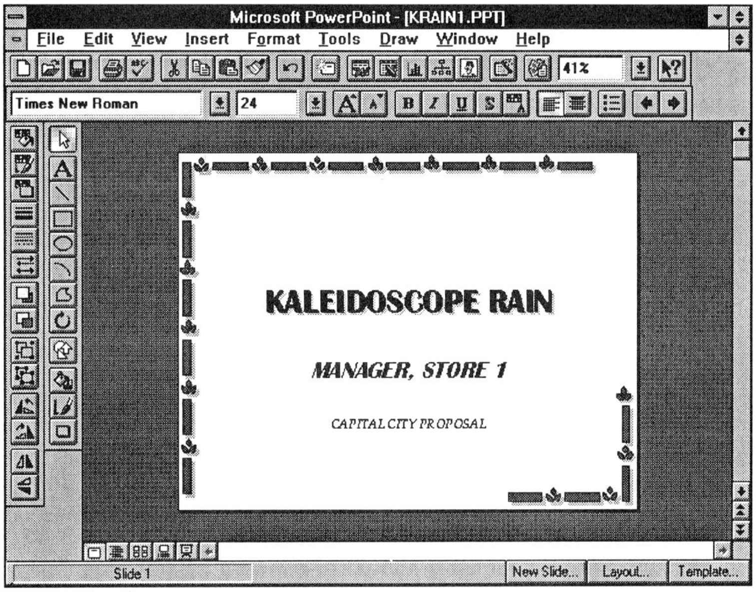

Figure 3 - 5

18. Save the presentation as **krain2.ppt**.

Text Alignment

You can change the way text aligns itself in a text block by changing the text alignment. Alignment commands affect paragraphs. You will need to press **ENTER** to create a new paragraph in a text block. Available alignments are *left*, *center*, *right*, and *justify*. Table 3 - 1 describes the effects of the alignment method.

Alignment method	Effect of Alignment Method on Text
Left	Text is lined up along the left margin of the text block.
Center	Text is lined up along the center of the text block.
Right	Text is lined up along the right margin of the text block.
Justify	Full lines of text are stretched across the text block so that both the left and right margins are lined up.

Table 3 - 1

To change the alignment of text:

- Select the paragraph or paragraphs you want to change.
- Choose **FORMAT/Alignment**.
- Click on the desired Alignment method.

  The selected alignment will be applied to the highlighted paragraphs.

ALTERNATIVE METHOD: *You can left align* 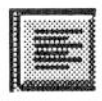 *or center align*  *text by clicking on the corresponding button on the Formatting toolbar.*

Activity 3.2: Changing the Alignment of Text

You look at the slides and decide that the titles would look better if they were left aligned. You will left align the title on two slides. Later, in *Activity 3.9: Working with the Slide Master*, you will left align the title on the Master Slide so that the title will automatically be left aligned without you having to do it on every slide.

1. After Activity 3.1 you should be on Slide 1 of the **krain2.ppt** presentation.
2. Use the **Next Slide** button to move to Slide 3.
3. Select the Title text block so that handles appear around the border (Figure 3 - 6).

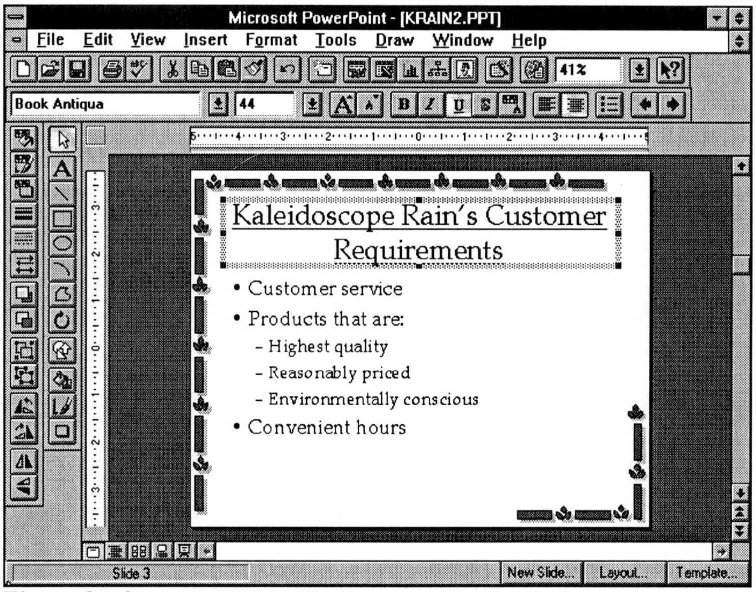

Figure 3 - 6

4. Choose **FORMAT/Alignment**, and then click on **Left**.

   The text in the title is left aligned.
5. Move to Slide 4.
6. Select the Title text block.

7. Click on the **Left Alignment** button on the Formatting toolbar.
8. Save the presentation using the same name.

Line Spacing

Line spacing is the space that *PowerPoint* allows between each line of text. A bulleted line of text is considered a paragraph. Paragraphs are separated by hard returns. Hard returns are inserted every time you press **ENTER**, instead of letting the text wordwrap on its own. You can control the spacing between lines and the spacing between paragraphs. If all the bullets do not fit on a slide, one of the changes you can make is to change the space between each line. Another scenario is a bullet slide with several closely spaced bullets. If you have the space on the slide, you can increase the spacing before and/or after the paragraph. This will increase the readability of the slide.

To change the line spacing or spacing before or after the paragraph:

- Select the text or text block you wish to change.
- Choose **FORMAT/Line spacing.**

  *The **Line Spacing** dialog box appears on the screen. There are three options: changing the line spacing, spacing before paragraph, and spacing after paragraph. The method for changing the spacing for each option is the same.*
- Click on the drop-down list box for measurement style to select the measurement. You can change line spacing by **lines** or by **points**.
- Click on the ↑ or ↓ on the spinner to increase or decrease the line spacing.

Activity 3.3: Changing the Line Spacing

Slides 2 and 9 of the **krain2.ppt** presentation have text that appear on the upper part of the slide. You will increase the spacing between paragraphs (bullets) to spread out the text on the slide. This will increase the readability of the slide.

1. After Activity 3.2 you should be on Slide 4 of the **krain2.ppt** presentation.
2. Move to Slide 2.
3. Select the bulleted text block so that handles appear around the border.
4. Choose **FORMAT/Line Spacing.**

   *The **Line Spacing** dialog box appears on the screen (Figure 3 - 7).*

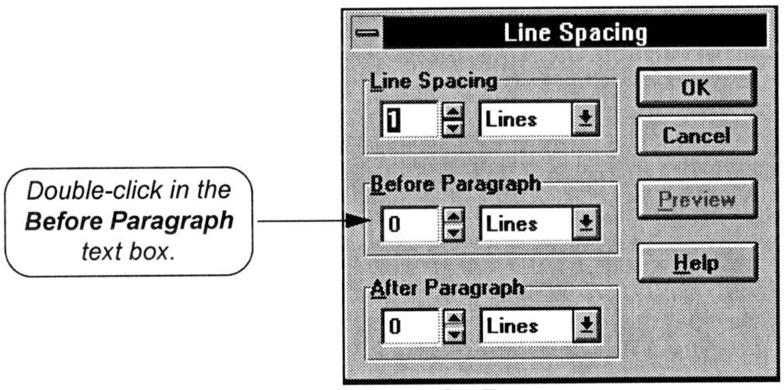

Figure 3 - 7

5. Double-click in the **Before Paragraph** text box so that **0.2** is highlighted.
6. Type: **.7**
7. Click on **OK** to return to the slide.

   The bulleted text is now spread out on the slide from top to bottom.
8. Use the vertical scroll bar to move to Slide 9.
9. Select the bulleted text block so that handles appear around the text border.
10. Choose **FORMAT/Line Spacing.**
11. Double-click in the **After Paragraph** text box so that **0** is highlighted.
12. Type: **1.3**
13. Click on **OK.**
14. Save the presentation using the same name.

Changing Case

You can change the case of text after you type it. For example, if you type text with initial caps and then decide to change the text to uppercase, you can use the *Change Case* feature to change the case of the text, rather than retyping the text. The options available for changing case are:

- Sentence case: The first letter is capitalized.
- lowercase: All the text is changed to lowercase.
- UPPERCASE: All the text is changed to uppercase.
- Title Case: All primary words are changed to initial caps. For example*, this is the title*, would be changed to *This Is the Title*. Words that would not be capitalized are: *a*, *and*, *the*, and *to*.
- tOGGLE cASE Uppercase letters are changed to lowercase and lowercase letters are changed to uppercase. For example, T*his Is the Title*, would be changed to *tHIS iS THE tITLE.*

To change the case of text:

- Select the text.
- Choose **FORMAT/Change Case.**

  *The **Change Case** dialog box appears.*
- Click on the button of the desired case change.
- Click on **OK.**

Activity 3.4: Changing the Case of Text

You decide that you want to capitalize all references of *Capital City* in the **krain2.ppt** presentation. There are two references that are not already uppercase. You will use the Change Case feature.

1. After Activity 3.3 you should be on Slide 9.
2. Highlight **Capital City** in the Title text block.
3. Select **FORMAT/Change Case.**

   *The **Change Case** dialog box appears on the screen (Figure 3 - 8).*

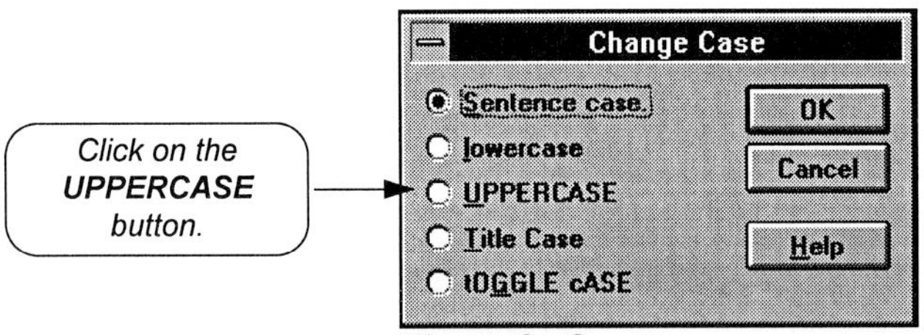

Figure 3 - 8

4. Click on the **UPPERCASE** button, and then click on **OK** to return to the slide.
5. Move to Slide 5.
6. Highlight **Capital City** in the second bullet.

7. Change the case to **UPPERCASE**.
8. Save the presentation using the same name.

Working with Bullets

The placeholder on a Bulleted text slide is already formatted to add text to the text block with a bullet preceding each paragraph. You may want to create a text block without a bullet or you may want to change the bullet symbol.

To turn bullets on or off:

- Select the text block you wish to change.
- Click on the **Bullet On/Off** button  on the Formatting toolbar.

  When the button is depressed, bullets are turned on. When the button is not depressed, bullets are turned off.

PROBLEM SOLVER: *If you are changing a preset placeholder, the bullets and indents have been preset for you. After turning off the bullets, you may need to use the Ruler to change the indent size so that the text will line up. If you are changing a text block created with the Text Tool or a Title or Subtitle placeholder, no indents will be predefined. When you turn bullets on in this type of text block, you will need to use the Ruler to add an indent to the text block so that the text will be set off from the bullet symbol. To view the ruler, select **VIEW/Ruler**.*

To change the bullet symbol:

- Select the paragraph or text block you wish to change.
- Choose **FORMAT/Bullet** from the Standard toolbar.

  *The **Bullet** dialog box appears on the screen.*
- Select the **font type** from the **Bullets From** list box.
- Click on the desired symbol from the symbols displayed in the **Bullet** dialog box.
- Click on **OK**.

  The bullet symbol for the selected text will be changed to the bullet symbol you selected.

Activity 3.5: Working with Bullets

You will create a numbered list for Slide 2. To do this you will need to turn bullets off, add the desired number, and then adjust the indent spacing. *PowerPoint* cannot create an automated numbered list. You will also change the bullet symbol for the sub-bullets on Slide 3.

1. After Activity 3.4 you should be on Slide 5.
2. Move to Slide 2.
3. Select the bulleted text block.

4. Click on the **Bullet On/Off** button on the Formatting toolbar.

   *The **Bullet On/Off** button is now raised, indicating that bullets have been turned off. The second line of each bulleted item has been indented, indicating that the hanging indent is still in place. You will use this hanging indent to create your numbered list.*
5. Select **VIEW/Ruler** so that the ruler appears on the screen.

6. Place the text cursor before the **C** of **Create** in the first bullet.
7. Type: **1.**
8. Press the **TAB** key.

   *Pressing the **TAB** key lines up the text of the first line with the text of the second line. The text would be easier to read if there were more space between the number and the text.*

9. Drag the bottom marker (bottom triangle) on the ruler over to **.6** (Figure 3 - 9).

   PROBLEM SOLVER: *Only the bottom marker should move to **.6**. If both the top and bottom marker move to **.6**, you pointed to the rectangle below the ruler. Make sure you point to the triangle about the rectangle before dragging to **.6**.*

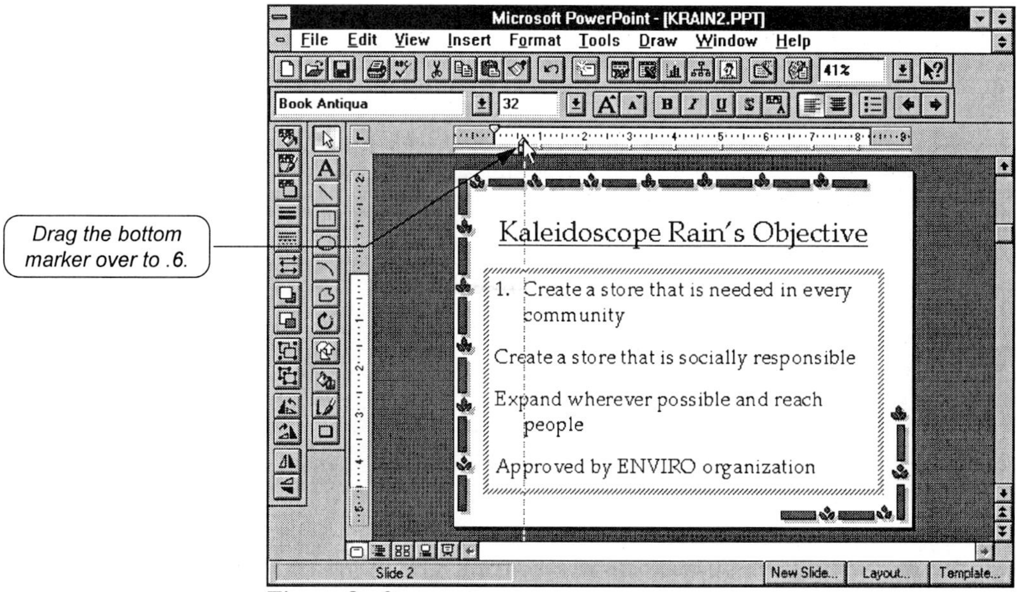

Figure 3 - 9

10. Place the text before the **C** of **Create** in the second bullet.
11. Type: **2.**
12. Press the **TAB** key.
13. Add a **3.** before the third bullet and a **4.** before the fourth bullet.

    Slide 2 should resemble Figure 3 - 10.

14. Move to Slide 3.
15. Highlight the subbullets of the second bullet.
16. Choose **FORMAT/Bullet**.

    *The **Bullet** dialog box appears on the screen (Figure 3 - 11).*

17. Select **Wingdings** in the **Bullets From** list box.

    The Wingdings characters will appear on the screen.

18. Click on the **3-D rectangle** (3rd column from the right, 3rd row). The symbol will enlarge so that you can see it (Figure 3 - 12).
19. Click on **OK** to select the bullet symbol and return to Slide 3.
20. Save the presentation using the same name.

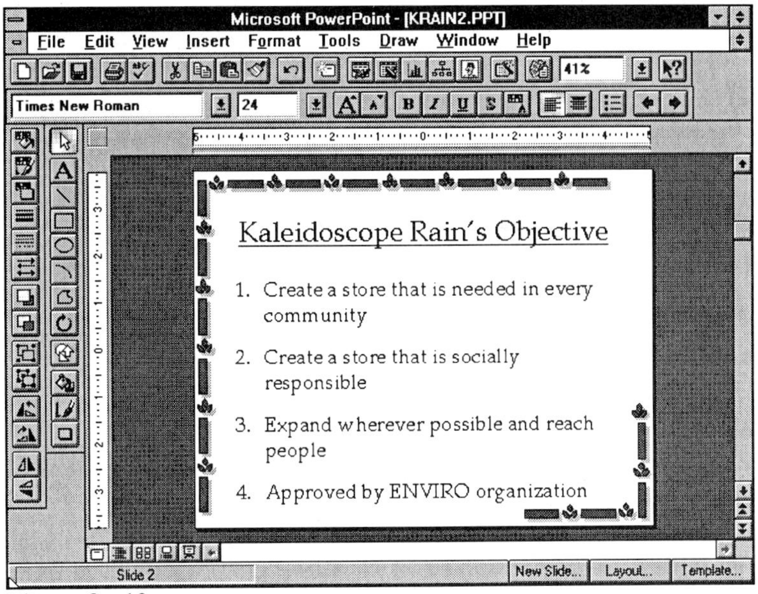

Figure 3 - 10

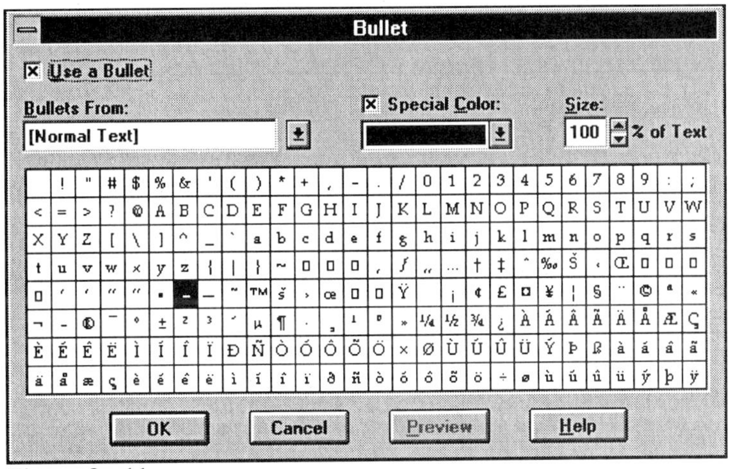

Figure 3 - 11

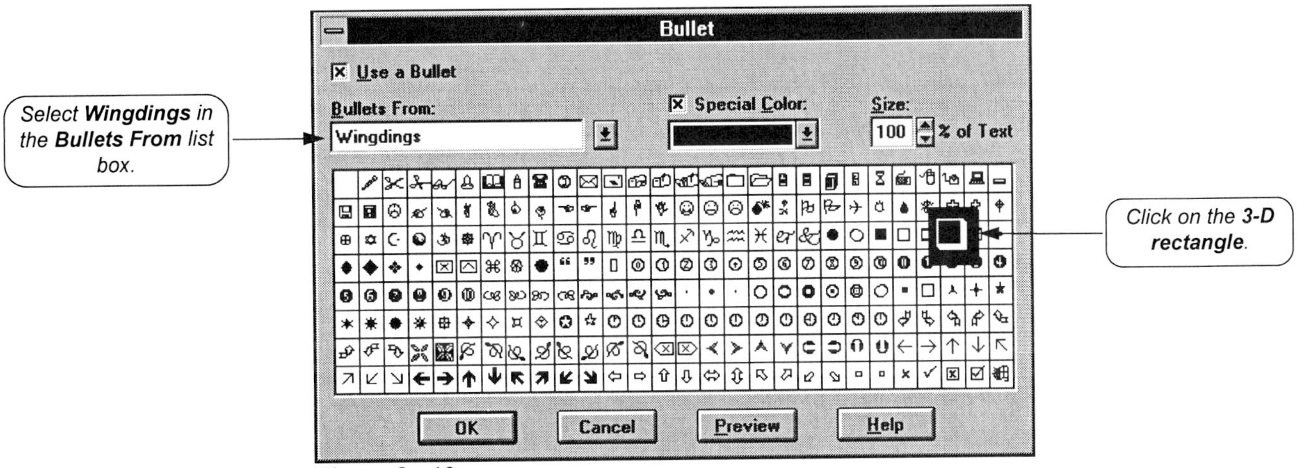

Figure 3 - 12

Size of Text Block

Once you have typed text into a text block, you can change the size of the text block so that the text appears on the screen the way that you want it to appear. When typing text into a text block, the text will continue to flow beyond the bottom border. You can then extend the height of the text block so that the text fits within the borders. Or after typing text into a text block, you may want to increase or decrease the width of the block.

To change the size of a text block:

- Select the text block so that handles appear around the border.
- Point to a handle until a two-tipped arrow appears on the screen.

HINT: *Point to a corner handle to change the height and width of the text block at the same time. Point to a middle handle to change either the height or the width.*

- Drag (click and hold the left mouse button down) the text block to the desired size, and then release the left mouse button.

Activity 3.6: Changing the Size of Text Blocks

Both text blocks on Slide 4 need to be changed. The text in both blocks extend past the boundaries. You will increase the boundaries so that the text fits within the boundaries. On Slide 5 you will change the size of the bulleted text block so that the text wordwraps differently.

1. After Activity 3.5 you should be on Slide 3.
2. Move to Slide 4.
3. Select the Title text block so that handles appear around the border.

   Notice that the size of the border fits only two lines of text.
4. Point to the middle handle of the right side of the text block until a two-tipped arrow appears (Figure 3 - 13).

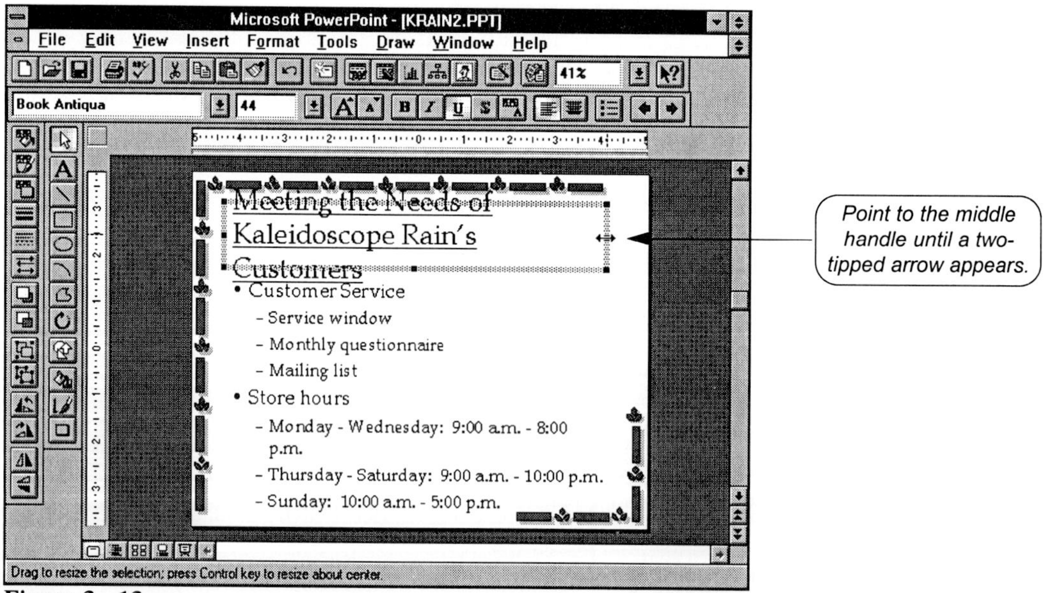

Figure 3 - 13

5. Drag the side of the text block to the end of the slide.

   The text from the third line should move up to line 2 so that the title is only two lines long.

6. Select the bulleted text block so that handles appear around the border.
7. Point to the middle handle on the bottom border until a two-tipped arrow appears.
8. Drag the border to the bottom of the slide.

   All the text should now fit within the borders of the text block.

9. Move to Slide 5.
10. Select the bulleted text block.
11. Point to the middle handle on the right border until a two-tipped arrow appears.
12. Drag the border to the left about an inch.

    *The text of the second bullet should wordwrap so that **CITY** is now on the second line.*

13. Save the presentation using the same name.

CHANGING THE LAYOUT OF A SLIDE

Once you have selected a slide layout and typed in text or added an object, you may want to change the layout of the slide. For example, there is an AutoLayout available for Text & Clip Art. This layout places text on the left side of the slide and the clip art on the right side of the slide. After placing the text and the clip art on the slide, you may look at the slide and decide that the text will look better on the right side of the slide. You can then change the AutoLayout for the slide to Clip Art & Text. This will swap the placement of the text and the clip art.

There are 21 slide layouts available. They are: Title Slide, Bulleted List, Graph, 2 Column Text, Text & Graph, Org Chart, Text & Clip Art, Graph & Text, Table, Clip Art & Text, Text & Object, Object, Text & 2 Objects, Object & Text, Object over Text, 2 Objects & Text, 2 Objects over Text, Text over Object, 4 Objects, Title Only, and Blank.

To change the layout of the slide:

- Choose **FORMAT/Slide Layout** or click on the **Layout** button  on the Status bar.

  *The **Slide Layout** dialog box appears on the screen.*

- Select the desired layout.

  NOTE: *If you are reapplying a layout, the prompt will read, **Reapply the current master styles** and the button to execute the action will be labeled **Reapply**. If you are selecting a different layout, the prompt will read, **Change the layout of the slide to** and the button to execute the action will be labeled **Apply**.*

- Click on the **Apply** button.

  The new layout will be applied to the slide.

Activity 3.7: Changing the Layout of a Slide

You want to add a graph to Slide 5. At the moment there is only a placeholder for text. You will change the layout of Slide 5 so that there is an added placeholder for a graph. You will actually add the graph to the slide in Lesson 4.

1. After Activity 3.6 you should be on Slide 5.

2. Select **FORMAT/Slide Layout** or click on the **Layout** button on the Status bar.

3. Select the **Graph & Text** layout (Figure 3 - 14).

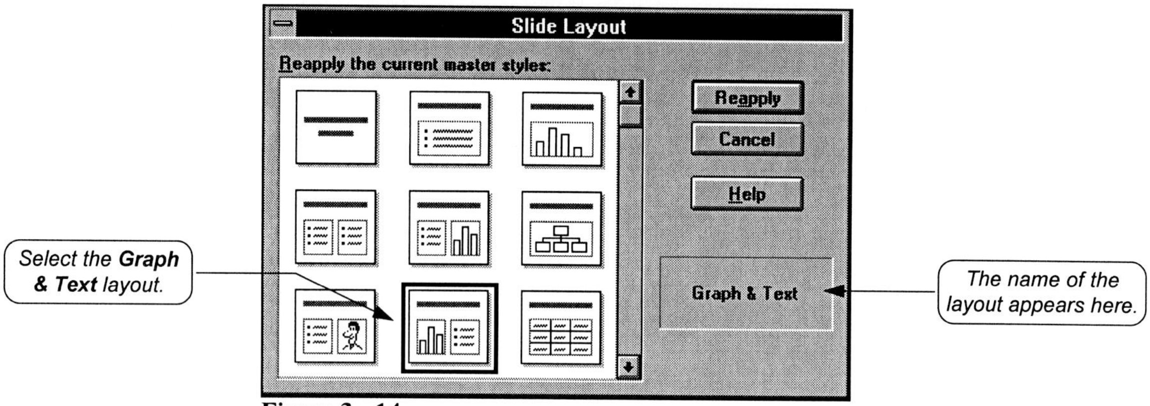

Figure 3 - 14

4. Click on the **Apply** button.

   The layout is applied to the slide. The original text now fits into the predetermined text block for this layout and there is a placeholder for a graph on the left side of the slide.

5. Save the presentation using the same name.

USING *POWERPOINT* MASTERS

PowerPoint has a master format for each view in *PowerPoint*. These masters hold the format for the title and text as well as the background of the presentation. If you make a change on the Master, such as changing a font or italicizing text, the change will affect every slide that is following the master. You can change the Master's format at any time as you are creating your presentation. Any items added to a Master need to be edited at the Master.

With Masters you can add page numbers, the time, or the date to the slides, and *PowerPoint* will keep track of the current time and date and the numbering for you. The time and date are often used for draft copies to keep track of the latest copy. The numbering feature is helpful, because if you change the order of your presentation, *PowerPoint* will keep track of the change and renumber the presentation.

To add slide numbers, the time, or the date to a Master:

- Display the desired master by selecting **VIEW/Master** and then clicking on the appropriate master selection (Slide Master, Outline Master, Handout Master, Notes Master).

  TIME SAVER: *A quick way to display the Master for each view is to press down the* ***SHIFT*** *key and then click on the appropriate view button. Tooltips will appear to guide you. The following table lists the correct button to click:*

Initial function	Function after pressing the SHIFT key
Slide View	Slide Master
Outline View	Outline Master
Slide Sorter View	Handout Master
Notes Pages View	Notes Master

Table 3 - 2

- Select **INSERT/Date** or **INSERT/Time** or **INSERT/Page Number**.

A text block with :: for time or // for date or ## for page number will appear in the middle of the slide.

NOTE: *Actual page numbers, times, and dates appear on the slides only during a Slide Show and on printed slides, handouts, and notes pages.*

- Move the text block to the desired location.
- Make any formatting changes (font or size change).
- Return to the desired view by clicking on the appropriate **View** button.

Activity 3.8: Adding a Page Number, Time and Date to the Handout Master

When you want to see the slides printed out, you use the Handouts printout because you can print up to six slides on a page. You will add a page number, time, and date to the Handout Master so that you can keep track of the latest printout.

1. After Activity 3.7 you should be on Slide 5.
2. Point to the **Slide Sorter View** button. Notice the Tooltip.
3. Press the **SHIFT** key down. Notice that the Tooltip changes to **Handout Master**.
4. Click on the **Slide Sorter View** button while you are pressing the **SHIFT** key down.

   The Handout Master will appear on the screen (Figure 3 - 15). The outlines show where the slides will be placed on the page for each different handout. You will place the page number, date, and time outside these outlines.

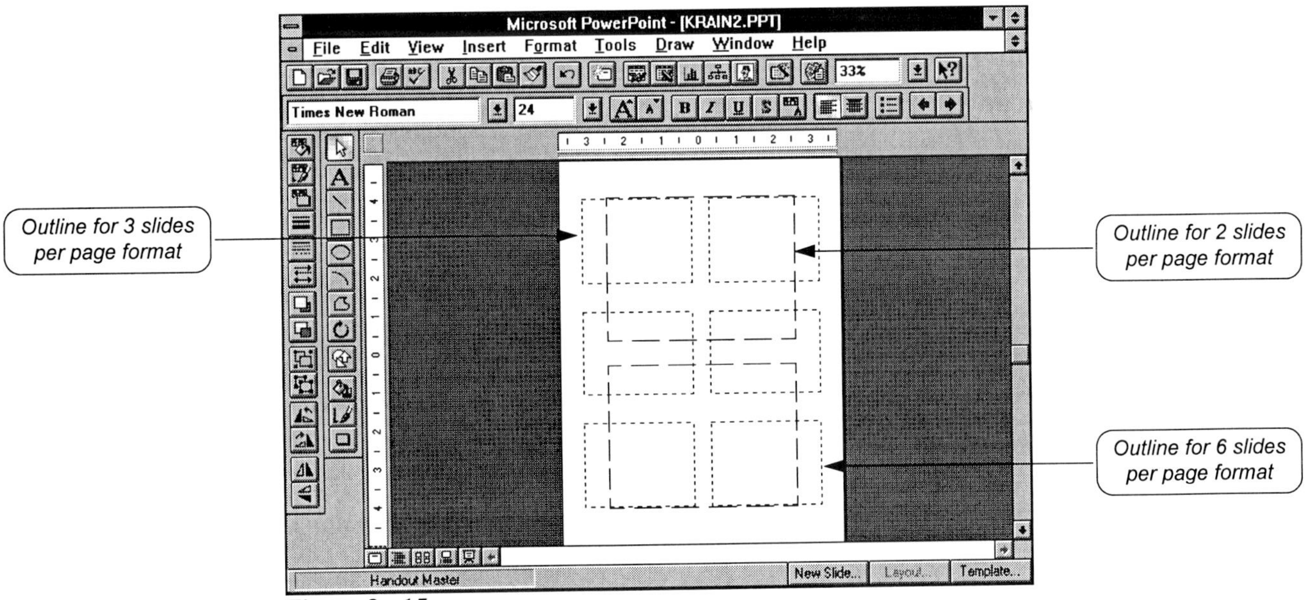

Figure 3 - 15

5. Choose **INSERT/Page Number**.

   A text box with the page number symbols (##) is placed in the middle of the Handout Master.

6. Point to the border of the text block, not on a handle. Drag the page number text block to the bottom right corner of the slide.
7. Select the page number text block again, if it is not selected.

8. Click on the **Decrease Font Size** button once to decrease the text size of the page number to **20 pt.**, and then deselect the text by clicking in a blank area of the screen.

   CAUTION: *If the text block is still selected when you insert the date, it will be inserted into the selected text block.*

9. Choose **INSERT/Date**.

   A text block with the date symbols (//) is placed in the middle of the Handout Master.

10. Drag the date text block to the bottom middle of the slide.
11. Decrease the text size to **20 pt.**, and then make sure the text block is not selected.
12. Choose **INSERT/Time**.

   A text box with the time symbols (::) is placed in the middle of the Handout Master.

13. Drag the time text block to the bottom left of the slide.
14. Decrease the text size to **20 pt.**, and then make sure the text block is not selected.

   Your Handout Master should resemble Figure 3 - 16. You will only see the symbols for page number, date, and time in the Handout Master. When you print the handouts, the actual page number, date, and time will appear on the printout.

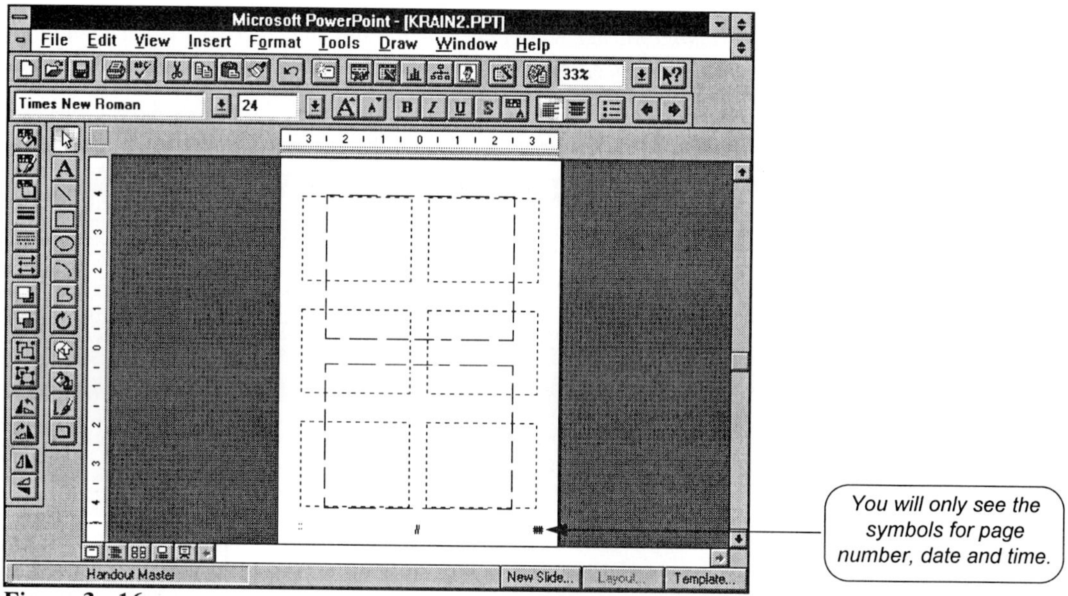

Figure 3 - 16

15. Save the presentation using the same name.
16. Return to Slide View by clicking on the **Slide View** button.
17. Select **FILE/Print**.
18. Select **Handouts (2 slides per page)** from the **Print What** list box.
19. Click on the **Black & White** check box so that an **X** appears.

   Remember, this is an on-screen presentation, so when you print you will need to change the print option to Black & White or Pure Black & White. Otherwise the printer will try to print the background of the presentation.

20. Click on **OK**.

There are nine slides in the presentation; the handout should be five pages long. On the bottom of the page from left to right should be the current time, current date, and the page number.

Using the Slide Master

Any changes that you want to appear on every slide should be created on the Slide Master. This way, you only have to make the change once. You can add drawing objects to your Slide Master, such as your company logo. Drawing objects are shapes, lines, or arcs created using *PowerPoint* tools. You can also add clip art to the Slide Master. You will add clip art to your presentation in Lesson 4.

To change a Slide Master:

- Select **VIEW/Master**.
- Click on **Slide Master**.

  The Slide Master appears on the screen. Notice the status bar reads, ***Slide Master****. Also notice the Title and Bulleted text placeholders. The Title placeholder reads,* ***Click to edit Master title style*** *and the Bulleted text placeholder reads,* ***Click to edit Master text styles****.*

  TIME SAVER: *Another way to get to the Slide Master is to press the* ***SHIFT*** *key down then click on the* ***Slide View*** *button. Notice the Tooltip when the* ***SHIFT*** *key is pressed down. It reads,* ***Slide Master****.*

- Make formatting changes, add a page number, date, or time, or add drawing objects such as a company logo.
- To return to Slide View, select **VIEW/Slides** or click on the **Slide View** button.

Not every slide has to follow the Slide Master. Individual slides can have their own color scheme, background colors, and font size and color. You can hide objects that appear on the Slide Master so that they don't appear on individuals slides. You might do this, for example, if you want the title slide to appear differently from the rest of the presentation. Any changes that are made to individual slides are retained if you decide to change the Slide Master or apply a new template.

To create a slide that differs from the Slide Master:

- Display the slide you want to change.
- Change the font, size, and color, or the background colors or the color schemes.

  Changes you make will not affect other slides in the presentation.

To hide drawing objects that appear on the Slide Master:

- Display the slide you want to change.
- Choose **FORMAT/Slide Background**.
- Click in the **Display Objects on This Slide** check box so that the **X** is removed.
- Click on the **Apply** button.

Activity 3.9: Working with the Slide Master

You want to change the text attributes for the whole presentation. You will do this at the Slide Master. You also do not want the background to show on the title slide. In Lesson 4 you will continue to work with the Slide Master by adding clip art to the Master.

1. After Activity 3.8 you should be on Slide 5.
2. Choose **VIEW/Master**, and then click on **Slide Master**.
3. Select the Title text block.
4. Click on the **Underline** button on the Formatting toolbar so that the button is no longer depressed.

   The underlining will be removed from the title.
5. Click on the **Bold** and the **Shadow** buttons on the Formatting toolbar. **Shadow** may already be depressed.
6. Click on the **Left Alignment** button on the Formatting toolbar.
7. Place the text cursor on the Second Level line in the Bulleted List text block.
8. Select **FORMAT/Bullet**.

   The Bullet dialog box appears.
9. Select **Wingdings** in the **Bullets From** list box.
10. Click on the diamond (4th column, 4th row), and then click on **OK**.

    The bullet shape of the second level is changed to the diamond.
11. Change the bullet shape for the Third Level to the square (24th column, 5th row) in the **Wingdings** font set. When you are finished making changes, the Slide Master should resemble Figure 3 - 17.

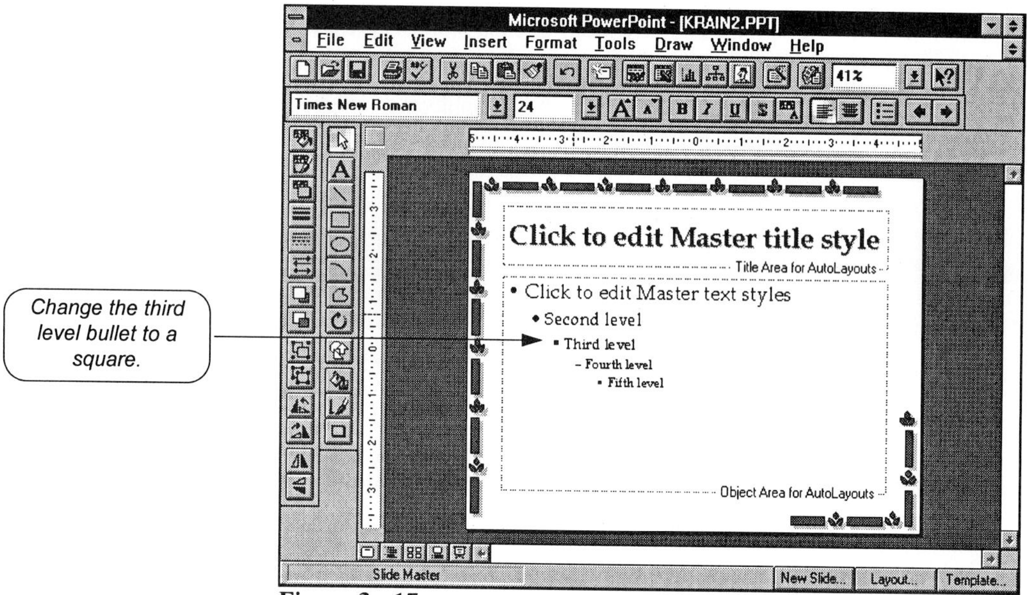

Figure 3 - 17

12. Return to Slide View.
13. Move through the presentation and view the results of your changes. When you are finished viewing the changes move to Slide 1.
14. Choose **FORMAT/Slide Background**.

    *The **Slide Background** dialog box appears on the screen (Figure 3 - 18).*
15. Click in the **Display Objects on This Slide** check box so that the **X** is removed.

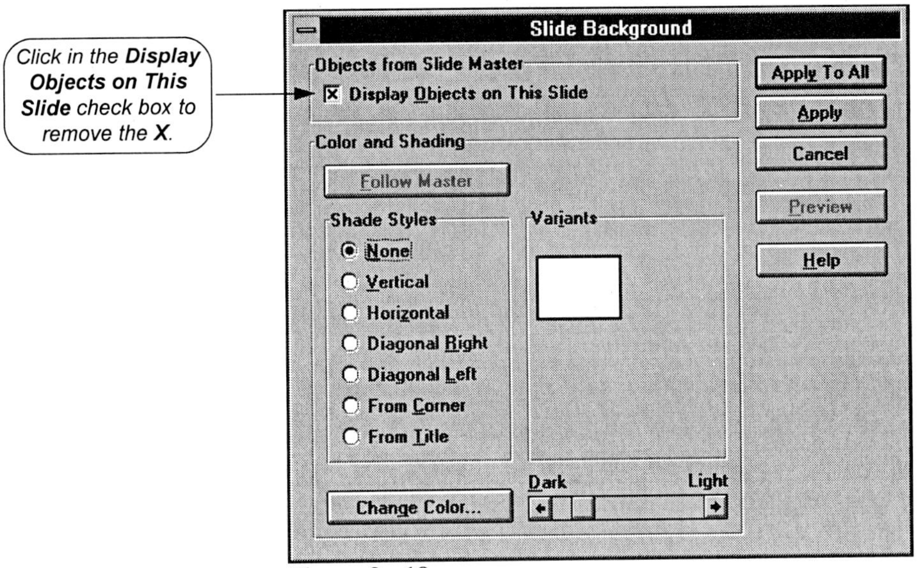

Figure 3 - 18

16. Click on the **Apply** button. You only want to make the change to the Title slide. If you click on the **Apply To All** button, the background objects would not show for the whole presentation.

    When you return to Slide 1, the background objects should be removed from the slide.

17. Move to Slide 2.

    The background objects still appear on this slide. Also the bullet changes that you made to the Master Slide did not effect this slide because you made your own changes to this slide.

18. Save the presentation using the same name.
19. Close the presentation.
20. Exit *PowerPoint*.

SUMMARY

In this chapter you completed basic tasks for formatting a presentation. You edited text attributes and changed the line spacing and case of text. You turned bullets off and changed the bullet symbol. You changed the size of a text block and changed the layout of a slide. You worked with the Master pages to format the whole presentation at one time. In Lesson 4 you will add application objects and clip art to your presentation. In Lesson 5 you will use the *PowerPoint* tools to add drawing objects to your presentation.

KEY TERMS

Bold
Bullet
Center Aligned
Change Case
Decrease Font Size
Handout Master
Increase Font Size
Italic
Left Aligned
Line Spacing
Notes Master
Object
Outline Master
Right Aligned
Shadow
Slide Background
Slide Layout
Slide Master
Text Attributes
Underline

INDEPENDENT PROJECTS

The four independent projects allow you to practice the basic skills involved in formatting presentations: formatting text, changing the layout of the slide, and using master pages. The independent exercises are continuations of those continued in Lesson 2. You will open those presentations saved at the end of Lesson 2 and format them using the topics covered in this Lesson.

Independent Project 3.1: Formatting a Presentation for History Class

In Independent Project 2.1 you edited the text of the **ellis1.ppt** presentation so that the information of the presentation is about Ellis Island. In this project you will format the **ellis2.ppt** presentation so that the delivery of the presentation will be more effective.

1. Open the *PowerPoint* program, if it is not already open.
2. Open the **ellis2.ppt** presentation.
3. Select **VIEW/Slides**, if you are not already in Slide View.
4. Select the title, **ELLIS ISLAND**, so that handles appear on the border.
5. Change the case to **Title Case**.
6. Use the **Increase Font Size** button twice to change the point size is **54 pt**.
7. Click on the **Bold** and the **Italic** buttons on the Formatting toolbar.
8. Select "**your name**" so that handles appear around the border.
9. Increase the font size to **40 pt**.
10. Click on the **Bold** button on the Formatting toolbar.
11. Select **VIEW/Master**, and then click on **Slide Master**.
12. Select the Title text block.
13. Click on the **Left Alignment** button on the Formatting toolbar.

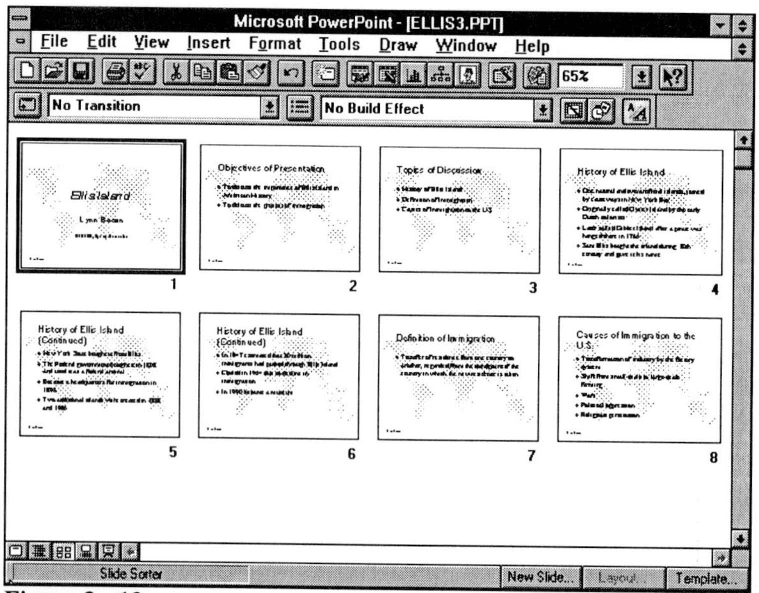

Figure 3 - 19

14. Place the text cursor in the Second Level of the Bulleted List text block.
15. Select **FORMAT/Bullet.**
16. Select the circle bullet symbol (6th column, 5th row) from the **(Normal Text)** font style, and then click on **OK**.
17. Drag the date text block from the bottom center of the slide to the top left corner of the slide.
18. Click on the **Slide Sorter View** button.
19. Save the presentation as **ellis3.ppt**. Your presentation should resemble Figure 3 - 19.
20. Print the presentation as **Handouts (2 slides per page)**. Remember to use the **Black & White** print option.
21. Close the presentation and exit *PowerPoint* or continue with the next project.

Independent Project 3.2: Formatting a Presentation for the Browning Museum

You have saved the presentation created in Independent Project 2.2 as **brown2.ppt**. You will open the **brown2.ppt** presentation, edit it with additional changes from Susan Whitney and the rest of the museum staff, and then format the presentation.

1. Open the *PowerPoint* program, if it is not already open.
2. Open the **brown2.ppt** presentation.
3. Click on the **Slide View** button at the bottom of the Slide Work Area.
4. Use the scroll box on the vertical scroll bar to move to Slide 1, if you are not already there.
5. Select the Title text block so that handles appear around the text border, and then select **FORMAT/Font**.
6. Select **Arial Rounded MT Bold** from the **Font list** box and **54** from the **Size** list box; then click on **OK**.
7. Select the Subtitle text block and click on the **Bold** button on the Formatting toolbar.
8. Use the **Next Slide** button to move to Slide 2.
9. Add the following line as the last bullet on Slide 2 (The Browning Museum Staff): **Elizabeth Kelly, Museum Shop Manager**
10. Select the bulleted text block so that handles appear around the border.
11. Point to the bottom middle handle of the text block until a two-tipped arrow appears and drag the bottom border of the text block to the bottom of the slide.
12. Change the text size to **30 pt**.
13. Use the **Next Slide** button to move to Slide 5.
14. Select the bulleted text block so that handles appear around the border.
15. Click in the **Size** text block so that the **32** is highlighted.
16. Type: **28** and press **ENTER**.
17. Point to the bottom middle handle of the text block until a two-tipped arrow appears; then drag the bottom border of the text block to the bottom of the slide.
18. Move to Slide 6 and repeat steps 14–17.
19. Move to Slide 3 (Statement of Purpose).

20. Select the bulleted text block.
21. Turn off the bullets.
22. Center align the text.
23. Increase the font size of the text to **40 pt**.
24. Point to the bottom middle handle of the bulleted text block until a two-tipped arrow appears.
25. Drag the bottom border of the text block up to the text.
26. Point to the border of the text block, not on a handle.
27. Drag the text block to the middle of the slide.
28. Switch to the Slide Master by pressing the **SHIFT** key down and clicking on the **Slide View** button.
29. Select **INSERT/Page Number**.
30. Point to the text border, not on a handle, and drag the page number to the bottom right corner of the slide.
31. Decrease the size of the page number to **12 pt**.
32. Make the Title text bold.
33. Click on the **Slide Sorter View** button.
34. Save the presentation as **brown3.ppt**. Your presentation should resemble Figure 3 - 20.

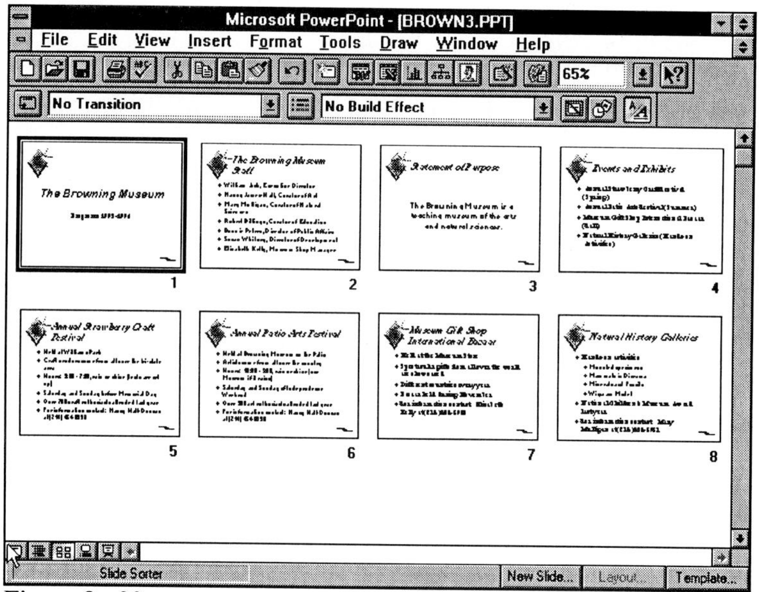

Figure 3 - 20

35. Print the presentation as **Handouts (2 slides per page)**. Remember to use the **Black & White** print option.
36. Close the presentation and exit *PowerPoint* or continue with the next project.

Independent Project 3.3: Formatting a Presentation for Julie's Travel Agency

In Independent Project 2.3, you edited and saved the **travel2.ppt** presentation. In this project you will format the **travel2.ppt** presentation.

1. Open the *PowerPoint* program, if it is not already open.
2. Open the **travel2.ppt** presentation.
3. Switch to Slide View if you are not already there.
4. Move to Slide 1.
5. Edit the Title on Slide 1 so that it has the **Bookman Old Style** font, **Bold** and **Italic** font styles, and a **54** pt. size.
6. Format the title's case to **UPPERCASE**.
7. Italicize the text block with **County Shopping Center** and **Pinebrook, NY**.
8. Move to Slide 4.
9. Change the size of the bulleted text to **30 pt**.
10. Change the line spacing of the bulleted text to **.8**.
11. Switch to the Slide Master.
12. Left align and Bold the Title.
13. Insert the date at the top right corner of the slide.
14. Decrease the size of the date to **12 pt**.
15. Insert a page number in the bottom right corner of the slide.
16. Decrease the size of the page number to **12 pt**.
17. Change the style of the bullets on each level to the airplane symbol (22nd column, 2nd row) found in the **Wingdings** font style.
18. Return to Slide View.
19. Move to Slide 3.
20. Change the layout of Slide 3 to **Text & Graph**. (You will add a graph in Independent Project 4.3).
21. Add a page number to the bottom right corner of the Handout Master.
22. Switch to Slide Sorter View.

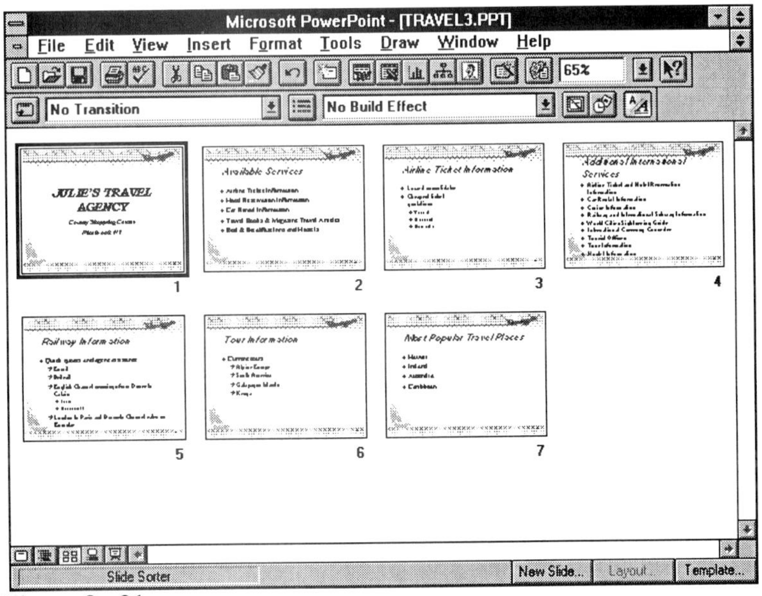

Figure 3 - 21

23. Save the presentation as **travel3.ppt**. Your presentation should resemble Figure 3 - 21.
24. Print the presentation as **Handouts (2 slides per page)**. Remember to use the **Black & White** print option.
25. Close the presentation and exit *PowerPoint* or continue with the next project.

Independent Project 3.4: Editing a Presentation for a Training Program

The **train2.ppt** presentation was edited and saved in Independent Project 2.4. You will format the **train2.ppt** presentation in this project.

1. Format the text on Slide 1 as follows:
   - Experiment with the font, font size, and font style.
   - Use the same font for the subtitles.
2. Put the date and page number on the Slide Master, Notes Master, and the Handout Master. You decide where to place the date and the page number.
3. Make the following changes on the Slide Master:
   - Left justify, Bold, and Shadow the Title.
   - Change the bullet symbols for each of the levels. You choose the symbols.
4. Format the text of the presentation as necessary. Use line spacing and changing the size of the text block as needed.
5. Save the presentation as **train3.ppt**. Your presentation should be similar to Figure 3 - 22 in Slide Sorter View.

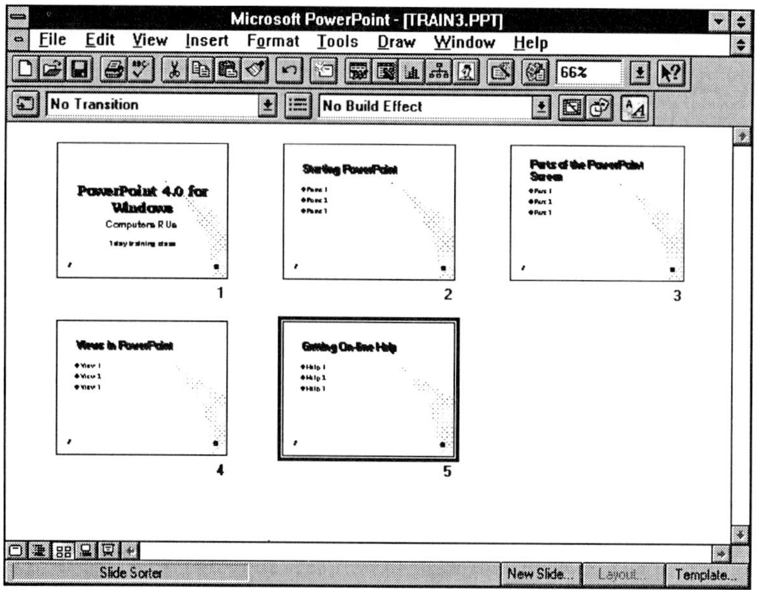

Figure 3 - 22

6. Print **Handouts (2 slides per page)**. Remember to use the **Black & White** print option.
7. Print the **Notes Page** for Slide 3.
8. Close the presentation and exit *PowerPoint.*

Lesson

4 Inserting Objects in a Presentation

Objectives

In this lesson you will learn how to:

- Insert clip art using a placeholder
- Insert clip art without using a placeholder
- Size clip art
- Move clip art
- Insert a *Word* table into a presentation
- Edit a *Word* table
- Insert a graph into a presentation
- Edit a graph

PROJECT DESCRIPTION

In Lesson 3, you formatted the **krain1.ppt** presentation. All the text has been entered into the presentation and formatted. In this lesson you will add application objects and clip art to the presentation. *PowerPoint* does not have the ability to create tables or graphs, so it uses the capability of Microsoft *Word*, Microsoft *Graph*, and Object Linking and Embedding to insert tables and graphs into the presentation. You will insert clip art images from the ClipArt Gallery into your presentation. When you are finished with this lesson, your presentation will resemble Figures 4 - 1 and 4 - 2.

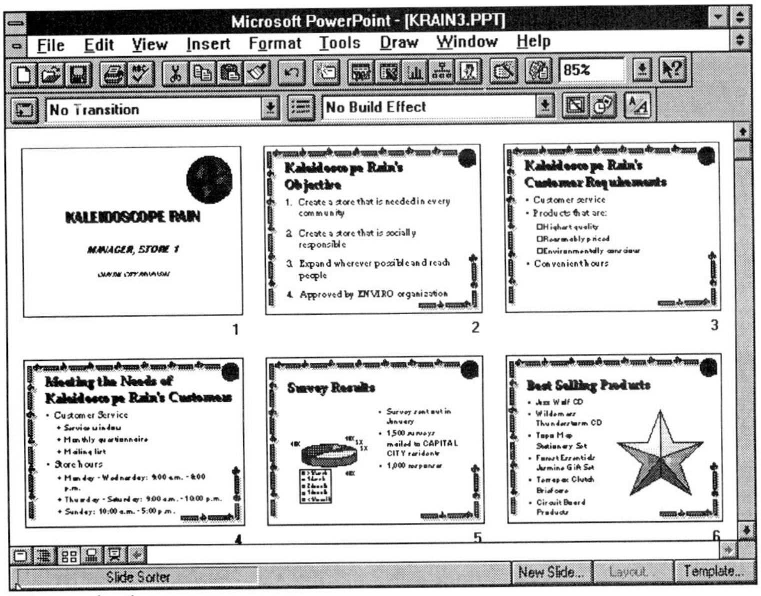

Figure 4 - 1

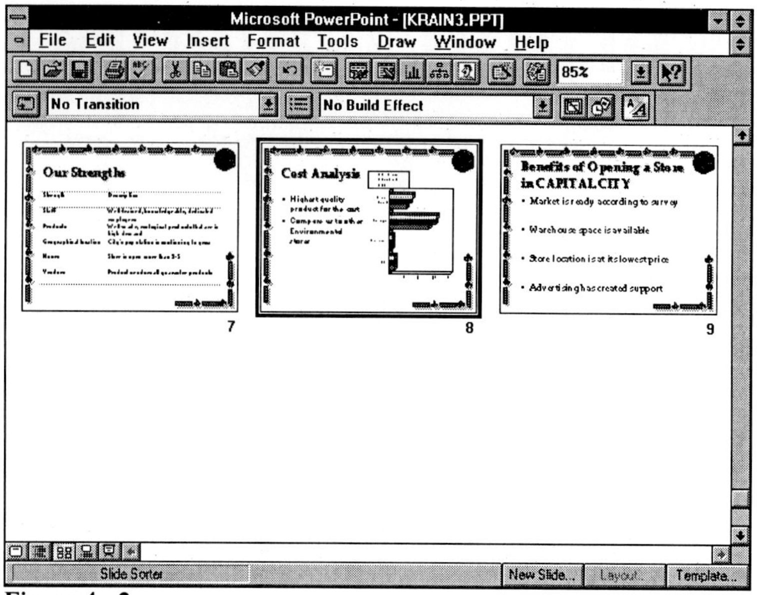

Figure 4 - 2

WHAT IS AN OBJECT?

In *PowerPoint* the term *object* refers to anything you work with in *PowerPoint.* It could be a simple piece of artwork created with the Drawing tools, a text block, a *Word* table, or a chart created in *Microsoft Graph.* Objects in a *PowerPoint* presentation are held in place by placeholders. Placeholders reserve space in the slide for the particular object type they're supposed to hold. They are movable and resizable within the boundaries of the slide. In this lesson you will focus on application objects and clip art objects. Application objects are pulled in from other software packages such as *Microsoft Word*, *Microsoft Excel* or *Microsoft Graph. PowerPoint* does not have the ability to create tables, spreadsheets or graphs, so its uses *Word*, *Excel* and *Graph* to insert these "application" objects into the presentation. In Lesson 5 you will learn about drawing objects. Drawing objects are created using the Drawing tools provided by *PowerPoint.*

WHAT IS AN EMBEDDED OBJECT?

Another term for application object is embedded object. An embedded object is one that is created by an object application, such as *Word* or *Microsoft Graph*, and inserted into your presentation using Object Linking and Embedding (OLE). Object Linking and Embedding (OLE) is a procedure developed by Windows to overcome the limitations of copying and pasting. OLE lets you create an ongoing connection between the data in the new location and the original data or the original application. Once the object is embedded, it becomes part of your *PowerPoint* presentation. When you double-click on the object, either a separate window belonging to the application you used to create the object opens in *PowerPoint* or some of the *PowerPoint* menus and toolbars are replaced by the ones in the object application.

You can add an embedded object to a *PowerPoint* presentation in several ways. You can create a slide using an AutoLayout that includes an object placeholder. You can click a button on the Standard toolbar, or you can use the **Insert Object** command from the **Insert** menu.

Some of the objects that you can embed in your *PowerPoint* presentation include:

- Text with special effects (*Microsoft WordArt*)
- Equations (*Microsoft Equation Editor*)

- Graphs (*Microsoft Graph*)
- Organizational charts (*Microsoft Organization Chart*)
- Tables (*Microsoft Word*)
- Worksheets (*Microsoft Excel*)

INSERTING CLIP ART

The *PowerPoint* ClipArt Gallery is a collection of more than 1,000 pieces of clip art that can be used to dress up your presentation. The ClipArt Gallery has a Find feature that helps locate the images you want. The ClipArt Gallery also has its own Help system to help you use the Gallery.

To insert clip art using a placeholder:

- Double-click on the clip art placeholder.

  The ClipArt Gallery appears.
- Select a category, and then use the vertical scroll bar to browse through the Gallery.
- Click on the desired picture.

  A selected picture will have a thick border around it. When a picture is selected, the category, picture description, and path for the picture will appear at the bottom of the dialog box.
- Click on **OK**.

  The clip art image will be placed on the slide using the dimensions of the placeholder.

To insert clip art without a placeholder:

- Select **INSERT/Clip Art** or click on the **Insert Clip Art** button  on the Standard toolbar.

  The ClipArt Gallery appears.
- Select a category and then use the vertical scroll bar to browse through the Gallery.
- Click on the desired picture, and then click on **OK**.

  The clip art image will be placed on the middle of the slide. You will need to size and move the image to the desired location.

To size clip art:

- Select the clip art so that handles appear around the border.
- Point to one of the handles.

  A two-tipped arrow will appear. Point to a corner handle to size the clip art both horizontally and vertically at the same time. Point to a middle handle to size either the height or the width.
- Drag the handle to its new location.

To move clip art:

- Point to the middle of the clip art image. It does not have to be selected first.
- Click and hold the left mouse button down.
- Drag the clip art image to its new location on the slide.

Activity 4.1: Inserting Clip Art into the krain2.ppt Presentation with a Placeholder

In this activity, you will add clip art to your presentation with a placeholder. The placeholder isn't on Slide 6 yet, so you will change the layout of the slide first. Then you will add the clip art to the slide.

1. Open *PowerPoint*, if it is not already open.
2. Open the **krain2.ppt** presentation.
3. Move to Slide 6.
4. Click on the **Layout** button on the Status bar.

   The Slide Layout dialog box appears.
5. Select the **Text & Clip Art** layout (Figure 4 - 3).

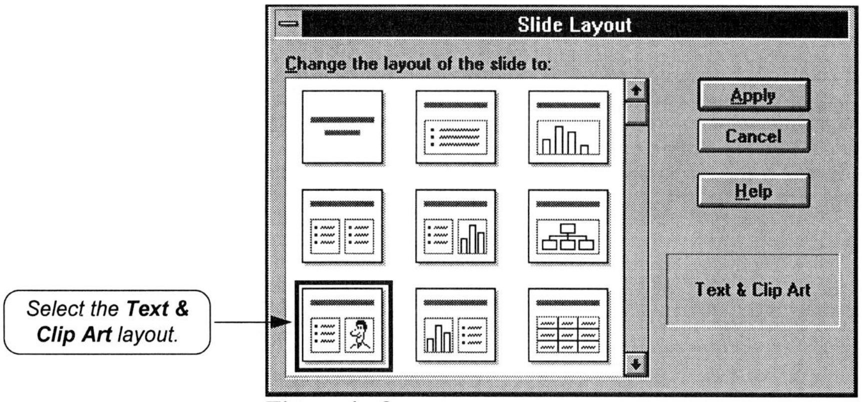

Figure 4 - 3

6. Click on **Apply**.

   The clip art placeholder is placed on the right side of Slide 6. The text is moved to the left side of the slide and overflows off the slide (Figure 4 - 4).

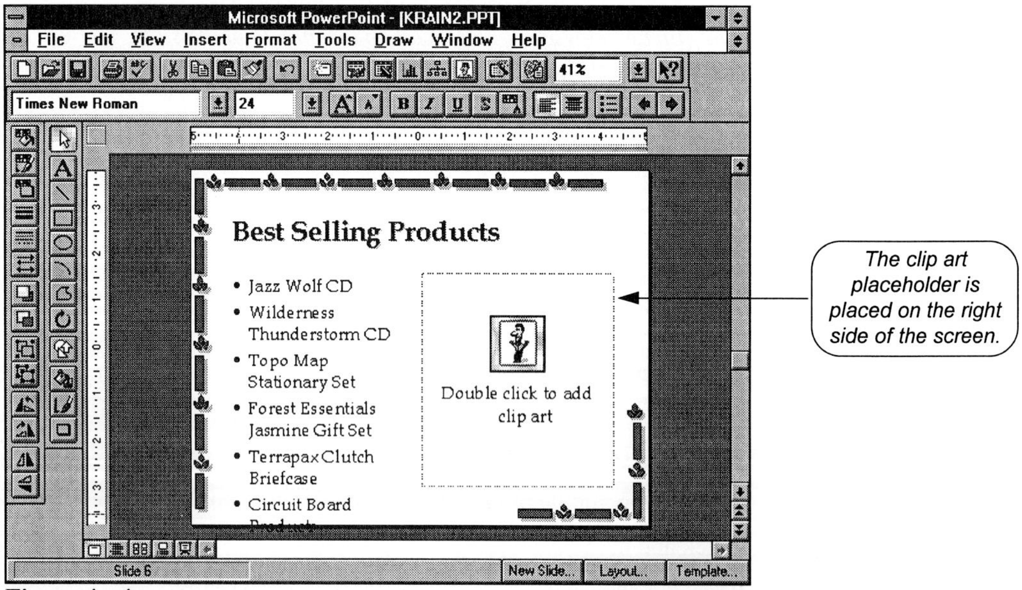

Figure 4 - 4

7. Select the text block so that handles appear on the border. Point to the border, not on a handle. Click and hold the left mouse button down, and drag the text block up on the slide until the last line of the text block fits on the slide.
8. Point to the bottom middle handle, and then drag the bottom of the text border to the bottom edge of the slide.

   When steps 7 and 8 are completed, your slide will resemble Figure 4 - 5.

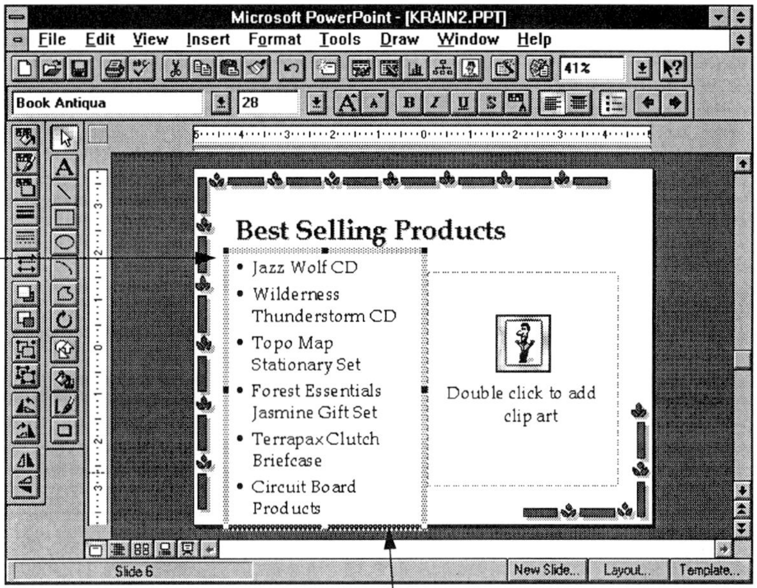

Figure 4 - 5

9. Double-click on the clip art placeholder.

   The Microsoft ClipArt Gallery appears on the screen (Figure 4 -6).

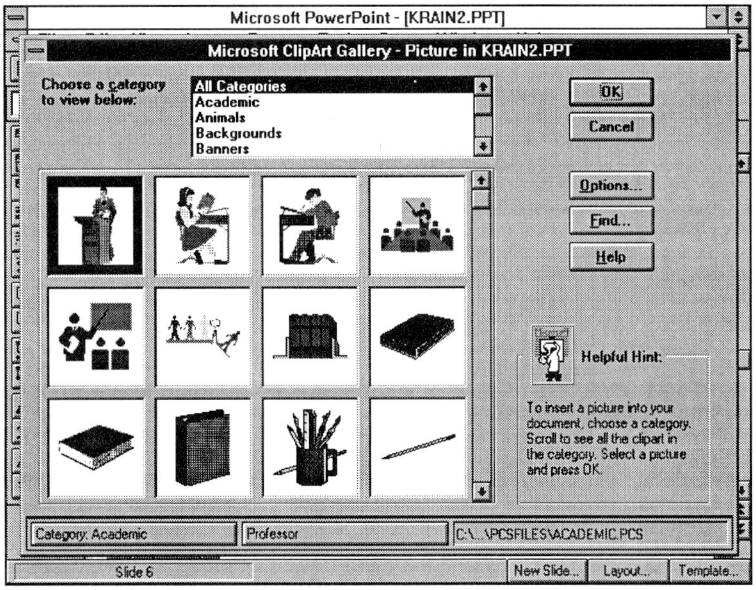

Figure 4 - 6

10. Click on the ↓ on the vertical scroll bar to see the images available in the ClipArt Gallery.

11. Click on the **Shapes** category in the **Category** list box. Use the ↓ on the vertical scroll bar to find the **Shapes** category. The categories are listed alphabetically.

✓ **PROBLEM SOLVER:** *It is possible to install PowerPoint without installing all of its clip art. If the Shapes category does not appear, talk to your instructor or lab assistant or select different clip art.*

12. Use the ↓ on the vertical scroll bar to move through the clip art images until you see a yellow 3-D star.

13. Click on the image.

    A thick border will appear around the clip art image, indicating that it is selected (Figure 4 - 7).

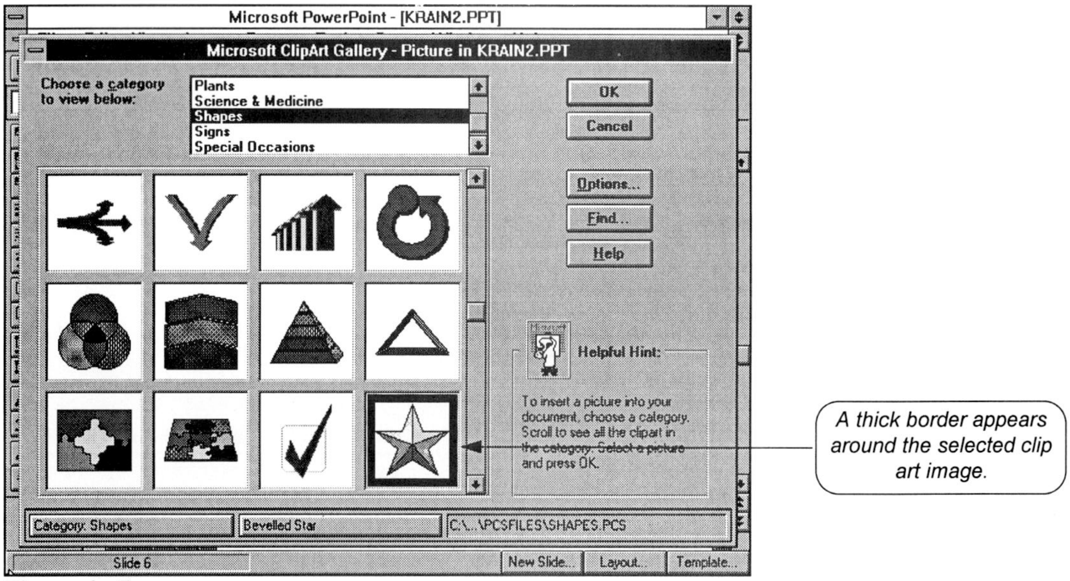

Figure 4 - 7

14. Click on **OK**.

    The star is placed on the slide in the clip art placeholder (Figure 4 -8).

Figure 4 - 8

15. Save the presentation as **krain3.ppt**.

Activity 4.2: Inserting Clip Art into the krain3.ppt Presentation without a Placeholder

In the last activity, you inserted clip art into a presentation with a clip art placeholder. In this activity you will add a clip art image to the presentation without using the clip art placeholder. You will add a picture of the earth to the Slide Master.

1. After Activity 4.1 you should be on Slide 6 of the **krain3.ppt** presentation.
2. Switch to the Slide Master.

HINT: *Use the **Slide View** button and the **SHIFT** key.*

3. Click on the **Insert Clip Art** button on the Standard toolbar.

   The Microsoft ClipArt Gallery appears.

4. Click on the **Find** button.

   *The **Find Picture** dialog box appears on the screen (Figure 4 - 9).*

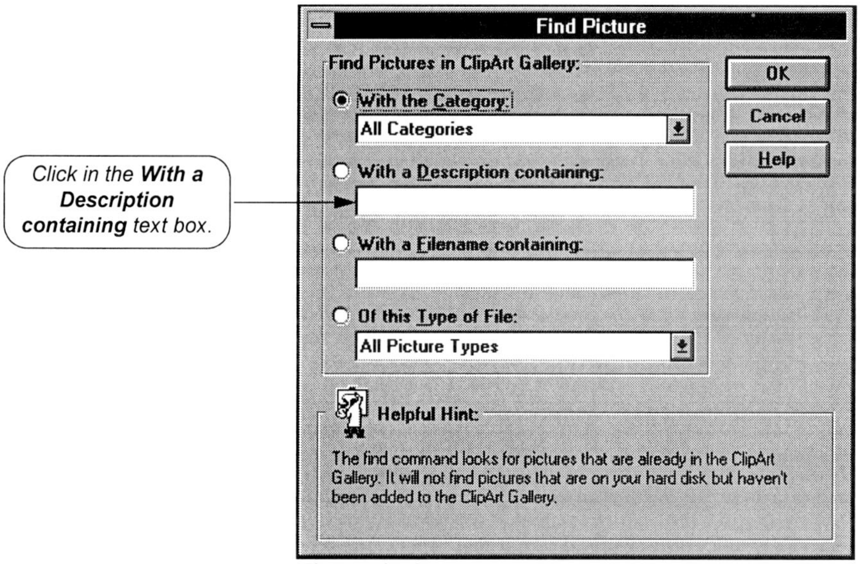

Figure 4 - 9

5. Click in the **With a Description containing** text box so that the text cursor appears and the button is marked.
6. Type: **world**

   Your screen should resemble Figure 4 - 10.

7. Click on **OK**.

   The clip art images with world in their description appear on the screen.

NOTE: *The clip art images of the world may vary on your screen. If Microsoft Works has been installed on your computer, your screen should match Figure 4 - 11. The first image with a green background is actually from Microsoft Works. Microsoft Works and PowerPoint share the same ClipArt Gallery.*

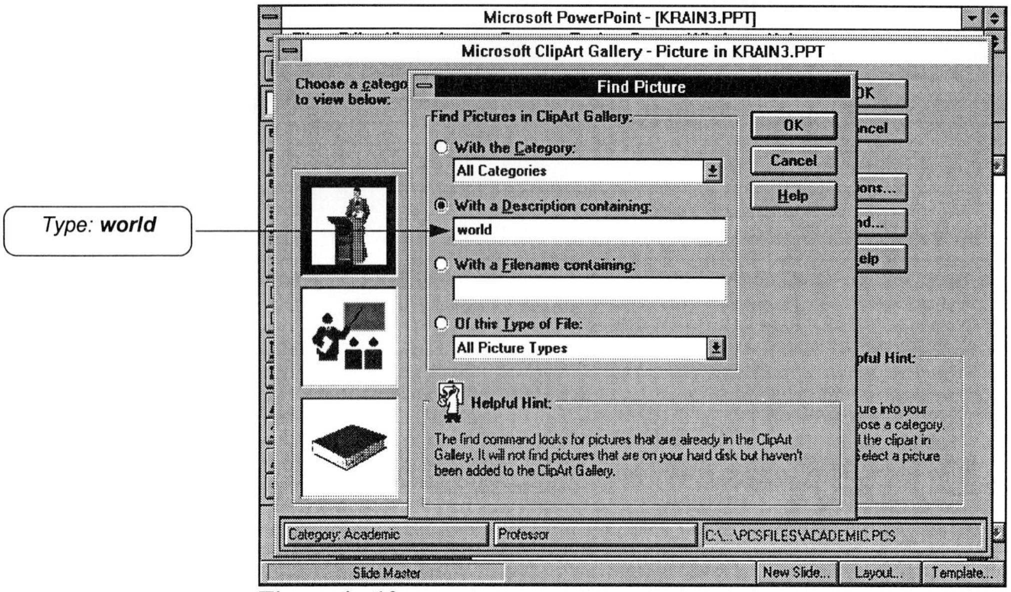

Figure 4 - 10

8. Click on the **World Globe (Western Hemisphere)** image.

   The description will appear in the middle of the Status bar (Figure 4 - 11).

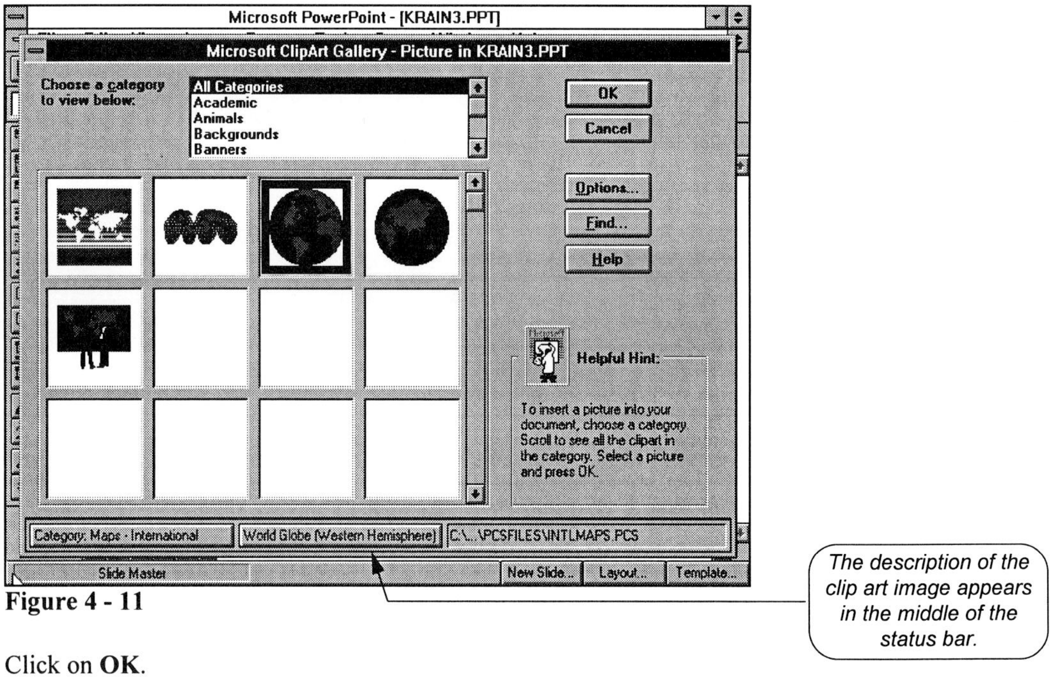

Figure 4 - 11

9. Click on **OK**.

   The clip art image is placed in the middle of the slide. You will size the image so that it is about 1/8 of the current size and then move it to the top right corner.

10. The clip art image should be selected already. Eight handles should appear around the image. Point to one of the corner handles. Click and hold the left mouse button down and drag the image to about 1/8 of its current size.

11. Point to the middle of the clip art image. Drag the globe to the top right corner of the slide.

    Your Slide Master should resemble Figure 4 - 12 when you are done.

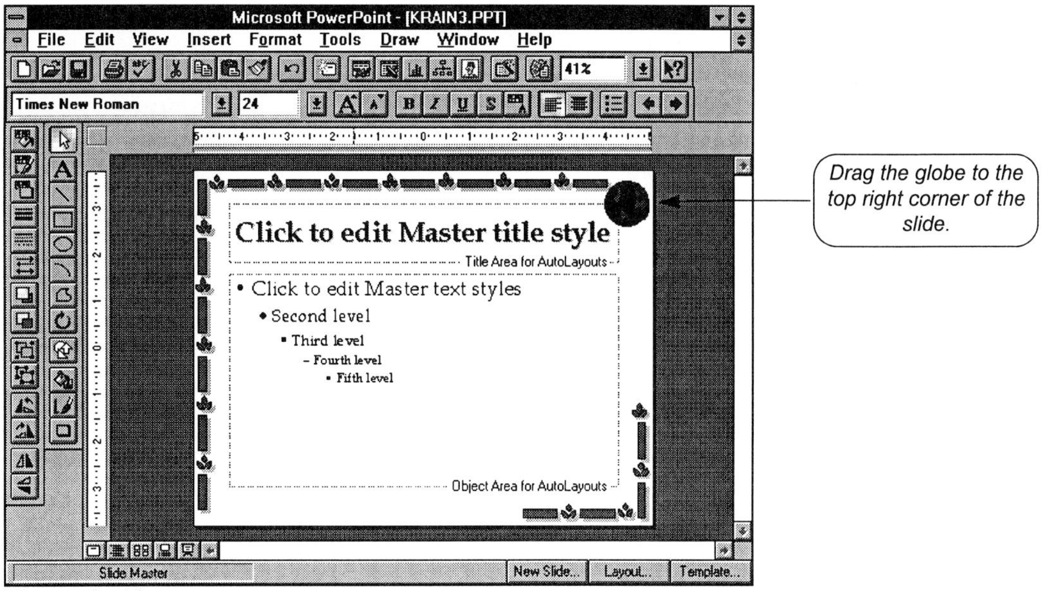

Figure 4 - 12

12. Return to Slide View.
13. Move through the presentation and look at the result of adding the clip art image to the Slide Master.
14. Move to Slide 1.

    The background objects and color scheme do not appear because you selected not to have them displayed at the end of Lesson 3.
15. Add the **World Globe (Western Hemisphere)** clip art image to Slide 1.
16. Size the image to about 1/4 of its current size.
17. Move the globe to the top right corner of the slide.
18. Save the presentation using the same name.

INSERTING A *WORD* TABLE

A table is a way to organize and communicate information. A table can be used to list a group of specific points with short notes beside them. A table can also be used for presenting a small set of data. A table allows you to use the row and column format to organize the data you want to present. The format of a table will be easily understood by your audience.

PowerPoint does not have the ability to create tables. You can, however, use the capabilities of *Word* to create a table. *Microsoft Word 6.0* needs to be installed on your computer for this topic to work. You will actually use the *Word* menus and functions to create the table and then insert it into *PowerPoint*. *PowerPoint* takes advantage of the compatibility of the *Microsoft Office* programs (*Word*, *Excel*, *PowerPoint*, *Access*) and the Object Linking and Embedding feature to create the table.

To create a new table:

- If there is a table placeholder, double-click on the table placeholder. If there is no placeholder, select **INSERT/Microsoft Word Table** or click on the **Insert Microsoft Word Table** button  on the Standard toolbar.

  *The **Insert Word Table** dialog box appears on the screen.*
- Type the number or use the spinner to enter the number of columns you want in your table.

- Type the number or use the spinner to enter the number of rows you want in your table.
- Click on **OK**.

  The Word table grid appears within the placeholder with rulers on the left side and top of the placeholder. The Title bar still says you are in PowerPoint; however, the Menu bar and toolbars are Word's Menu bar and toolbars.
- Use the *Word* tools and menus to create the table.
- Click anywhere on the slide, outside the placeholder, to return to *PowerPoint.*

To edit a *Word* table:

- Double-click on the *Word* table to enable the *Word* Menu bar and toolbars.

Activity 4.3: Inserting a Word Table into the krain3.ppt Presentation

In this activity, you will use the *Microsoft Word* program to insert a table into the **krain3.ppt** presentation. Slide 7 (*Our Strengths*) already has a table placeholder on it. You will use this placeholder to add a table to the slide.

1. After Activity 4.2 you should be on Slide 1 of the **krain3.ppt** presentation.
2. Move to Slide 7.
3. Double-click on the table placeholder.

   *The **Insert Word Table** dialog box appears on the screen (Figure 4 - 13).*

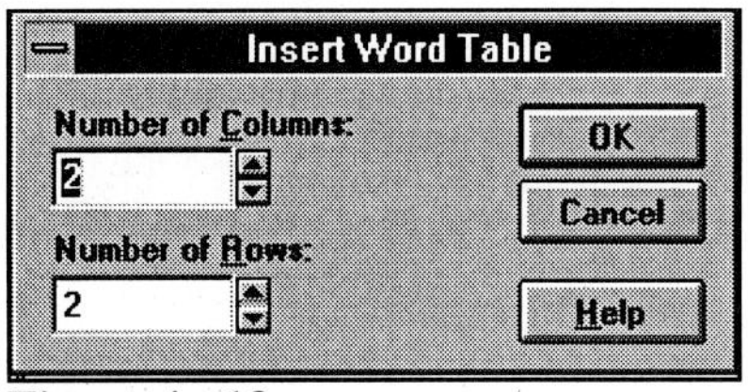

Figure 4 - 13

4. Enter **2** in the **Number of Columns** text box if it is not already there.
5. Enter **6** in the **Number of Rows** text box, and then click on **OK**.

   A table with a border around the outside and two rulers (top and left side) appears on the screen. Even though the Title bar reads PowerPoint, the Menu bar and toolbars are from Word, not PowerPoint (Figure 4 - 14).
6. Enter the following information into the table. Use the **TAB** key to move to the right one cell (or from the end of one row to the beginning of the next) and the **SHIFT+TAB** keys to move to the left one cell. You can also use the arrow keys to move from cell to cell.

Strength	**Description**
Staff	**Well-trained, knowledgeable, dedicated employees**
Products	**Well-made, ecological products that are in high demand**
Geographic Location	**Area's population is continuing to grow**
Hours	**Store is open more than 9-5**
Vendors	**Product vendors all guarantee products**

You are still in PowerPoint.

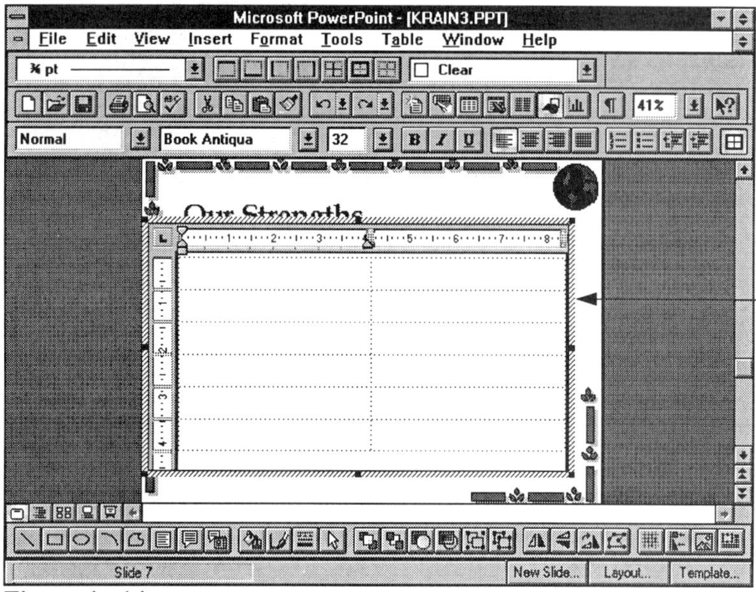

Menu bar and toolbars are from Word.

A table with a border and two rulers appears on the screen.

Figure 4 - 14

After typing in the text, your screen should resemble Figure 4 - 15. The text is too large to fit on the screen. You will select the entire table and change the size of the text and select an AutoFormat.

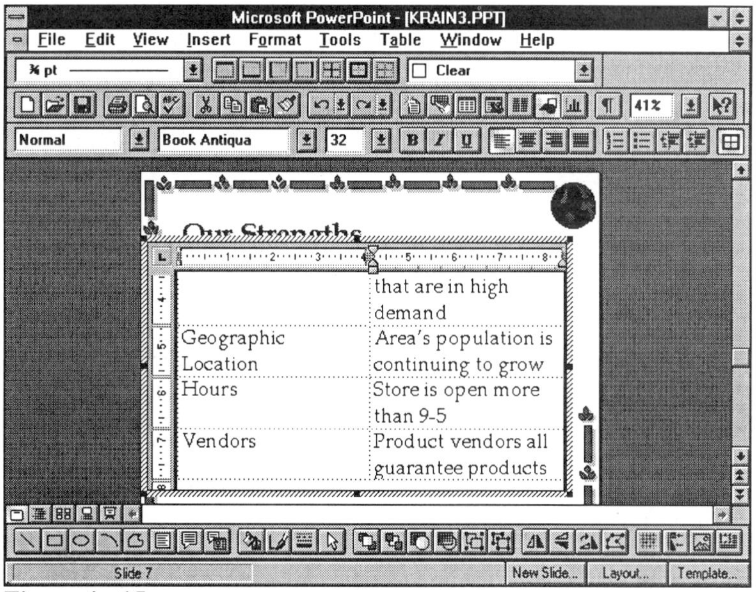

Figure 4 - 15

7. Choose **TABLE/Select Table**.

   You are using Word to create the table. ***TABLE/Select Table*** *and* ***TABLE/Table AutoFormat*** *are Word commands not PowerPoint commands.*

8. Use the Formatting toolbar to change the size of the text to **20 pt**.

9. Choose **TABLE/Table AutoFormat**.

   The ***Table AutoFormat*** *dialog box appears on the screen (Figure 4 - 16).*

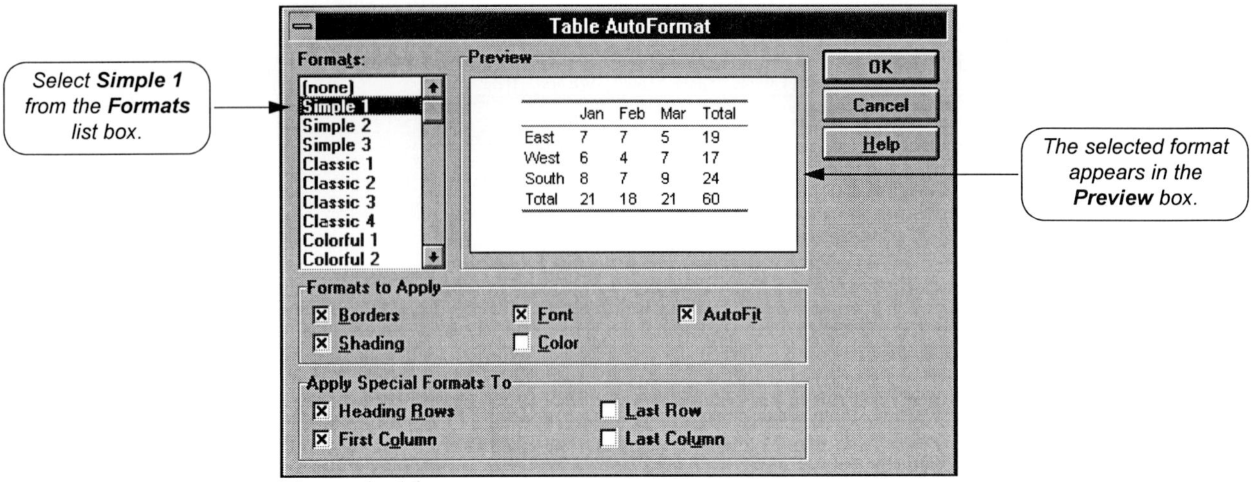

Figure 4 - 16

10. Select **Simple 1** from the **Formats** list box, and then click on **OK**.

    You return to the Word table. The table should still be selected.

11. Click in one of the cells so that the entire table is no longer selected and move to Row 1.
12. Click outside the *Word* table on a blank area of the slide.

    The table is placed on the slide within the original placeholder boundaries. Your slide should resemble Figure 4 - 17. Now you will make one editing change to the table.

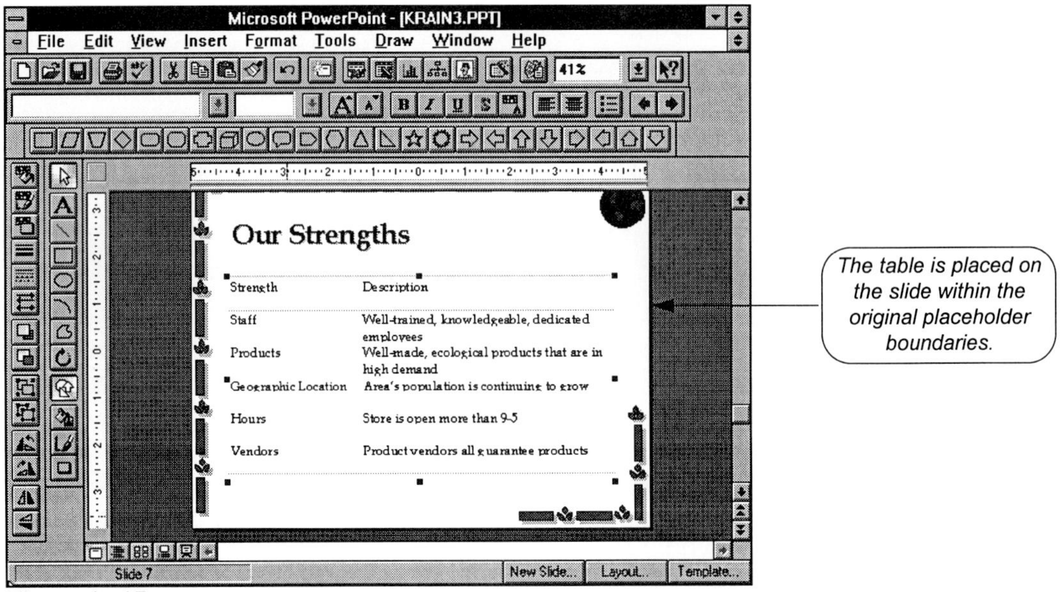

Figure 4 - 17

13. Double-click on the *Word* table.

    The border outside the table and the rulers return as well as the Word Menu bar and toolbars.

14. Change **Area's** in the third description to **City's**.
15. Return to the *PowerPoint* presentation.

    ***Area's** has been changed to **City's**.*

16. Save the presentation using the same name.

INSERTING A GRAPH

A graph (also called a chart) is a graphical representation of data. A graph is a useful tool in presentations. Your audience will not want to read lengthy data, even if it is in an organized table format. A graph allows you to take the data and graphically show comparisons, trends, progress, growth, decline or change. The basic graph formats are the pie, bar, and line graphs. Pie graphs are good graphs for showing parts of a whole. Percentages are easily represented using the pie graph. Bar graphs are good graphs for comparisons. Your audience will be able to scan the sizes of the bars for comparisons. Line graphs are good for changes over time. Lines easily show the ups and downs of data.

As with tables, *PowerPoint* does not have the capability of adding a graph to a slide. It does, however, use the capability of *Microsoft Graph 5.0,* a separate charting program for creating graphs.

Graphing Terms and Definitions

There are several terms and definitions that are important to understand before inserting a graph into a presentation. Table 4 - 1 lists these terms and definitions:

Term	Definition
pie graph	A pie graph, just like a pie, is a circle divided into slices. Pie graphs let you show how the parts make up the whole.
bar graph	A bar graph shows columns of data. Bar graphs are used to graphically compare items of information.
horizontal bar graph	A horizontal bar graph switches the data from the x and y axes changing the orientation of the graph. The labels appear on the y-axis.
x-axis	The horizontal axis of a graph.
y-axis	The vertical axis of a graph.
legend	The legend shows what each series of data represents.
label	The label is text that identifies the data.
value	Values are the data or numbers.

Table 4 - 1

To insert a graph:

- If the slide has a graph placeholder, double-click on the placeholder. If there is no placeholder on the slide, select **INSERT/Microsoft Graph** or click on the **Insert Graph** button on the Standard toolbar.

  A graph charting sample data will appear within a border with the datasheet with the sample data appearing above the graph. As with inserting the Word table, the Title bar still says you are in PowerPoint; however, the Menu bar and toolbar are from Microsoft Graph.

- Delete the current sample data and enter your own data.
- Close the datasheet.
- Select a chart type.
- Select a format.
- Format labels as necessary.
- Format the legend as necessary.
- Click anywhere on the slide, outside the placeholder, to return to *PowerPoint.*

To edit a graph:

- Double-click on the graph to enable the *Microsoft Graph* Menu bar and toolbar.

Activity 4.4: Inserting a Pie Graph into the krain3.ppt Presentation

In this activity, you will use the *Microsoft Graph* program to insert a pie graph into the **krain3.ppt** presentation. Both Slide 5 and Slide 8 have placeholders for graphs. You will insert a pie graph on Slide 5.

1. After Activity 4.3 you should be on Slide 7 of the **krain3.ppt** presentation.
2. Move to Slide 5.
3. Double-click on the graph placeholder.

   A graph appears in the placeholder with a datasheet above the graph (Figure 4 - 18).
4. Highlight the sample data and labels and press the **DELETE** key.

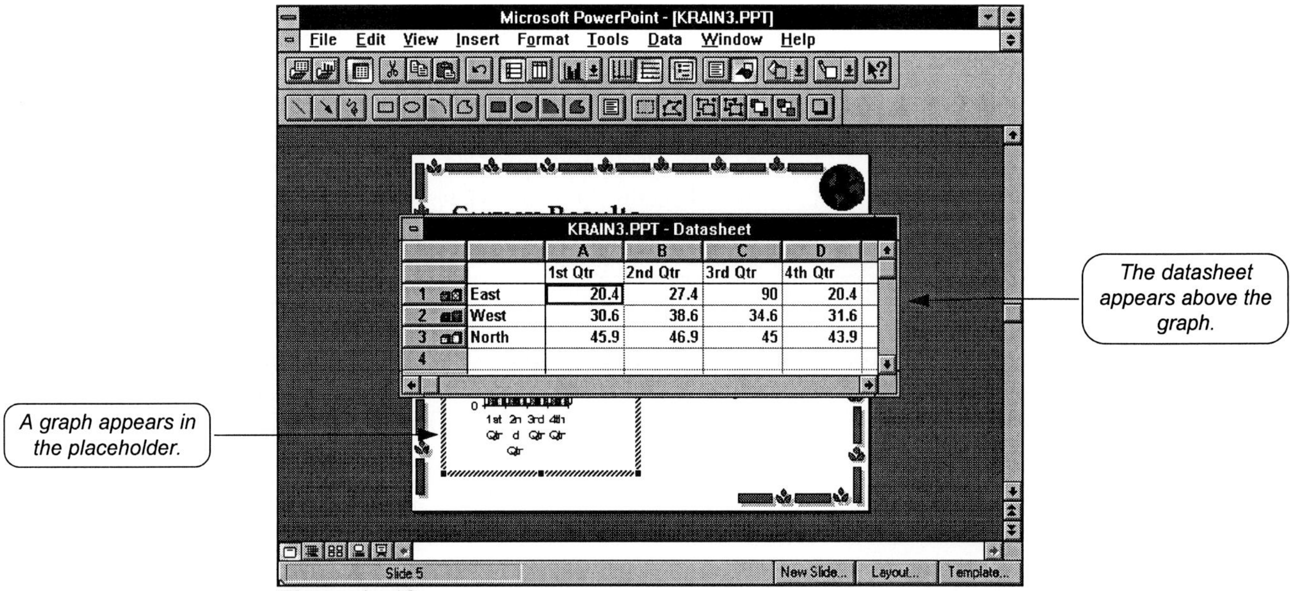

Figure 4 - 18

5. Choose **FORMAT/Chart Type**.

   *The **Chart Type** dialog box appears on the screen (Figure 4 - 19).*

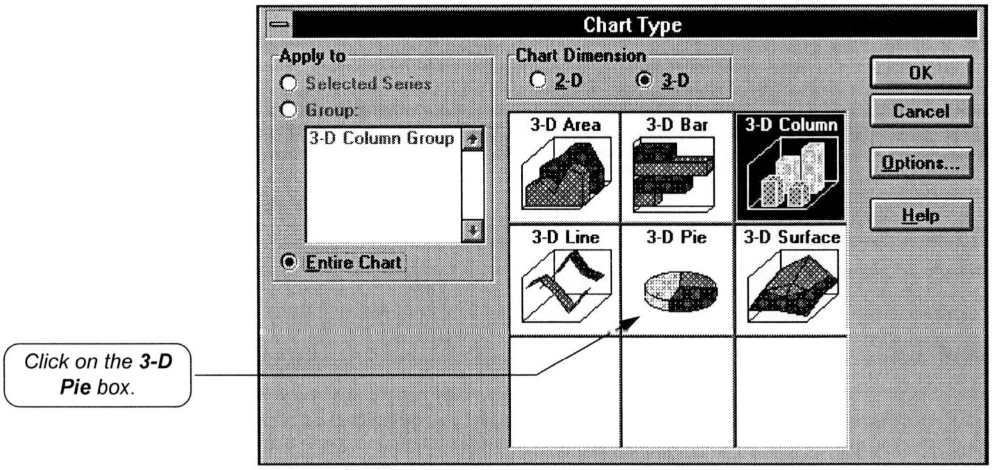

Figure 4 - 19

6. Click on the **3-D Pie** box and then click on **OK**.

   The datasheet labels change to indicate pie rather than bar data (Figure 4 - 20).

The datasheet labels change to indicate Pie rather than Bar data.

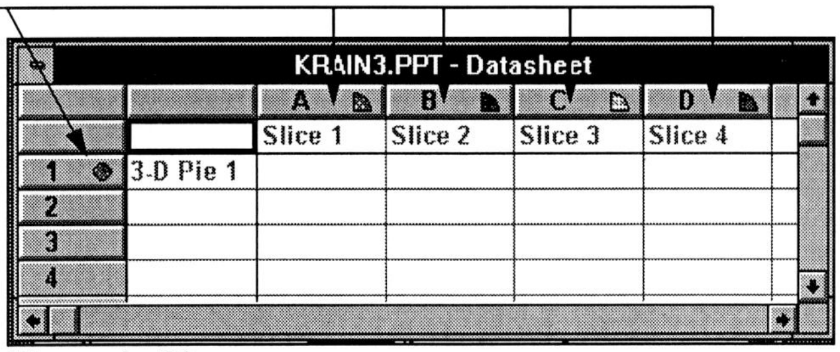

Figure 4 - 20

7. *Slice 1*, *Slice 2*, *Slice 3*, etc. should appear in gray print in each of the cells. Enter the labels listed below from left to right typing over the existing labels (*Slice 1*, *Slice 2*, *Slice 3*, etc.). Use the **TAB** key to move to the right. Use the **SHIFT+TAB** keys to move to the left. Or use the arrows keys.

   >1/week

   1/week

   2/month

   1/month

   <1/month

8. Enter the following values under each of the labels in the second row from left to right beginning in cell **A1**.

   50

   50

   400

   400

   100

   Your datasheet should resemble Figure 4 - 21.

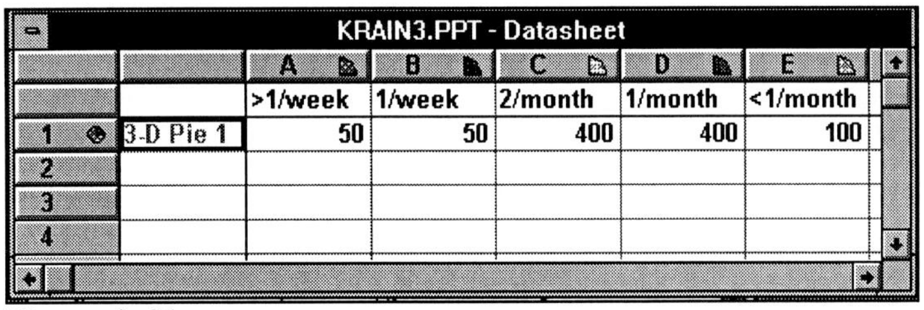

Change the size of the datasheet by dragging the frame on the right side until the E slice appears.

Figure 4 -21

PROBLEM SOLVER: *The datasheet's right margin has been extended so that all slices could be included in Figure 4 -21. On your screen, you may only be able to see 4 slices of data at once. You can change the size of the datasheet by pointing to the right frame (the gray border around the outside of the datasheet) and dragging it to the right until the E slice appears.*

9. Close the datasheet by clicking on the **Control** menu in the top left corner of the datasheet and then clicking on **Close**.

The datasheet will be removed from the screen and you will be able to see your graph. The graph is not complete yet. You will resize and move the legend, and then select an AutoFormat for the pie graph.

10. Click on the legend so that handles appear around the border.
11. Point to the left middle handle. Drag the left side until **month** in the last item appears on one line (Figure 4 - 22).

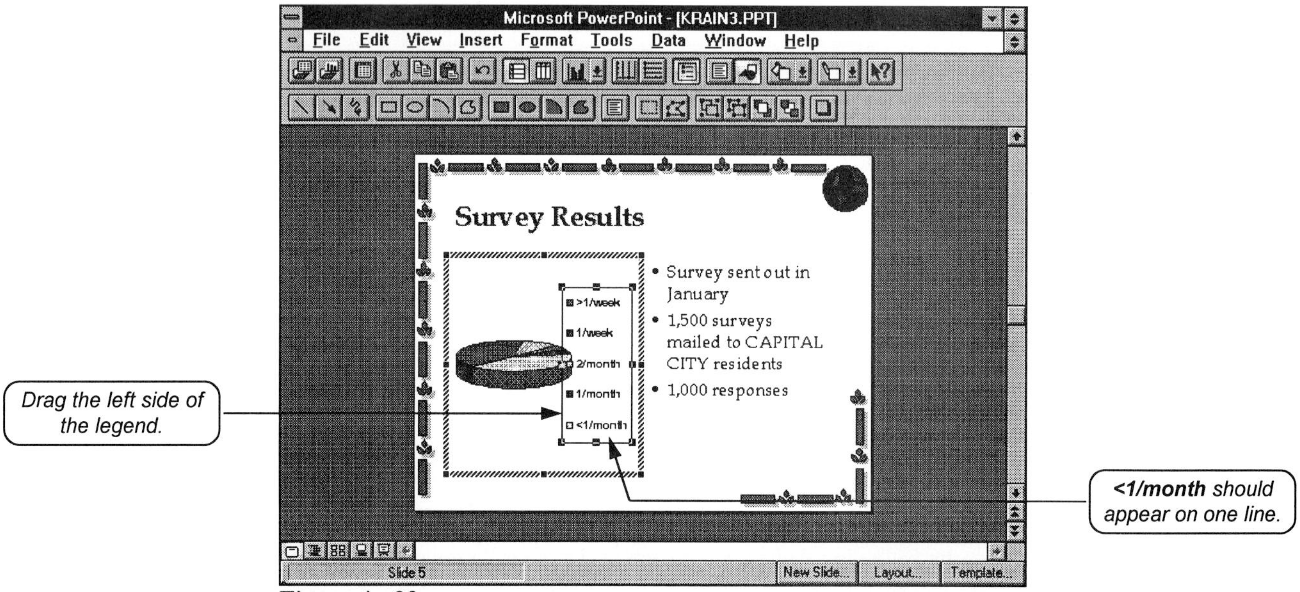

Figure 4 - 22

12. Point to the top middle handle and drag the top side down until the legend box is about half its current size (Figure 4 - 23).

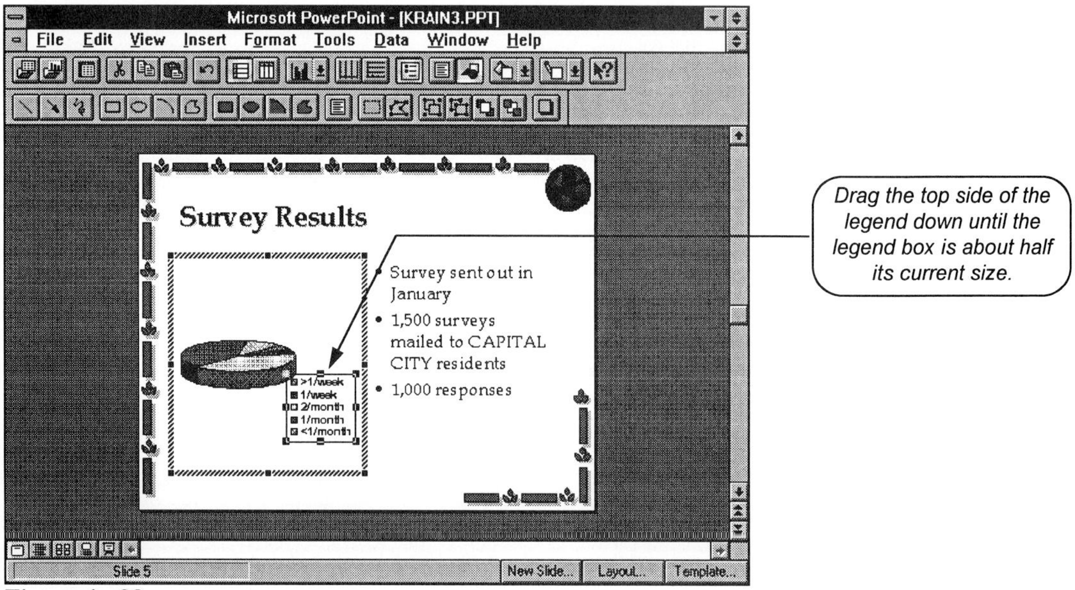

Figure 4 - 23

13. Move the legend to the bottom left corner inside the graph border.

14. Choose **FORMAT/AutoFormat.**

    *The **AutoFormat** dialog box appears on the screen (Figure 4 - 24).*

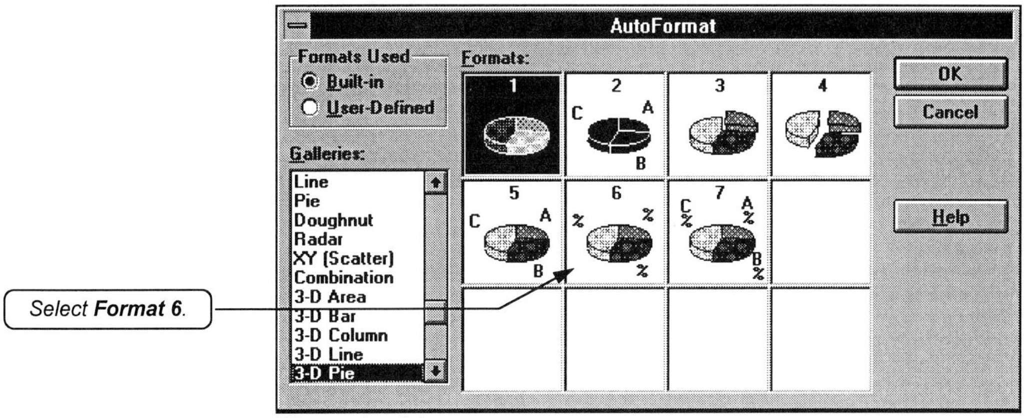

Figure 4 - 24

15. Select **Format 6**. Only the percent values are showing in this format.
16. Click on **OK**.

    The pie is resized with the percentages showing around the pie (Figure 4 - 25).

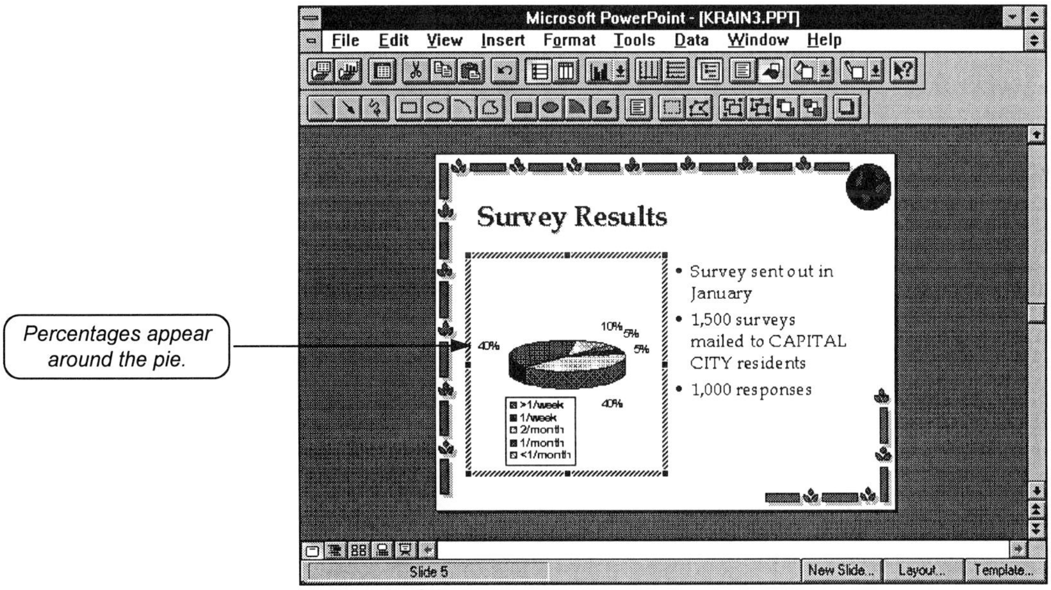

Figure 4 - 25

17. Return to *PowerPoint* by clicking on a blank area of the slide.
18. Save the presentation using the same name.

Activity 4.5: Inserting a Bar Graph into the krain3.ppt Presentation

In this activity, you will use the *Microsoft Graph* program to insert a bar graph into the **krain3.ppt** presentation. Both Slide 5 and Slide 8 have placeholders for graphs. You will insert a bar graph on Slide 8.

1. After Activity 4.3 you should be on Slide 5 of the **krain3.ppt** presentation.
2. Move to Slide 8.
3. Double-click on the graph placeholder.
4. Highlight and delete the sample data and labels in the datasheet.
5. Type the following labels in the first column. Gray **3-D Colum** labels appear in these cells.

   KR

   EcoWorld

   Mr. Green's

   Your datasheet should resemble Figure 4 - 26.

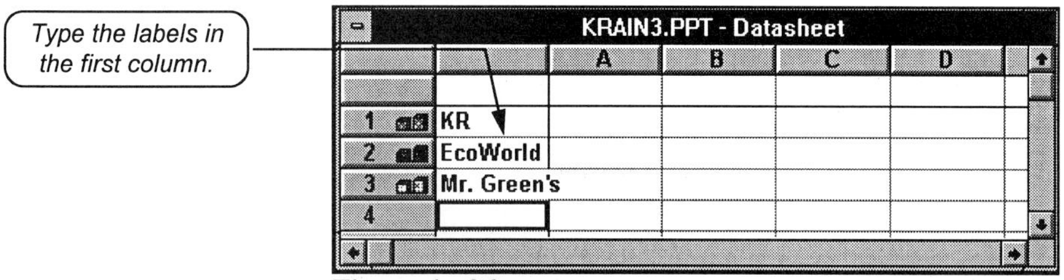

Figure 4 - 26

6. Type the following labels into the first row under the column headings, **A**, **B**, **C**, and **D**:

   CDs

   Stationary

   Terrapax

   Circuit Board

   Your datasheet should resemble Figure 4 - 27.

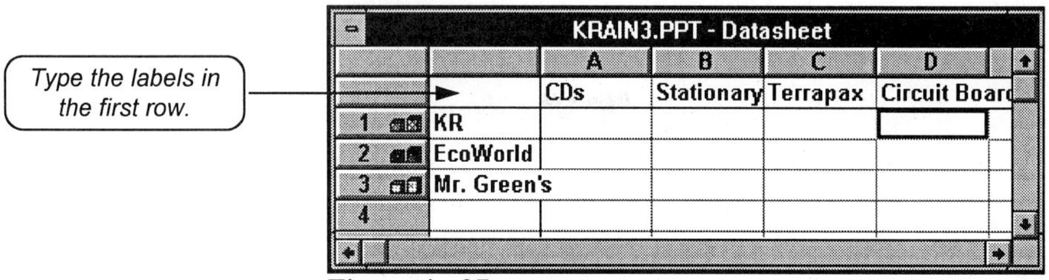

Figure 4 - 27

PROBLEM SOLVER: *Even though the complete labels do not show in the cells, they are there. They will appear on the graph. Text overflows to the next cell unless there is already something in the cell to the right in which case it is truncated.*

7. Enter the following values in the indicated columns:

A	B	C	D
15.98	**7.98**	**130**	**55**
16.5	**8.59**	**150**	**65**
16.55	**8.75**	**155**	**75**

Your datasheet should resemble Figure 4 - 28.

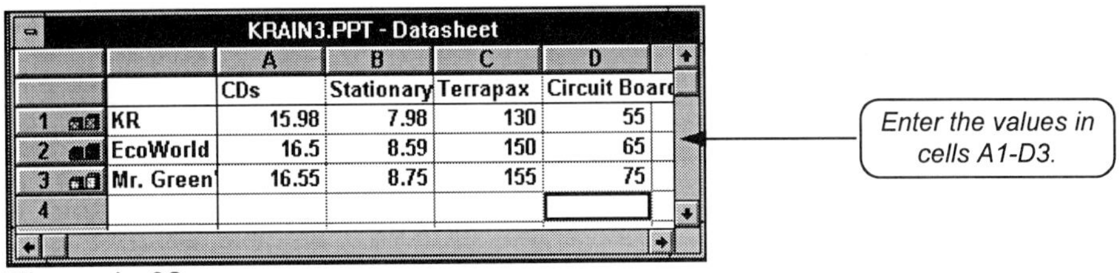

Figure 4 - 28

8. Close the datasheet.

   You will see the graph on the slide with the Microsoft Graph toolbars showing (Figure 4 - 29). Your graph will need some formatting. You will resize the graph area so that there is more space for the graph. Then you will select a chart type that will allow the labels to show. Then you will resize and move the legend.

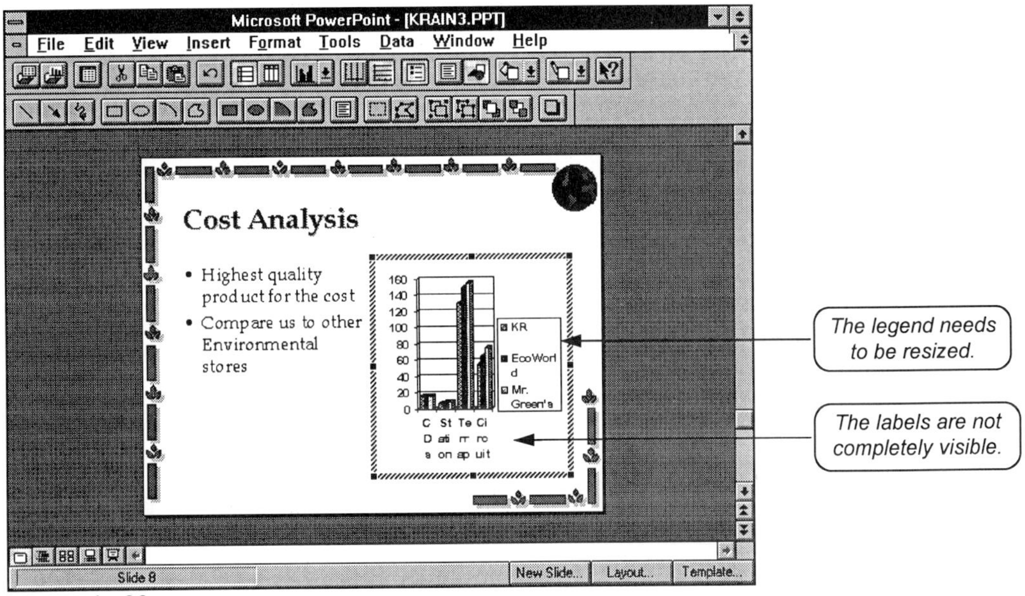

Figure 4 - 29

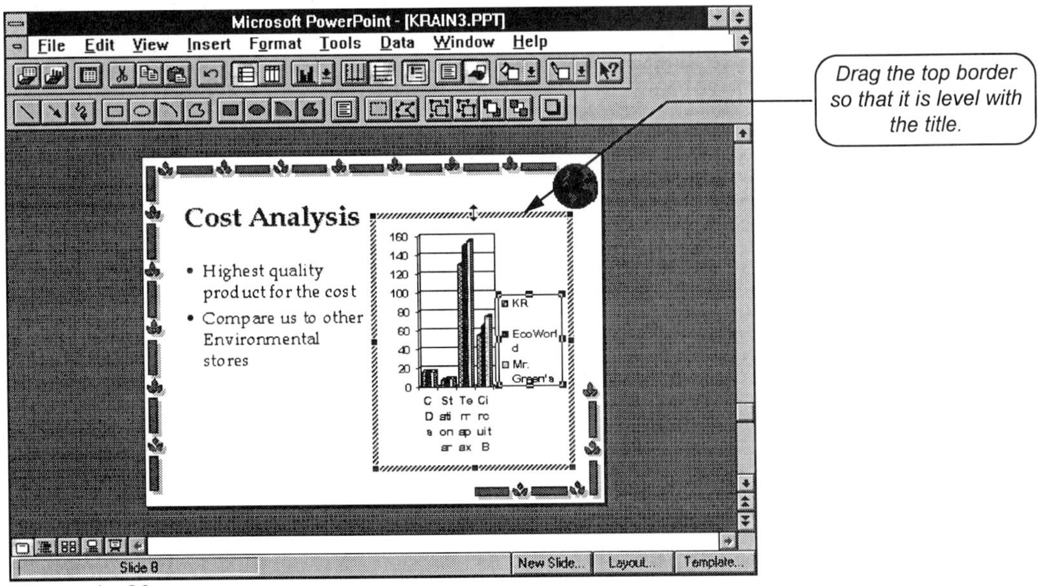

Figure 4 - 30

9. Point to the top middle handle of the graph border, and then drag the border so that it is level with the title (Figure 4 - 30).
10. Choose **FORMAT/Chart Type.**

    *The **Chart Type** dialog box appears.*
11. Select **3-D Bar**, and then click on **OK**.

    The orientation of the bars change to horizontal, showing the product labels along the vertical axis (y-axis).
12. Click on the legend so that it is selected.
13. Increase the width so that each label is on one line.
14. Decrease the height so that there is very little space between the legend items.
15. Move the legend to the top left corner of the graph area.
16. Choose **FORMAT/AutoFormat**.

    *The **AutoFormat** dialog box appears.*
17. Select **Format 1**, and then click on **OK**.

    The graph is almost formatted. The y-axis labels are too large to fit on one line (Figure 4 - 31). You will change the size of the labels so that they fit on one line.

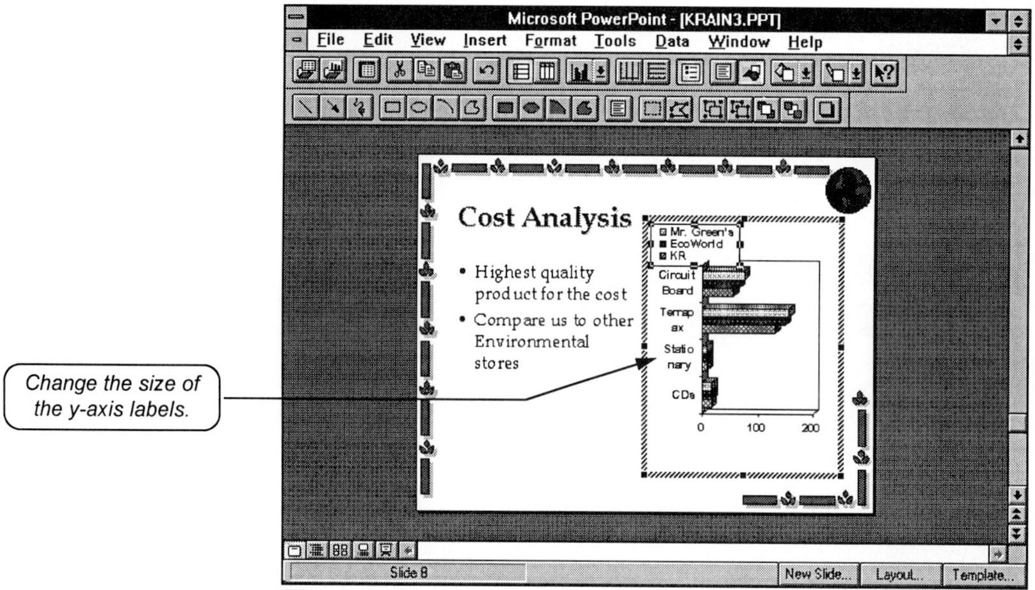

Figure 4 - 31

18. Point to the y-axis labels and double-click.

    *The **Format Axis** dialog box appears on the screen (Figure 4 - 32).*
19. Click on the **Font** tab.

    The Font formatting information will appear (Figure 4-33).
20. Change the size of the text to **12** in the **Size** list box, and then click on **OK**.

    PROBLEM SOLVER: ***Stationary*** *may still appear on two lines. If this happens, adjust the size of the graph block by pointing to the left middle handle and dragging it a small distance to the left.*

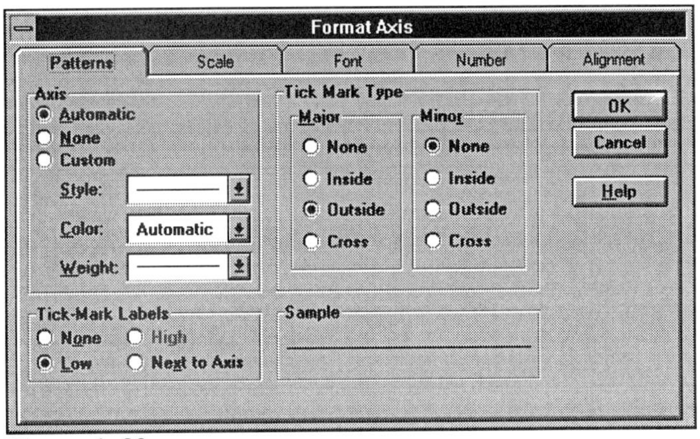

Figure 4 -32

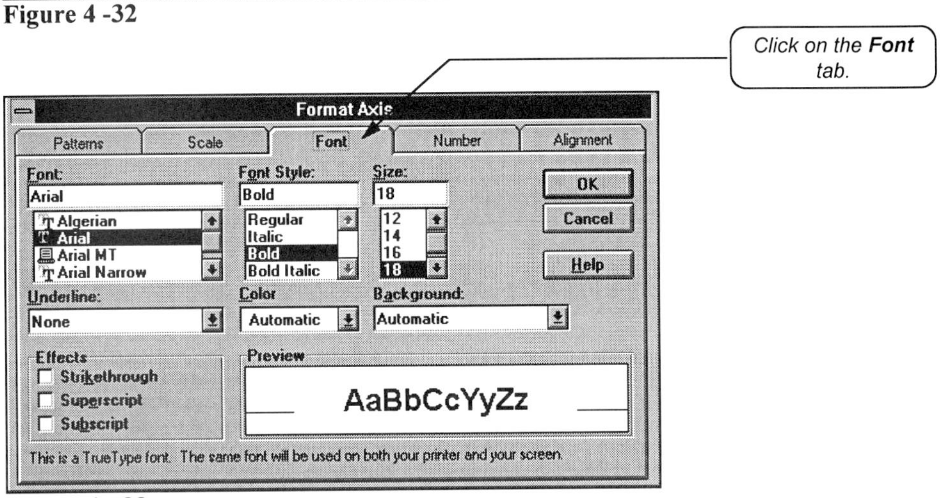

Figure 4 - 33

21. Change the size of the x-axis labels to **12 pt** by following steps 18-20.
22. Change the size of the legend labels to **12 pt** by following steps 18-20.

When your graph is completed, it should resemble Figure 4 - 34.

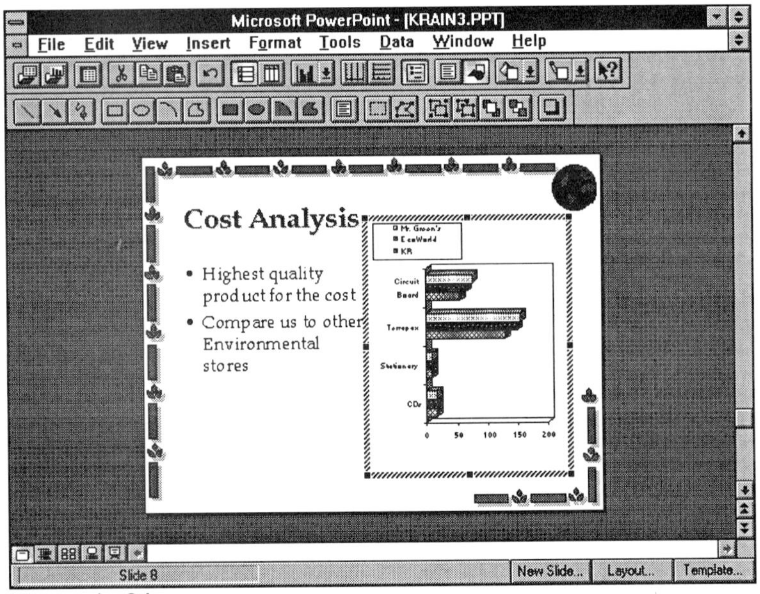

Figure 4 - 34

23. Return to the slide by clicking on a blank area of the slide.
24. Save the presentation using the same name.
25. Close the presentation.
26. Exit *PowerPoint*.

SUMMARY

In this lesson, you inserted application objects and clip art into a presentation. You inserted clip art into a presentation with and without a placeholder. You sized and moved the clip art when you did not use the placeholder. You also inserted a *Word* table and a pie and bar graph using *Microsoft Graph* into the presentation. In Lesson 5, you will learn about creating drawing objects using the *PowerPoint* tools.

KEY TERMS

Application Objects
AutoFormat
Chart Type
Clip Art
ClipArt Gallery
Datasheet
Embedding
Find Feature
Graph
Labels
Legend
Moving
Object Linking and Embedding (OLE)
Objects
Placeholder
Sizing
Table
X-axis
Y-axis

INDEPENDENT PROJECTS

The four independent projects allow you to practice the basic skills involved in inserting objects into presentations. You will insert clip art, tables, and graphs into the presentations that have been created, edited, and formatted in the last three lessons.

Independent Project 4.1: Inserting a Word Table into the ellis3.ppt Presentation

In Independent Project 3.1, you formatted the **ellis2.ppt** presentation so that the delivery of the presentation would be more effective. In this project, you will add a *Word* table to the end of the **ellis3.ppt** presentation that lists specific information about immigrants that entered the United States.

1. Open the *PowerPoint* program, if it is not already open.
2. Open the **ellis3.ppt** presentation.
3. Switch to Slide View, if necessary.
4. Move to Slide 8, the last slide in the presentation.
5. Add a new slide to the presentation with a **Table** layout.
6. Add the following title to Slide 9: **Immigration from 1820-1920**
7. Double-click on the Table placeholder.
8. Enter **2** columns and **6** rows into the **Insert Word Table** dialog box, and then click on **OK**.
9. Enter the following information into the table:

Area	**Number of People**
Asia	**6,019**

Europe	**37,101**
Australia and New Zealand	**147**
Africa	**334**
South America	**13,068**

10. Choose **TABLE/Select Table.**
11. Change the size of the text to **28 pt**.
12. Choose **TABLE/Table AutoFormat**.
13. Select the **Simple 1** format, and then click on **OK**.
14. Return to the *PowerPoint* presentation by clicking on a blank area of the slide.
15. Double-click on the *Word* table.
16. Change the first column heading to **Area of the World**.
17. Return to the *PowerPoint* presentation.
18. Save the presentation as **ellis4.ppt**. Slide 9 should resemble Figure 4 - 35.

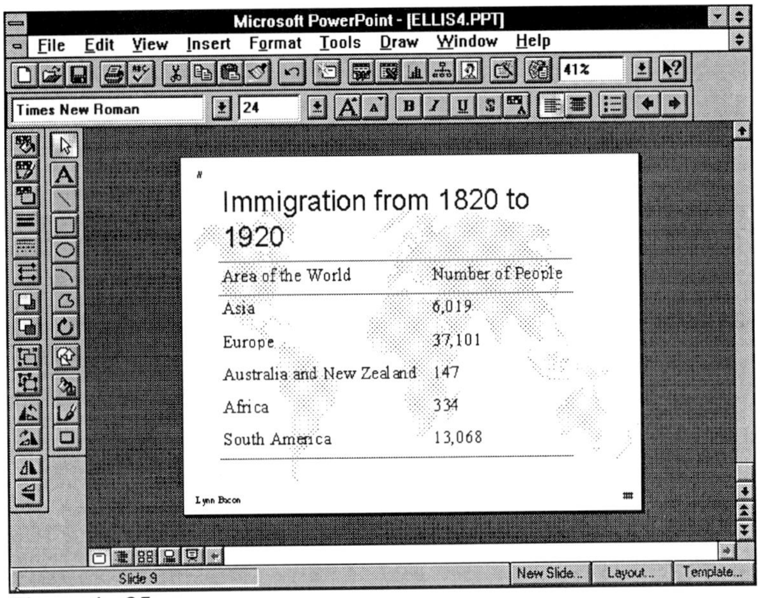

Figure 4 - 35

19. Print **Slide 9** using the **Black & White** print option.
20. Close the presentation and exit *PowerPoint* or continue with the next project.

Independent Project 4.2: Adding Clip Art to the brown3.ppt Presentation

In Independent Project 3.2, you formatted the **brown2.ppt**. In this project, you will add clip art to the **brown3.ppt** presentation. You will add clip art to the Title slide without using a placeholder and to Slide 3 (<u>Statement of Purpose</u>) using a clip art placeholder.

1. Open the *PowerPoint* program, if it is not already open.
2. Open the **brown3.ppt** presentation.
3. Switch to Slide View, if necessary.

4. Move to Slide 3.
5. Change the layout of the slide to **Text & Clip Art**.
6. Double-click on the clip art placeholder.
7. Select the **Academic** category.
8. Select the **Seminar** image.

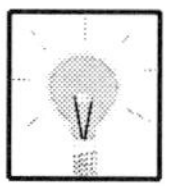

HINT: *Look at the Status bar as you click on pictures to find the correct picture.*

9. Click on **OK**.

The clip art image is placed on the slide within the boundaries of the placeholder (Figure 4 - 36).

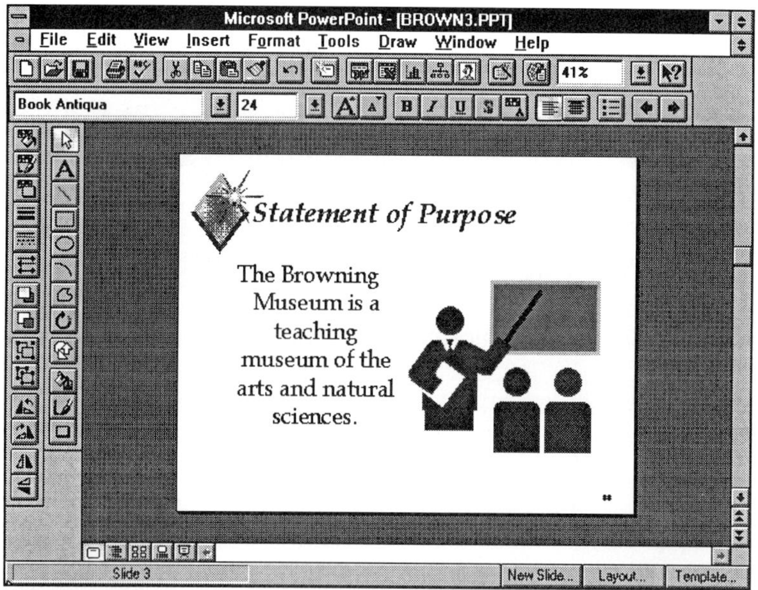

Figure 4 - 36

10. Move to Slide 1.

11. Click on the **Insert Clip Art** button on the Standard toolbar.
12. Select the **Plants** category.
13. Select the **Lily** image, and then click on **OK**.

The lily is placed on the middle of the slide. You will size it, and then move it to the top right corner of the slide.

14. Decrease the size of the lily to ½ its current size.
15. Move the lily to the top right corner of the slide. Slide 1 should resemble Figure 4 - 37.
16. Save the presentation as **brown4.ppt**.
17. Print Slide 1 and 3 using the **Black & White** print option.
18. Close the presentation and exit *PowerPoint* or continue with the next project.

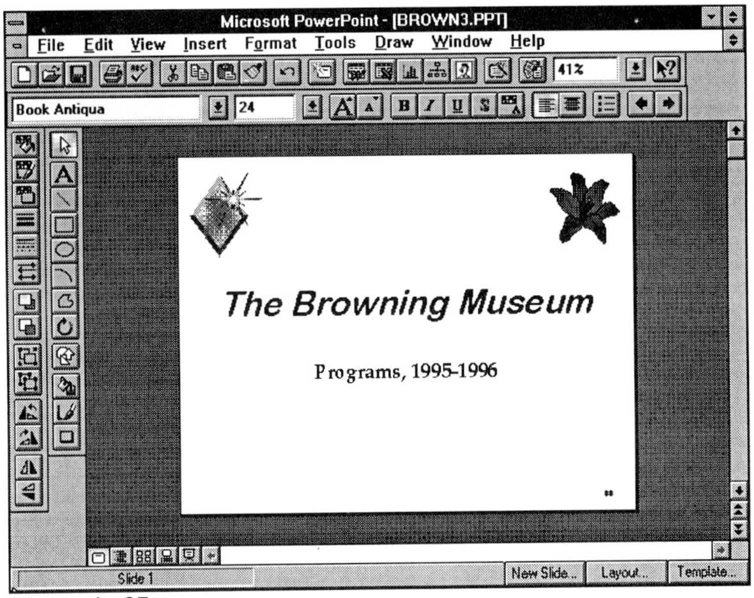

Figure 4 - 37

Independent Project 4.3: Adding a Graph to the travel3.ppt Presentation

In Independent Project 3.3, you formatted the **travel2.ppt** presentation. In this project you will add a graph to the **travel3.ppt** presentation. There is already a graph placeholder on Slide 3 (<u>Airline Ticket Information</u>). You will add a graph comparing ticket quotations.

1. Open the *PowerPoint* program, if it is not already open.
2. Open the **travel3.ppt** presentation.
3. Switch to Slide View, if necessary.
4. Move to Slide 3.
5. Double-click on the graph placeholder.
6. Delete the sample data and labels in the datasheet.
7. Enter the following labels in the first column where there is gray text (<u>3-D Colum</u>).

   1 **Julie's**

   2 **Travel the World**

   3 **Global Travel**

8. Enter the following labels in the first row as indicated:

A	B	C
Tourist	**Discount**	**Domestic**

9. Enter the following values into the datasheet as indicated:

	A	B	C
1	**200**	**400**	**300**
2	**300**	**500**	**400**
3	**350**	**450**	**350**

10. Highlight Column D down to the third row.
11. Choose **EDIT/Delete.**
12. Click on the **Entire Column** button, and then click on **OK.**

    The sample data had four series of data. Even though there are no values in the column now, you still need to do steps 10-12 to clear the column.

13. Close the datasheet.
14. Change the chart type to **3-D Bar.**
15. Edit the legend so that the text is **12 pt.**
16. Adjust the size of the legend as necessary and move it to the bottom left corner of the graph box.
17. Change the AutoFormat to the first format (no lines in the background frame).
18. Change the size of the x-axis and y-axis labels to **12 pt.**
19. Move the legend to the top left or top right corner.
20. Return to the *PowerPoint* presentation.
21. Save the presentation as **travel4.ppt**. Slide 3 should resemble Figure 4 - 38.

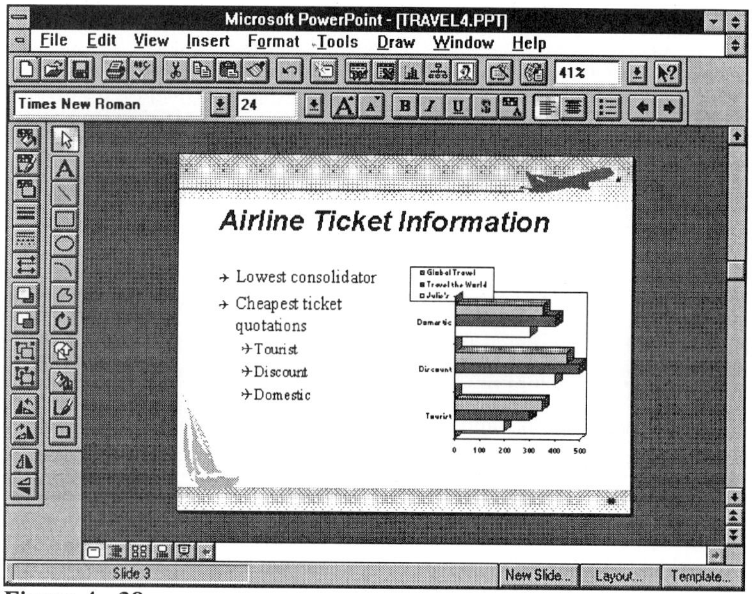

Figure 4 - 38

22. Print Slide 3 using the **Black & White** print option.
23. Close the presentation and exit *PowerPoint* or continue with the next project.

Independent Project 4.4: Adding Clip Art and a Word Table to the train3.ppt Presentation

In Independent Project 3.4 you formatted the **train2.ppt** presentation and saved it as **train3.ppt.** In this project, you will add a clip art image to the slide master and add a slide with a *Word* table listing formatting effects and their definitions.

1. Open the **train3.ppt** presentation.

2. Add a computer symbol of your choice to the Slide Master in the top right corner.
3. Do not show the background objects on the Title slide.
4. Add a larger version of the computer symbol you chose for the Slide Master to the Title slide.
5. Add a new slide to the end of the presentation with the **Table** layout.
6. Entitle the slide: **Formatting in PowerPoint**
7. Create a 2 column by 8 row table.
8. Use the following labels in the left column of the table:

   Formatting Feature

   Bold

   Italic

   Underline

   Shadow

   Increase Font Size

   Decrease Font Size

   Bullet On/Off
9. Enter the following text as the heading for the second column: **Definition**
10. Read Lesson 3 to find the information you will enter in the second column.
11. Decrease text size so that the entire table fits on the slide.
12. Use a **Table AutoFormat** to format the table.
13. Save the presentation as **train4.ppt**. The structure of your presentation should resemble Figure 4 - 39.

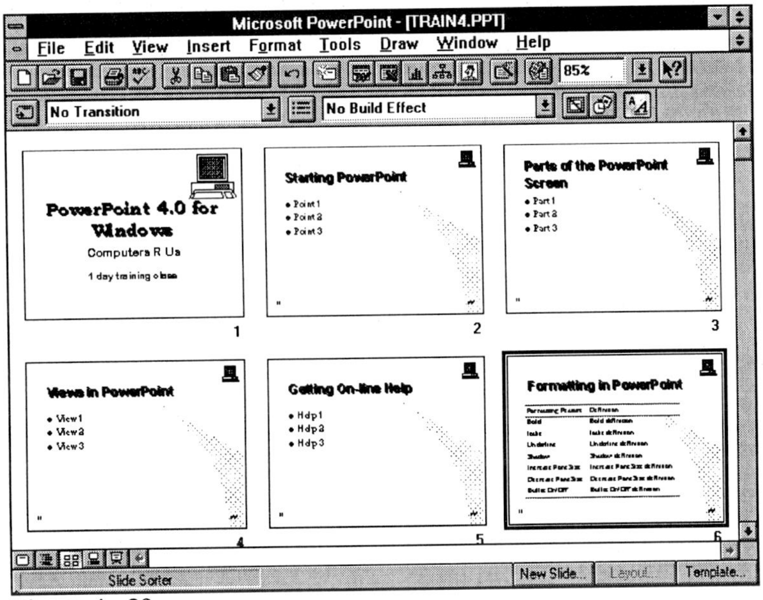

Figure 4 - 39

14. Print **Handouts (2 slides per page)** using the **Black & White** print option.

Lesson 5

Using Drawing Tools in a Presentation

Objectives

In this lesson you will learn how to:

- Add text to a slide using the Text tool
- Create a drawing object
- Move a drawing object
- Size a drawing object
- Size a line
- Copy a drawing object
- Delete a drawing object
- Change the attributes of a drawing object
- Change the color and attributes of a line
- Change the color of text
- Copy attributes from one drawing object to another
- Add an AutoShape to a slide
- Add text to an AutoShape
- Change the size of text within an AutoShape
- Change the AutoShape

PROJECT DESCRIPTION

In Lesson 4, you added application objects and clip art to the **krain2.ppt** presentation. In this lesson you will use the drawing tools available in *PowerPoint* to create drawing objects. The old saying, "A picture is worth a thousand words" is a true statement, especially for presentations. If the slides in your presentation are all text slides, your audience will lose interest. Drawings help to illustrate points, as well as keep the attention of your audience. When you are finished with this lesson, Slides 5, 7, and 9 will resemble Figure 5 - 1.

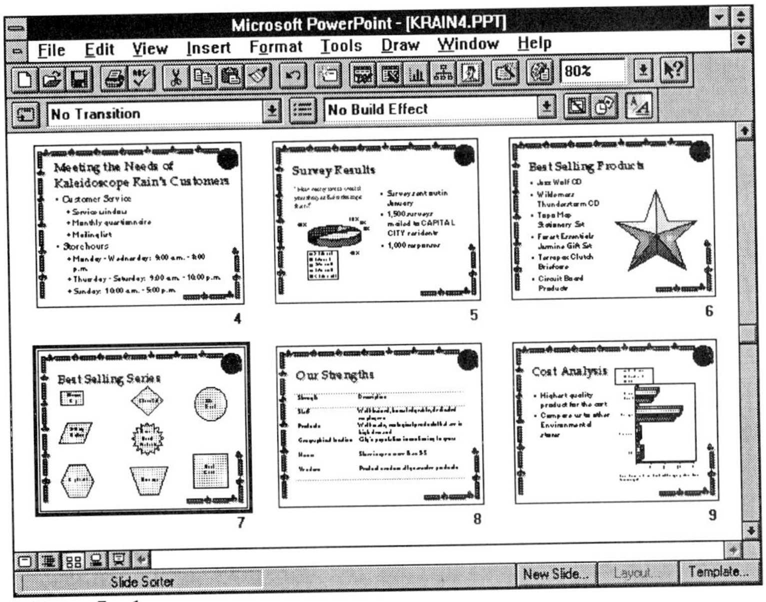

Figure 5 - 1

THE DRAWING TOOLS

The Drawing toolbars have all the tools available for drawing objects in Slide View and Notes Pages View. The Drawing toolbars are located to the left of the Slide Work Area and are used to add drawing objects to slides. The available tools on the Drawing toolbar are listed and defined in Table 5 - 1.

Button	Tool Name	Description
	*Selection Tool*	Used to select objects
	*Text Tool*	Used to create text
	*Line Tool*	Used to create lines
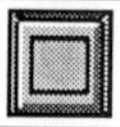	*Rectangle Tool*	Used to create rectangles and squares
	*Ellipse Tool*	Used to create ellipses and circles
	*Arc Tool*	Used to create arcs
	*Freeform Tool*	Used to create polygons, polylines or freehand lines
	*Free Rotate Tool*	Allows you to rotate to any angle
	*AutoShapes*	Shows or hides the AutoShapes toolbar
	*Fill On/Off*	Turns the fill of an object on or off
	*Line On/Off*	Turns the line for an object on or off
	*Shadow On/Off*	Turns the shadow for an object on or off

Table 5 - 1

To add text using the Text tool:

- Click on the **Text Tool** button on the Drawing toolbar.

  When you move the mouse pointer to the slide, a text cursor will appear.
- Drag a box on the screen.

  This box is the text block. When you type text, it will conform to the size of the text block.
- Type the desired text.

To create a drawing object:

- Click on the **Drawing Tool** button for the object you wish to create.
- Position the crosshair pointer where you want the object to start on the slide.
- Press and hold the left mouse button down, and then drag the pointer to where you want the object to end (diagonally across from the start point) and release the mouse button.

NOTE: *You can draw symmetrical objects by holding down the* ***SHIFT*** *key before releasing the mouse button while drawing. Using the Rectangle Tool, you can draw a square. Using the Ellipse Tool, you can draw a circle. Using the Line Tool, you can draw horizontal, vertical, or 45-degree lines.*

Activity 5.1: Adding Drawing Objects to the krain3.ppt Presentation

In this activity, you will use the Text Tool to add text to the two graphs that were created in Lesson 4. Then you will begin a diagram using the Drawing Tools to illustrate the Circuit Board products.

1. Open *PowerPoint*, if it is not already open.
2. Open the **krain3.ppt** presentation.
3. Move to Slide 5 (Survey Results).
4. Click on the **Text Tool** button on the Drawing toolbar.
5. Move the text cursor below the title and above the graph, and then drag a text block across the area (Figure 5 - 2).

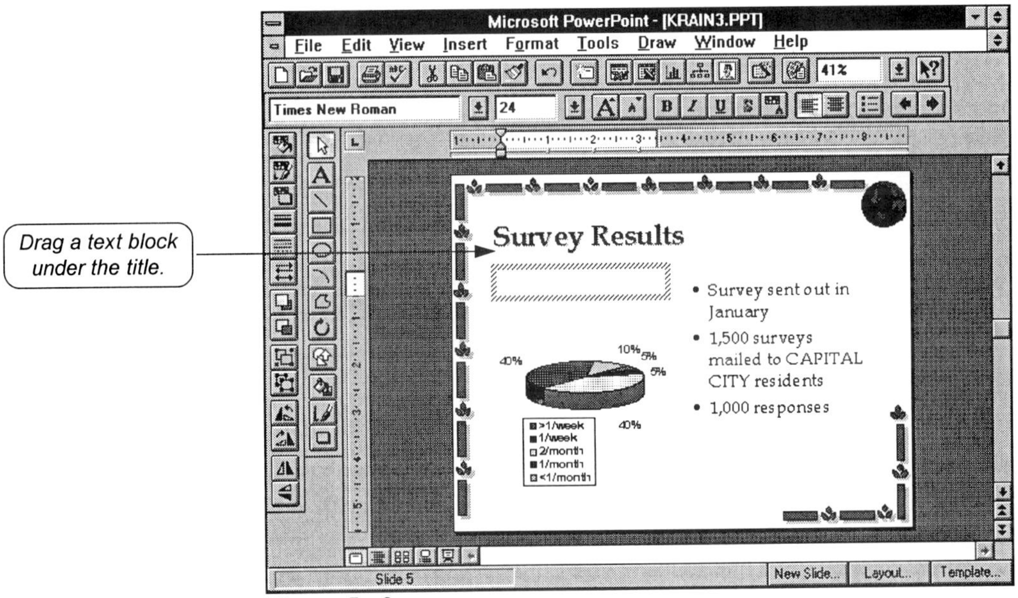

Figure 5 - 2

The text block appears with a flashing text cursor at the left margin of the text block.

6. Type the following text in the text box: **"How many times would you shop at Kaleidoscope Rain?"**

PROBLEM SOLVER: *The text on your screen may wordwrap differently because your text block may be a different size than the one used in Figure 5 - 2. It is okay if your text wordwraps differently.*

7. Deselect the text block by clicking on a blank area of the screen.

Slide 5 should resemble Figure 5 - 3.

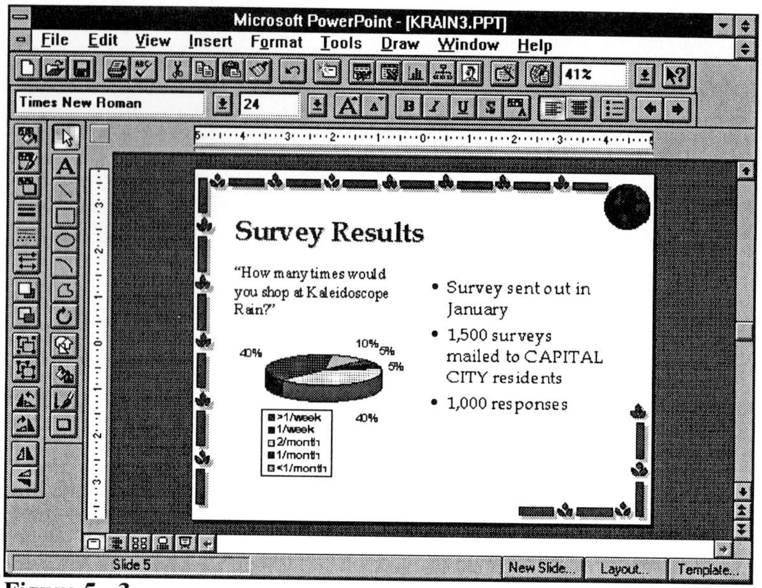

Figure 5 - 3

8. Move to Slide 8 (Cost Analysis).
9. Click on the **Text Tool** button on the Drawing toolbar.
10. Drag a text block below the bar graph (Figure 5 - 4).

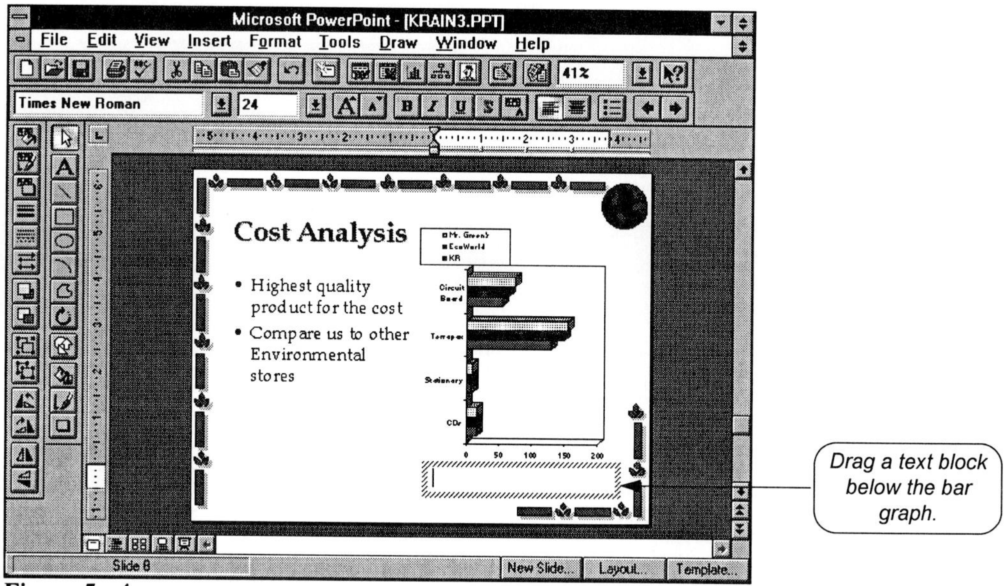

Figure 5 - 4

11. Type the following text in the text block: **Note: Values for Circuit Board and Terrapax products have been averaged.**

    NOTE: *Your text may wordwrap differently because of the size of the text block.*

12. Select the text block border so that handles appear and change the size of the text to **12 pt**.
13. Deselect the text block.

    Slide 8 should resemble Figure 5 - 5.

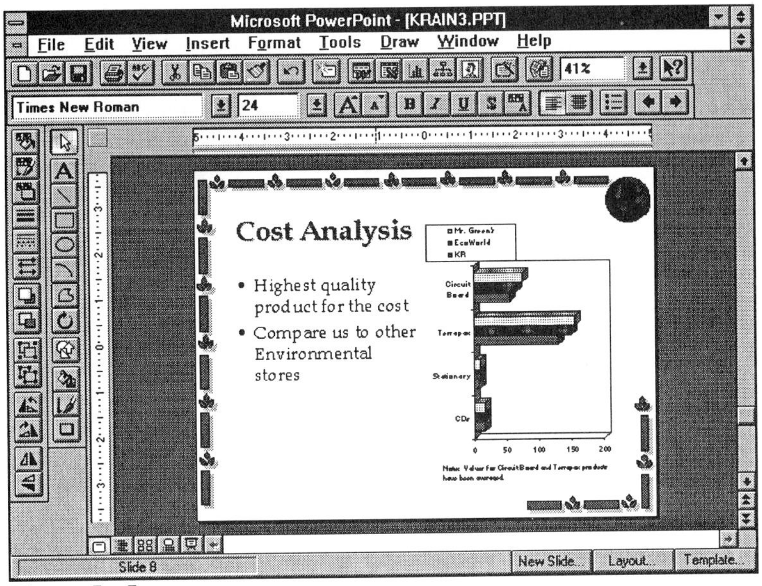

Figure 5 - 5

14. Save the presentation as **krain4.ppt**.
15. Move to Slide 6 (Best Selling Products).
16. Add a new slide to the presentation using the **Title Only** layout.
17. Add the following title to the presentation: **Best Selling Series**

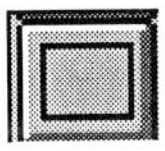

18. Click on the **Rectangle Tool** button on the Drawing toolbar.

    *The **Rectangle Tool** button is depressed.*
19. Move the mouse pointer under the title.

    The mouse pointer changes to a crosshair indicating that you are creating a drawing object.
20. Click and hold the left mouse button down, drag down and to the right about 2 inches, and then release the left mouse button.

    A rectangle will be drawn on your screen (Figure 5 - 6).

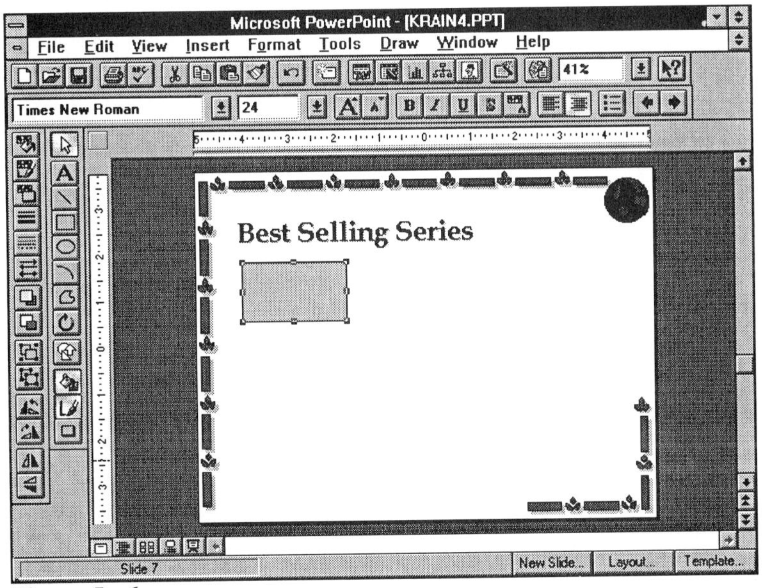

Figure 5 - 6

21. Draw a square in the bottom right corner of the slide using the **Rectangle Tool**. Before releasing the left mouse button, press the **SHIFT** key down. This will constrain the rectangle to a square (Figure 5 - 7).

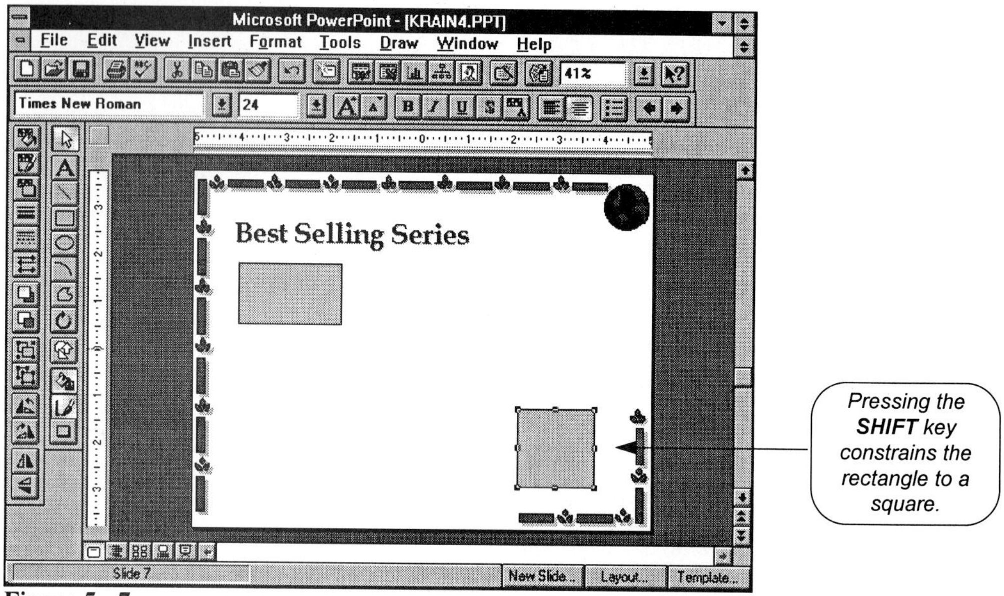

Figure 5 - 7

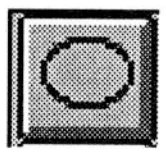

22. Click on the **Ellipse Tool** button on the Drawing toolbar.

    *The **Ellipse Tool** button is depressed.*

23. Draw an ellipse in the bottom left corner of the slide.
24. Draw a circle in the top right corner of the slide using the **Ellipse Tool**. Before releasing the left mouse button, press the **SHIFT** key down. This will constrain the ellipse to a circle (Figure 5 - 8).

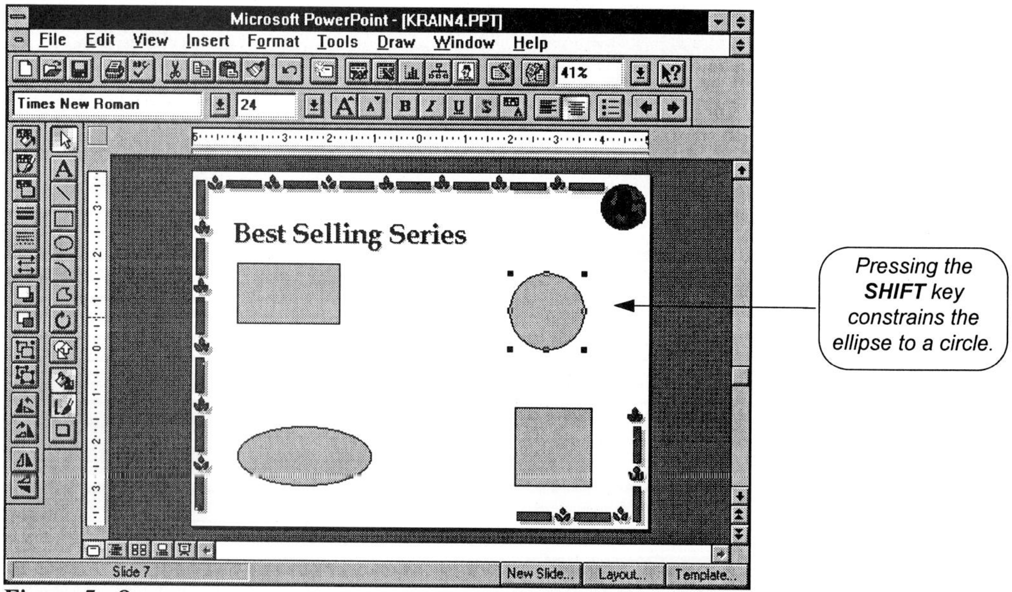

Figure 5 - 8

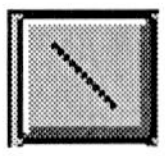

25. Click on the **Line Tool** button on the Drawing toolbar.

    *The **Line Tool** button is depressed.*

26. Point to the middle of the right side of the rectangle (Figure 5 - 9).

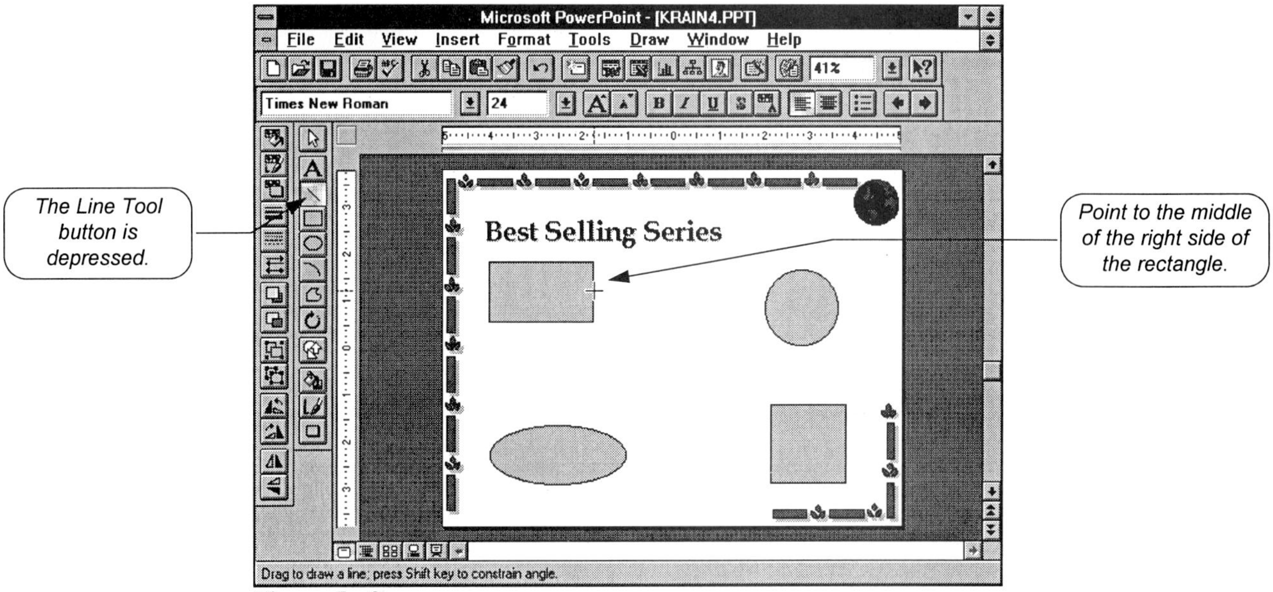

Figure 5 - 9

27. Click and hold the left mouse button down. Move to the middle of the left side of the square and then release the left mouse button.

    A line will be drawn connecting the rectangle and the square (Figure 5 - 10).

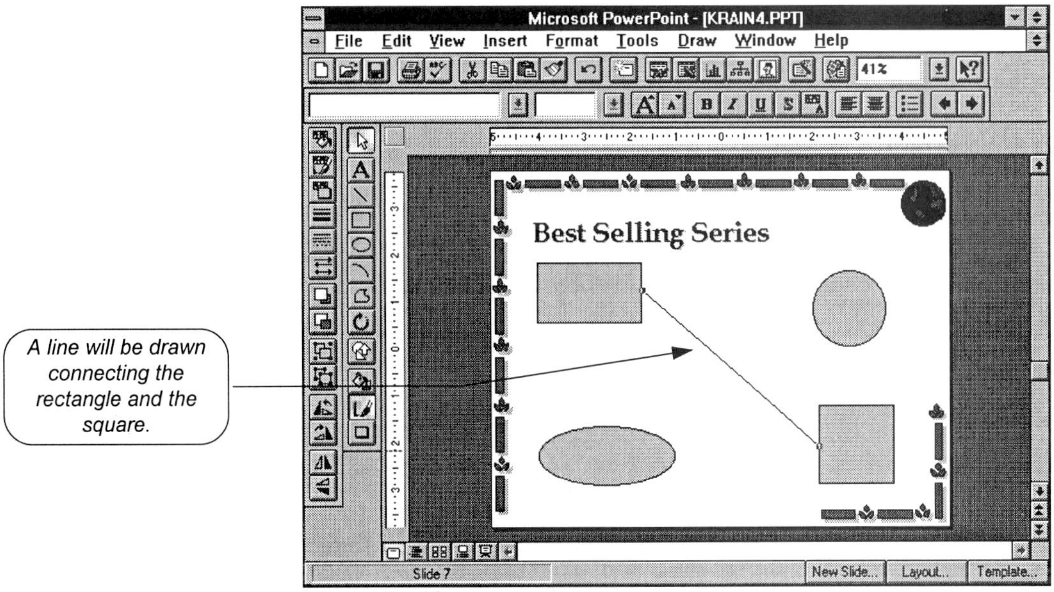

Figure 5 - 10

28. Draw a line connecting the ellipse to the circle.

    Your Slide 7 should resemble Figure 5 - 11.

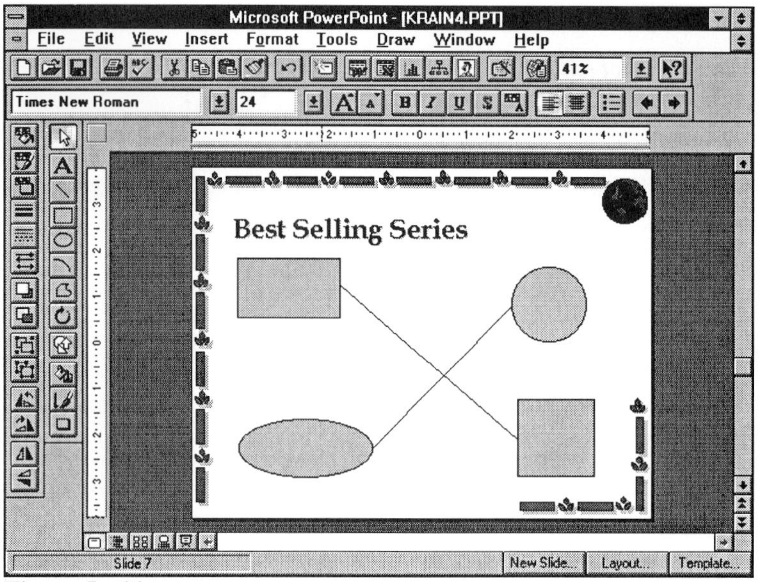

Figure 5 - 11

29. Save your presentation using the same name.

EDITING DRAWING OBJECTS

The Drawing+ toolbar is the second Drawing toolbar available in *PowerPoint*. The tools on this toolbar are used to edit or modify the drawing objects that you add to your slide using the Drawing toolbar. The tools on the Drawing+ toolbar are listed and defined in Table 5 - 2.

Button	Tool Name	Description
	Fill Color	Selects the fill color for an object
	Line Color	Selects the color of the line for an object
	Shadow Color	Selects the shadow color for an object
	Line Style	Select the line style for a line or object
	Dashed Lines	Creates dashed lines
	Arrowheads	Adds arrowheads to lines
	Bring Forward	Brings an object forward
	Send Backward	Sends an object backward
	Group	Groups objects together
	Ungroup	Ungroups objects
	Rotate Left	Rotates an object 90 degrees to the left
	Rotate Right	Rotates an object 90 degrees to the right
	Flip Horizontal	Flips an object horizontally
	Flip Vertical	Flips an object vertically

Table 5 - 2

To move an object:

- Point to the middle of the object.
- Drag the object to its new location.

To size an object:

- Select the object so that handles appear around the object.
- Point to one of the handles.

  Corner handles will size both the height and the width proportionately. Middle handles will size either the height or the width. A two-tipped arrow will appear.
- Drag the handle until the object is its new size.

To size a line:

- Point to the line and click once.

  Two handles will appear, one on each end of the line.
- Point to one of the handles.

  A crosshair will appear 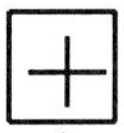 .
- Drag the end of the line to its new location.

To copy an object:

- Select the object you wish to copy.
- Choose **EDIT/Copy** or click on the **Copy** button  on the Standard toolbar.

  A copy of the object is placed on the clipboard.
- Choose **EDIT/Paste** or click on the **Paste** button  on the Standard toolbar.

  A copy of the object is placed on the slide.

To delete an object:

- Select the object you wish to delete.
- Choose **EDIT/Cut**, click the **Cut** button  on the Standard toolbar, or press the **DELETE** key.

  The selected object is deleted. When the Cut option is used, a copy of the cut item is placed on the clipboard.

Activity 5.2: Moving, Copying, Sizing, and Deleting Drawing Objects in the krain4.ppt Presentation

In this activity, you will continue to work with Slide 7 of the **krain4.ppt** presentation. In Activity 5.1 you placed a rectangle, square, ellipse, and circle on a slide. Then you drew lines to connect the rectangle to the square and the ellipse to the circle. In this activity, you will edit the drawing objects by moving, copying, sizing, and deleting them.

1. After Activity 5.1 you should be on Slide 7 of the **krain4.ppt** presentation.
2. Select the rectangle so that handles appear around the object.

   You will decrease the size of the rectangle. The corner handles size both the height and the width at the same time. Middle handles size either the height or the width.

3. Point to the top left corner handle so that a two-tipped arrow appears (Figure 5 - 12).

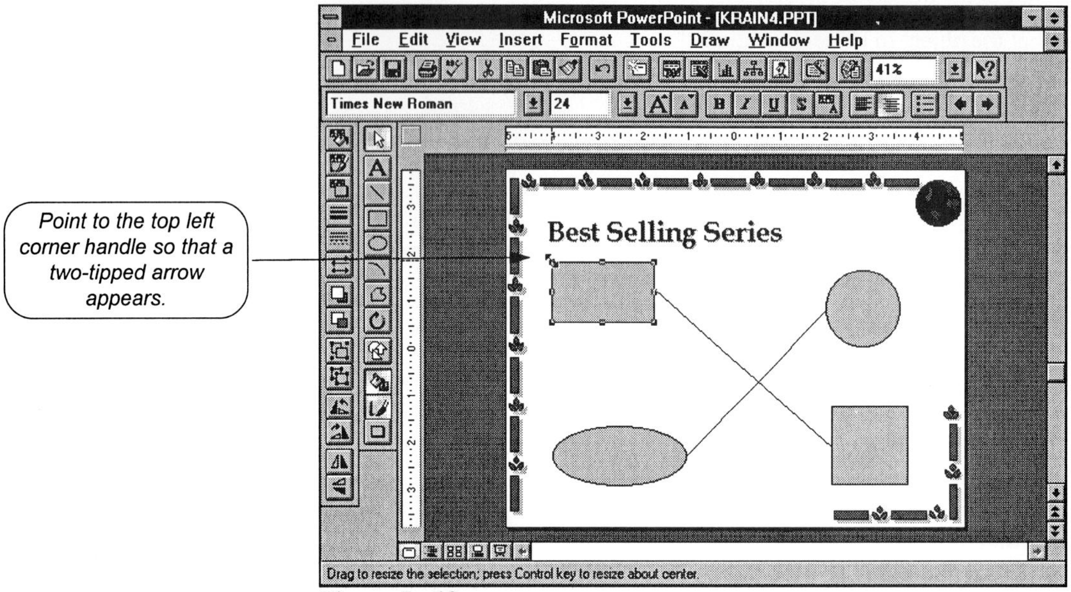

Figure 5 - 12

4. Click and hold the left mouse button down and drag the rectangle to half its current size; then release the left mouse button.

   Next you will move the rectangle under the title.

5. Point to the middle of the rectangle. The rectangle does not need to be selected.
6. Click and hold the left mouse button down, drag the rectangle to its new location, and then release the left mouse button (Figure 5 - 13).

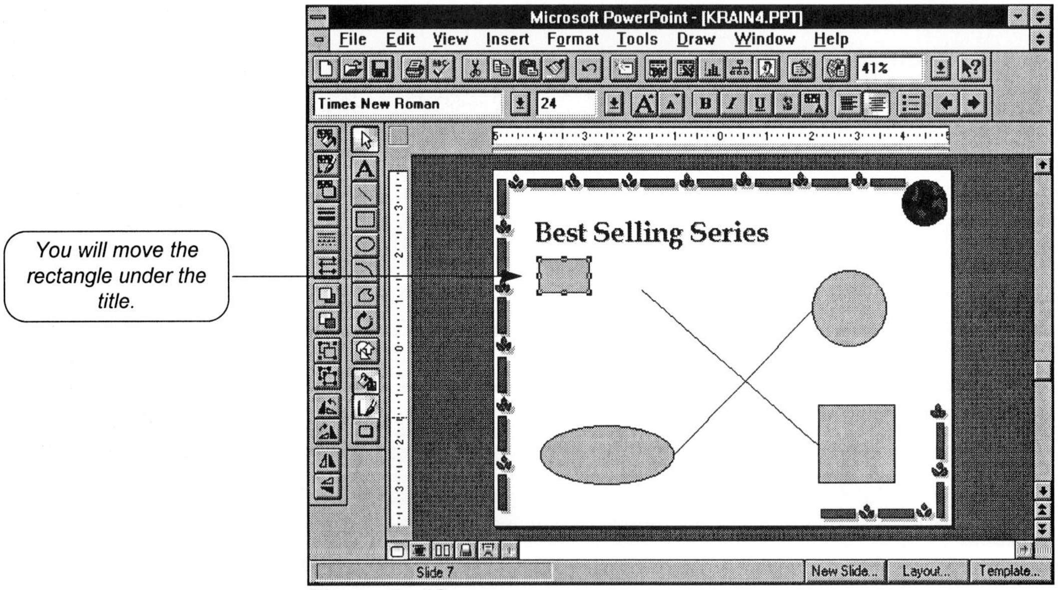

Figure 5 - 13

7. Decrease the size of the ellipse to half of its current size, and then move it to the bottom left corner of the screen (Figure 5 - 14).

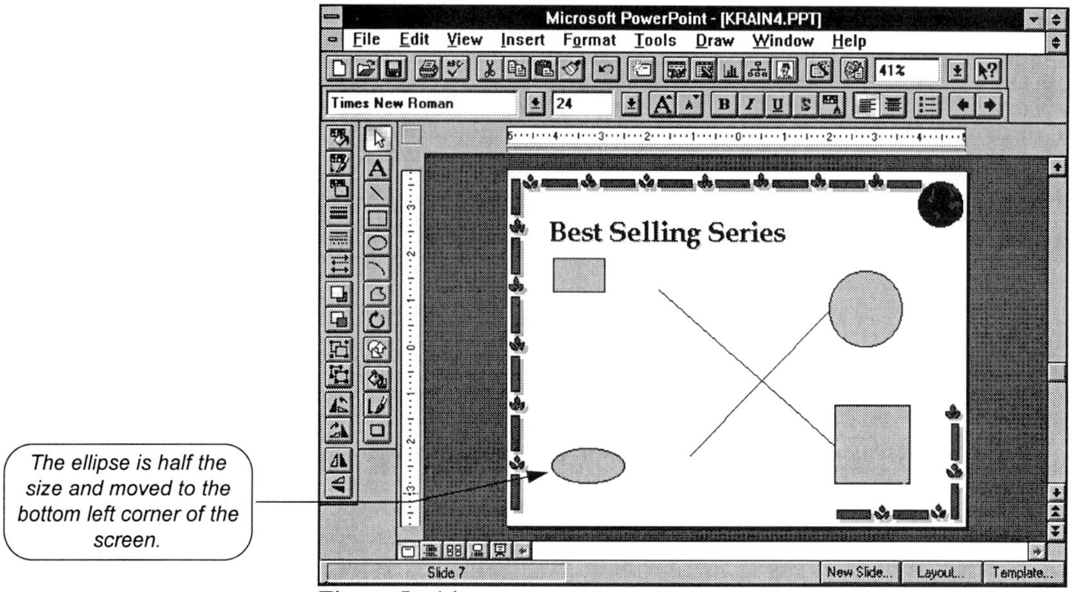

Figure 5 - 14

8. Move the circle and the square further into the top right and bottom right corners of the slide.

   You will move the lines that were connecting the rectangle and square and ellipse and circle so that they are connecting the objects again.

9. Select the line that was connecting the rectangle and the square.

   Two handles will appear, one on each end of the line.

10. Point to the handle that isn't connected to the rectangle.

    A crosshair appears.

11. Click and hold the left mouse button down, drag the line to the middle of the right side of the rectangle, and then release the left mouse button.

12. Connect the other side of the line to the square (Figure 5-15).

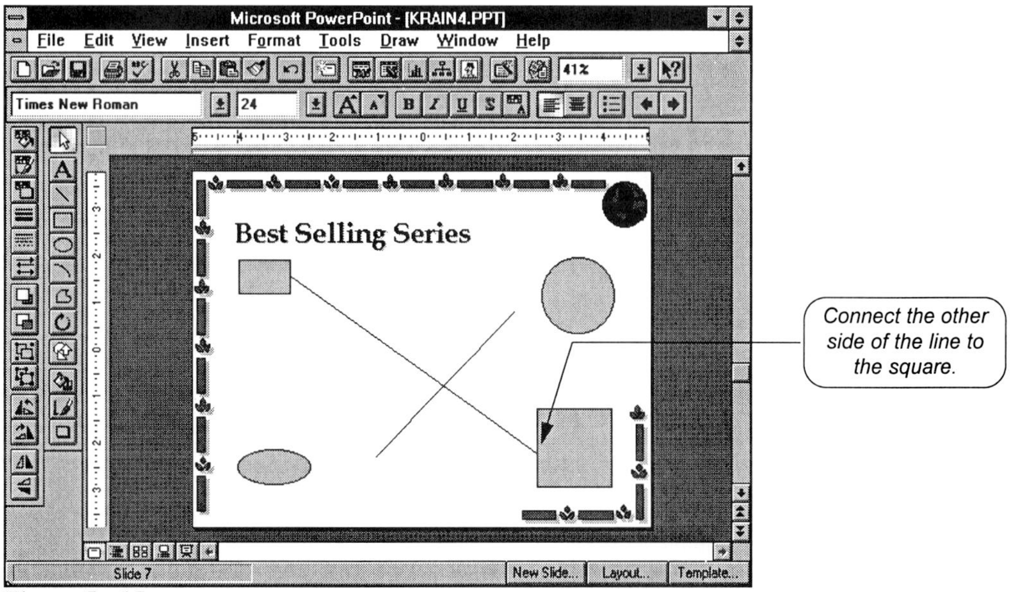

Figure 5 - 15

13. As you did with the line that is connecting the rectangle and the square, increase the size of the line that was connecting the ellipse and the circle so that it is once again connecting the two objects.

    You will copy the circle and move it on top of where the lines cross.

14. Select the circle so that handles appear around the object.

15. Choose **EDIT/Copy** or click on the **Copy** button on the Standard toolbar.

    A copy of the circle is placed on the clipboard.

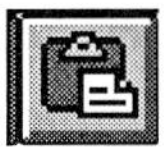

16. Choose **EDIT/Paste** or click on the **Paste** button on the Standard toolbar.
17. Move the copied circle over the point where the lines cross (Figure 5 - 16).

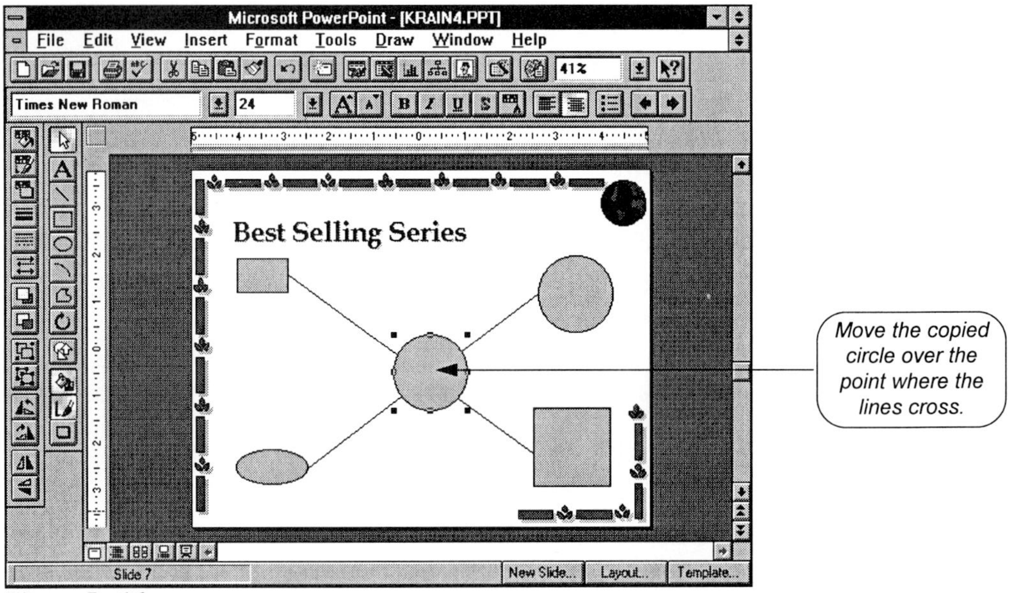

Figure 5 - 16

18. Choose **EDIT/Paste** again.

    The circle will remain on the clipboard until you copy or cut another object. Another copy of the circle is placed on the slide.

19. Move the copy of the circle between the rectangle and the ellipse (Figure 5 - 17).

    You will delete the ellipse and replace it with the circle that you just moved.

20. Select the ellipse.
21. Press the **DELETE** key.

    The ellipse is removed from the slide.

22. Move the circle that was just moved so that it replaces the ellipse (Figure 5 - 18).
23. Save the presentation using the same name.

Changing the Attributes of a Drawing Object

Once you have drawn objects on a slide, you will want to change the way the object looks. The way the object looks is defined by its attributes. Attributes are features of an object that you can manipulate using the *PowerPoint* tools including line, fill, shadow, embossing, color, and shape.

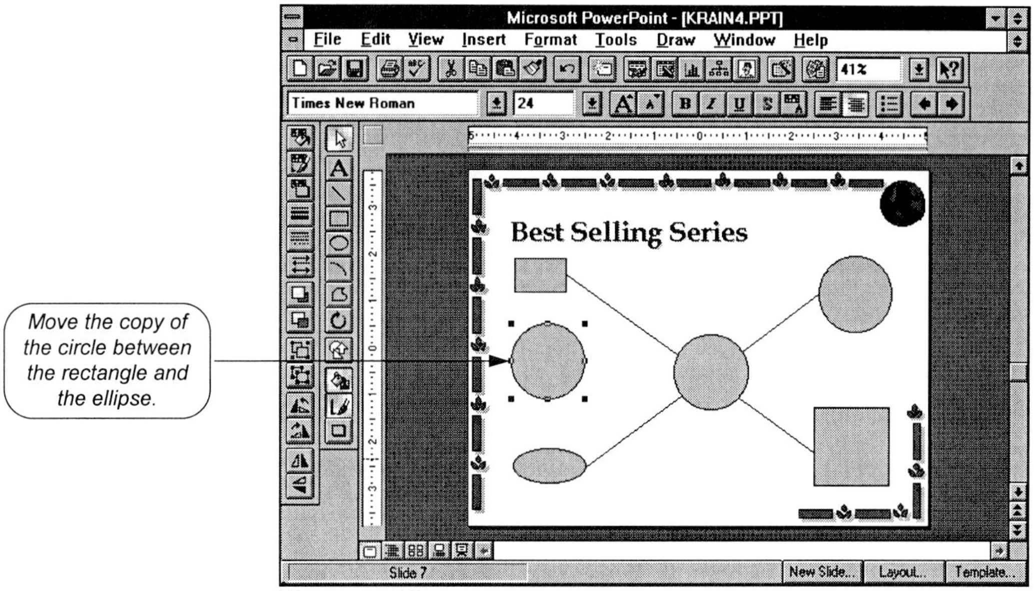

Figure 5 - 17

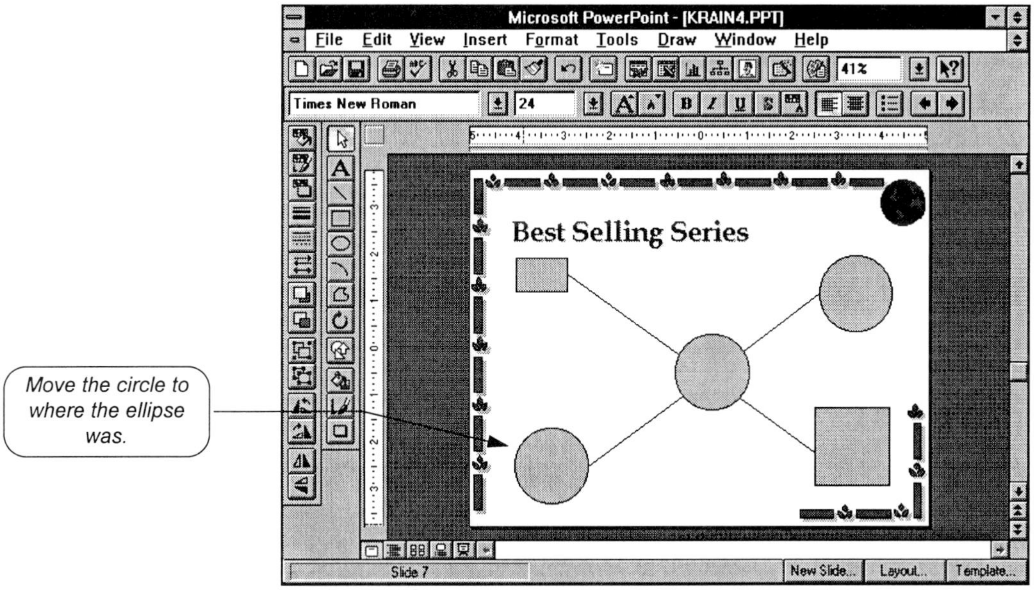

Figure 5 - 18

To change the attributes of an object:

- Select the object you wish to change.

  If the object you select has the fill and line of the object turned on, the corresponding buttons will be depressed on the Drawing toolbar .
- Click on the **Fill Color** or **Line Color** button on the Drawing+ toolbar.

  A pop-up dialog box appears below the button with options for changing the color of the fill or line.
- Click on the desired color.

PROBLEM SOLVER: *If the desired color does not appear, click on **Other Color**. The **Other Color** dialog box will appear on the screen. Click on the desired color, and then click on **OK**.*

To change the color of a line:

- Select the line you wish to change.
- Click on the **Line Color** button on the Drawing+ toolbar.

  A pop-up dialog box appears below the button with options for changing the color of the line.
- Click on the desired color.

  PROBLEM SOLVER: *If the desired color does not appear, click on* ***Other Color****. The* ***Other Color*** *dialog box will appear on the screen. Click on the desired color, and then click on* ***OK****.*

To change the attributes of a line:

- Select the line you wish to change.
- Click on either the **Line Style**, **Dashed Lines**, or **Arrowheads** buttons on the Drawing+ toolbar.

  A pop-up dialog box will appear for each choice with selections.
- Click on the desired attribute.

  The attribute will be applied to the line.

To change the color of text:

- Select the text you wish to change so that handles appear around the text block.
- Click on the **Text Color** button on the Formatting toolbar.

  A pop-up dialog box appears below the button with options for changing the color of the text.
- Click on the desired color.

  PROBLEM SOLVER: *If the desired color does not appear, click on* ***Other Color****. The* ***Other Color*** *dialog box will appear on the screen. Click on the desired color, and then click on* ***OK****.*

To copy attributes from one object to another:

- Click on the object that has the desired attributes.
- Click on the **Format Painter** button on the Standard toolbar.

  The mouse pointer appears with a paint brush attached to it.
- Point to the object you wish to copy the attributes to and click once.

  The attributes of the first object are copied to the second object.

Activity 5.3: Changing the Attributes of Drawing Objects in the krain4.ppt Presentation

In this activity, you will change the color and style attributes of objects, lines, and text in the **krain4.ppt** presentation.

1. After Activity 5.2 you should be on Slide 7 of the **krain4.ppt** presentation.
2. Move to Slide 5.
3. Select the text block, **"How many times would you shop at Kaleidoscope Rain?"**, so that handles appear around the text border.

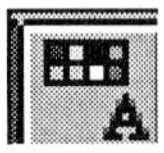

4. Click on the **Text Color** button on the Formatting toolbar.

   A pop-up menu appears with several color choices (Figure 5 - 19).

Figure 5 - 19

5. If purple appears in the color choices given, click on the purple square.
6. If purple is not one of the color choices, click on **Other Color**.

   *The **Other Color** dialog box appears on the screen (Figure 5 - 20).*

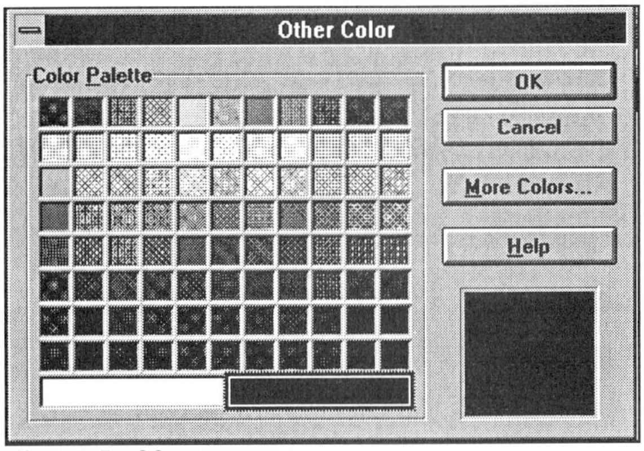

Figure 5 - 20

7. Click on the desired shade of purple, and then click on **OK**.
8. Move to Slide 7.
9. Select the rectangle.

10. Click on the **Fill Color** button on the Drawing+ toolbar.
11. Click on **Other Color**.

    *The **Other Color** dialog box appears.*
12. Click on the first shade in the red column (Figure 5 - 21), and then click on **OK**.

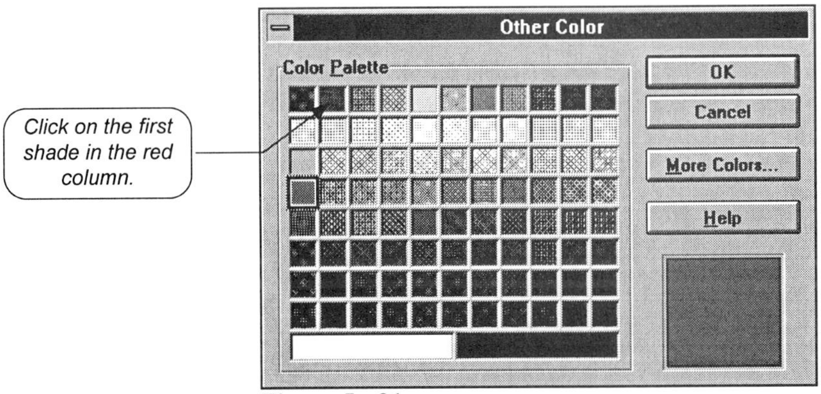

Figure 5 - 21

The rectangle changes to the selected color. You will now use the ***Format Painter*** *option to copy the attributes from the rectangle to the rest of the objects.*

13. Select the rectangle if it is not already selected.

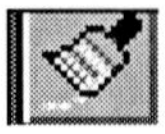

14. Click on the **Format Painter** button on the Standard toolbar.

    When you move the mouse pointer onto the Slide Work Area, you will see that a paint brush is attached to the mouse pointer (Figure 5 - 22).

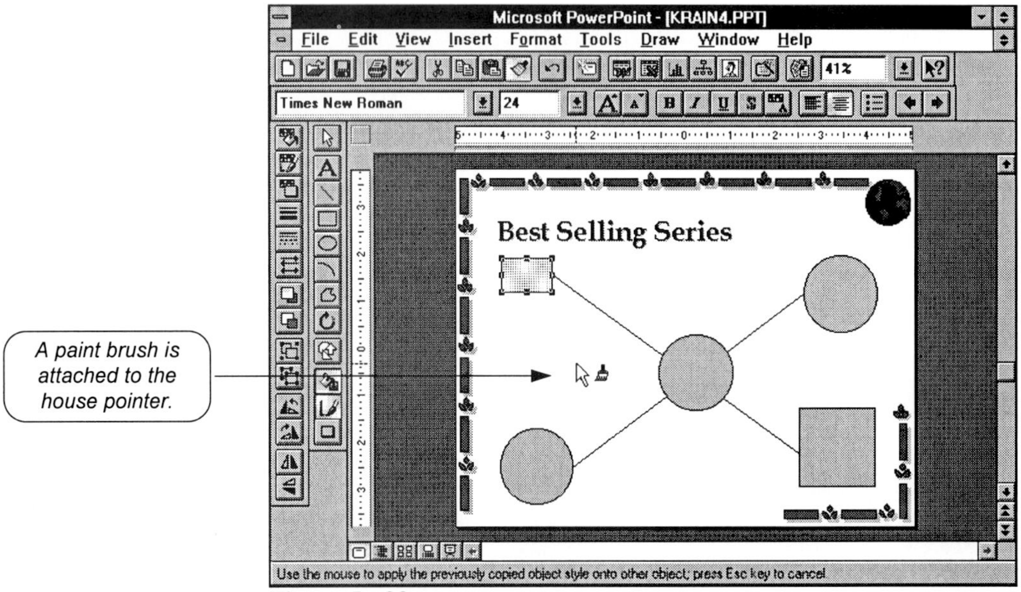

Figure 5 - 22

15. Point to the square and click once.

    The color of the square changes to the brighter shade of red.

16. Change the color of the remaining circles by clicking on the **Format Painter** button first, then clicking on each circle.

17. Select the line connecting the rectangle and the square.

18. Click on the **Line Color** button on the Drawing+ toolbar.

    A pop-up dialog box appears (Figure 5 -23).

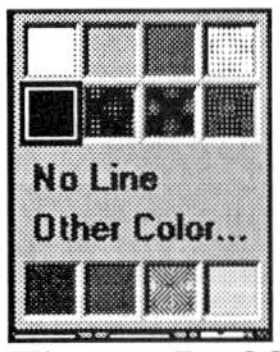

Figure 5 - 23

19. Click on **Other Color**.

    The ***Other Color*** *dialog box appears.*

20. Click on the seventh shade of blue in the blue column (Figure 5 - 24), and then click on **OK**.

    Now that you have changed the color of the line, you will change the attributes for the line. You will change the line width, the dashed effect, and the arrowhead style of the line.

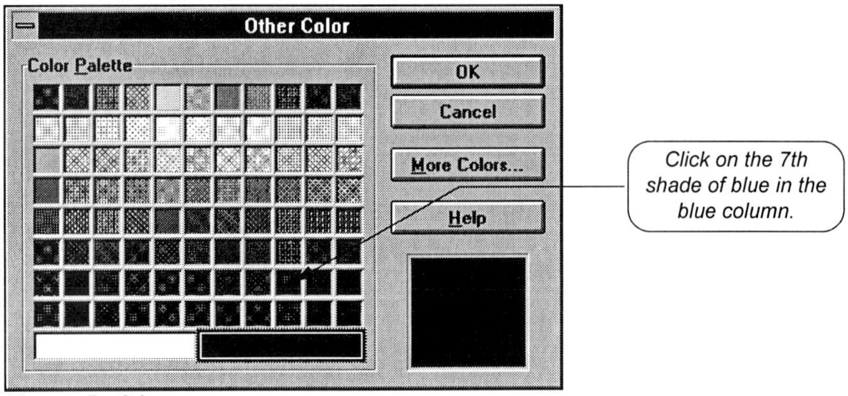

Figure 5 - 24

21. Click on the **Line Style** button on the Drawing+ toolbar.

    A pop-up dialog box appears with line width styles (Figure 5 - 25).

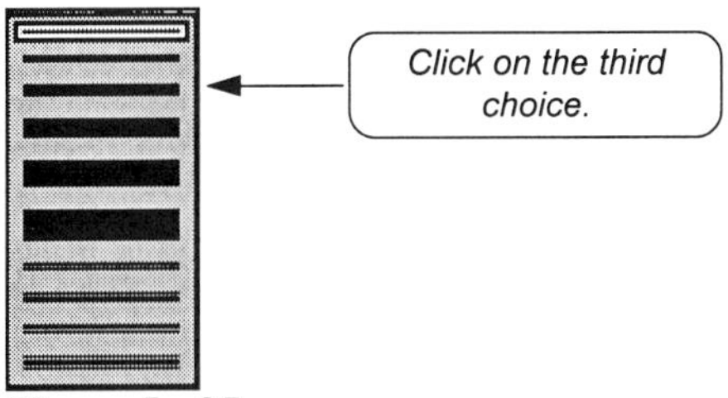

Figure 5 - 25

22. Click on the third choice.

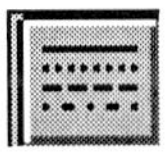

23. Click on the **Dashed Lines** button on the Drawing+ toolbar.

    A pop-up dialog box appears with dashed line styles (Figure 5 - 26).

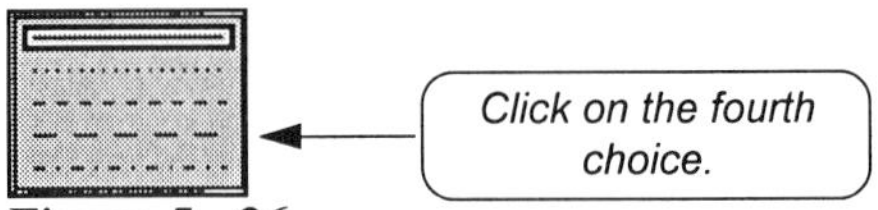

Figure 5 - 26

24. Click on the fourth choice.

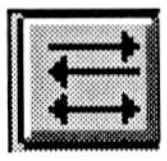

25. Click on the **Arrowheads** button on the Drawing+ toolbar.

    A pop-up dialog box appears with arrowhead styles (Figure 5 - 27).

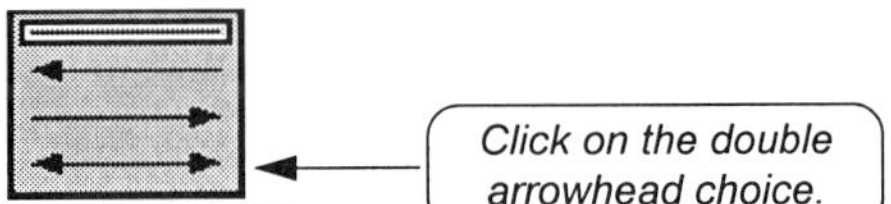

Figure 5 - 27

26. Click on the double arrowhead choice (fourth).
27. Use the **Format Painter** button on the Standard toolbar to copy the attributes of the line that is connecting the rectangle and the square to the line that is connecting the circles.
28. Save the presentation using the same name.

USING AUTOSHAPES

AutoShapes are shapes that are used often in drawing. Rather than having you draw the shapes or go to the ClipArt Gallery to find the shapes, *PowerPoint* has provided these shapes in the AutoShapes toolbar.

Text can be inserted into AutoShapes. Very often in drawing, you will want to draw a shape and place text inside the shape. With AutoShapes it is an easier process to add and edit text.

To access the AutoShapes toolbar, click on the **AutoShapes** button on the Drawing toolbar. The AutoShapes toolbar can be moved anywhere on the screen. See Table 5 - 3.

Button	Description
	Rectangle Tool
	Parallelogram Tool
	Trapezoid Tool
	Diamond Tool
	Rounded Rectangle Tool
	Octagon Tool
	Cross Tool
	Cube Tool
	Ellipse Tool
	Balloon Tool
	Pentagon Tool
	Hexagon Tool
	Isosceles Triangle Tool
	Right Triangle Tool
	Star Tool
	Seal Tool
	Thin Right Arrow Tool
	Thin Left Arrow Tool
	Thin Up Arrow Tool
	Thin Down Arrow Tool
	Thick Right Arrow Tool
	Thick Left Arrow Tool
	Thick Up Arrow Tool
	Thick Down Arrow Tool

Table 5 - 3

To add an AutoShape to a slide:

- Click on the **AutoShapes** button  on the Drawing toolbar if the AutoShapes toolbar does not appear on the screen.
- Move the AutoShapes toolbar to a different location if it is blocking the slide by pointing to the Title bar of the toolbar and dragging it to its new location.
- Click on the desired **AutoShape** button.
- Move the crosshair to the point on the slide where you would like the shape to begin.
- Press the left mouse button down and drag the shape on the screen.

  An outline of the shape appears as you are dragging.
- Release the left mouse button.

NOTE: *To create a symmetrical shape, press the* ***SHIFT*** *key down before releasing the left mouse button.*

To add text to an AutoShape:

- Select the desired AutoShape.
- Begin typing text.

To change the size of text within an AutoShape:

- Select the AutoShape with the text you wish to change so that handles appear around the border.
- Change the size of text using the **Font Size** text box, or the **Increase Font Size** button, or the **Decrease Font Size** button on the Formatting toolbar.

To change the AutoShape:

- Select the AutoShape you wish to change.
- Choose **DRAW/Change AutoShape**.

  A pop-up dialog box appears with AutoShape selections.
- Click on the desired AutoShape.

Activity 5.4: Adding AutoShapes to the krain4.ppt Presentation

In this activity, you will continue working with Slide 7 of the **krain4.ppt** presentation. You will add several AutoShapes to the slide, change several of the existing shapes, and then you will add text to the AutoShapes.

1. After Activity 5.3 you should be on Slide 7 of the **krain4.ppt** presentation.

2. If the AutoShapes toolbar is not showing on your screen, click on the **AutoShapes** button on the Drawing toolbar.

   The AutoShapes toolbar can appear in several places in the Slide Work Area (Figure 5 - 28). You will move the AutoShapes toolbar under the Formatting toolbar so that it does not cover any of the Slide Work Area. The toolbar will change shape as you move it under the Formatting toolbar.

   NOTE: *If the AutoShapes toolbar is already under the Formatting toolbar, skip to Step 5.*

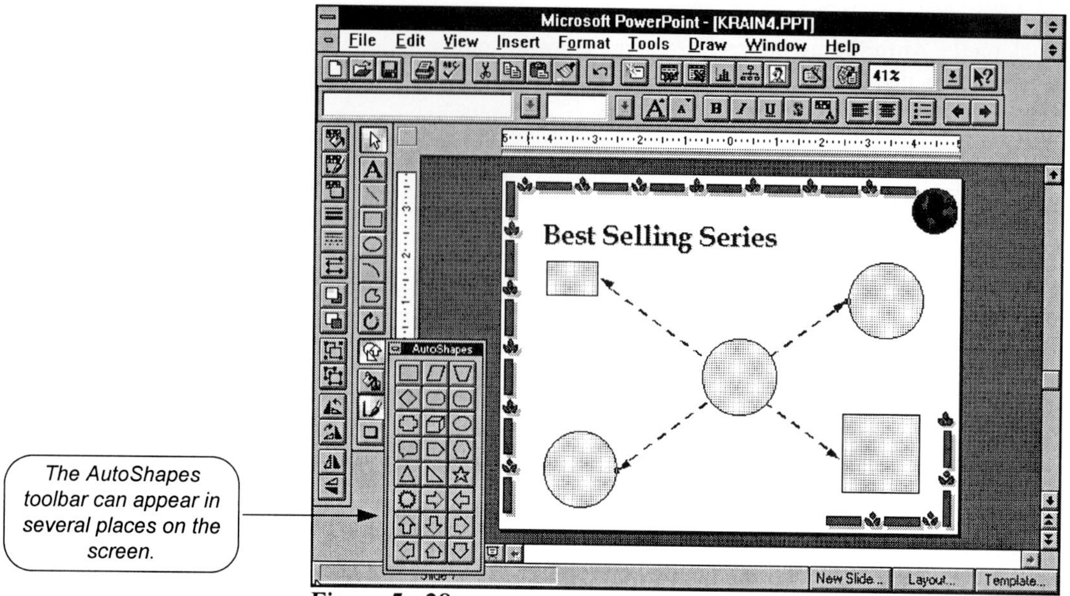

Figure 5 - 28

3. Point to the Title bar of the AutoShapes toolbar (Figure 5 - 29).

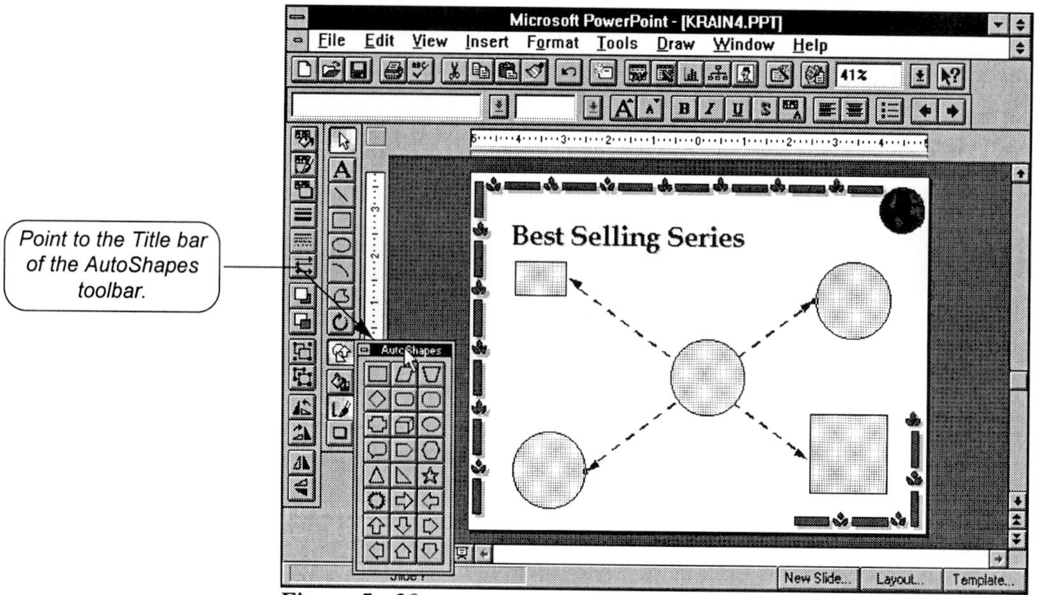

Figure 5 - 29

4. Drag the AutoShapes toolbar under the Formatting toolbar until a long rectangle appears below the Formatting toolbar (Figure 5 - 30), and then release the mouse button.

   The AutoShapes toolbar will be placed horizontally under the Formatting toolbar (Figure 5 - 31).

5. Click on the **Parallelogram** tool on the AutoShapes toolbar.

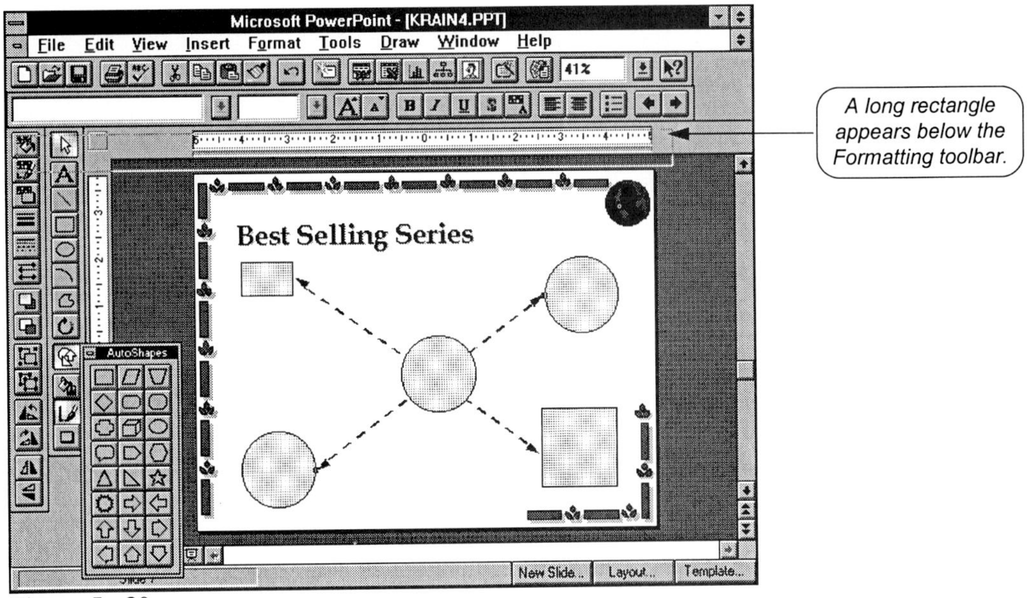

Figure 5 - 30

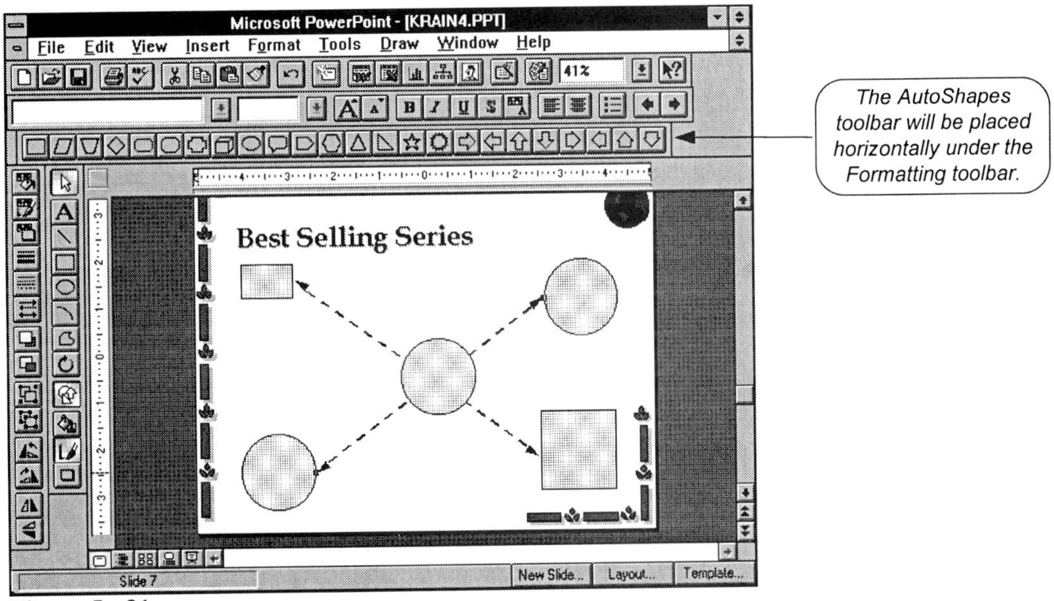

Figure 5 - 31

6. Draw a parallelogram on the left side of the screen between the rectangle and the circle (bottom left).

   A parallelogram is placed on the slide with the original color scheme used when the other objects were drawn on the slide.

7. Click on the **Diamond** tool on the AutoShapes toolbar.
8. Draw a diamond under the title between the rectangle and the circle (top right).
9. Click on the **Trapezoid** tool on the AutoShapes toolbar and draw a trapezoid between the circle (bottom left) and the square at the bottom of the slide.

   Your Slide 7 should resemble Figure 5 - 32.

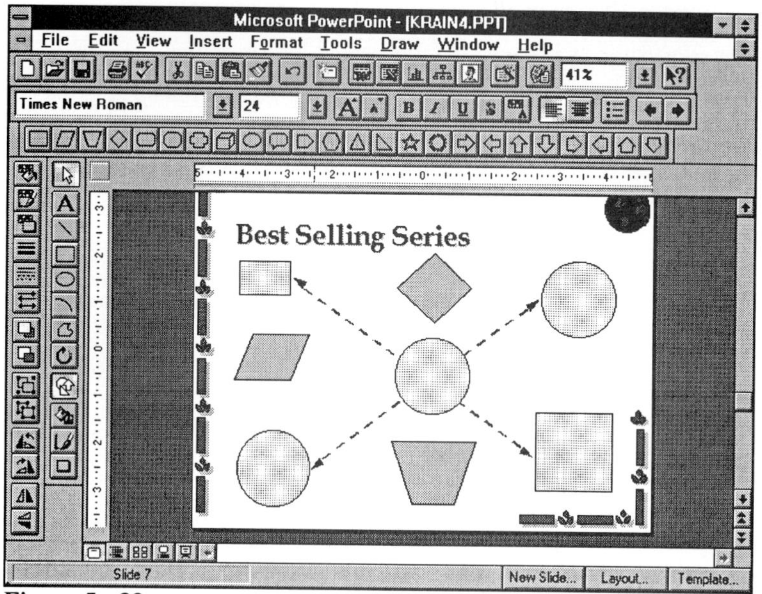

Figure 5 - 32

10. Select the circle in the middle of the slide.
11. Choose **DRAW/Change AutoShape**.

    A submenu of AutoShape choices appears (Figure 5 - 33).

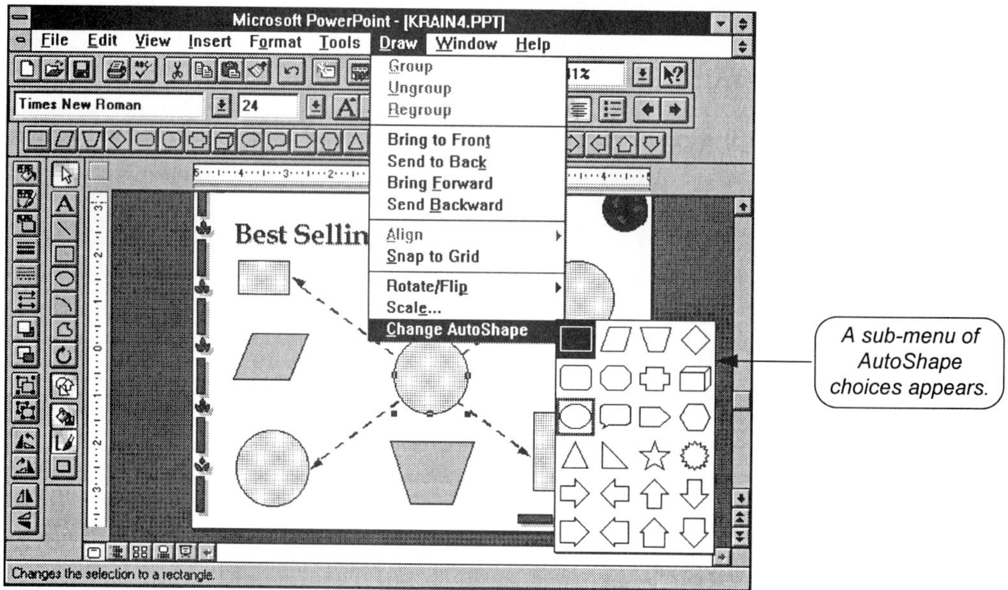

Figure 5 - 33

12. Select the **Seal** AutoShape (4th column, 4th row).

    The circle changes to a seal.

13. Change the circle in the bottom left corner of the slide to a **hexagon**.

14. Use the **Format Painter** button on the Standard toolbar to change the attributes of the objects that were added to the slide to the brighter red color scheme.
15. Select the **Seal** AutoShape.
16. Type: **Circuit**
17. Press **ENTER**.
18. Type: **Board**
19. Press **ENTER**.
20. Type: **Products**

    The text, ***Circuit Board Products*** *is added to the Seal AutoShape using center justification. A text border appears around the AutoShape (Figure 5 - 34).*

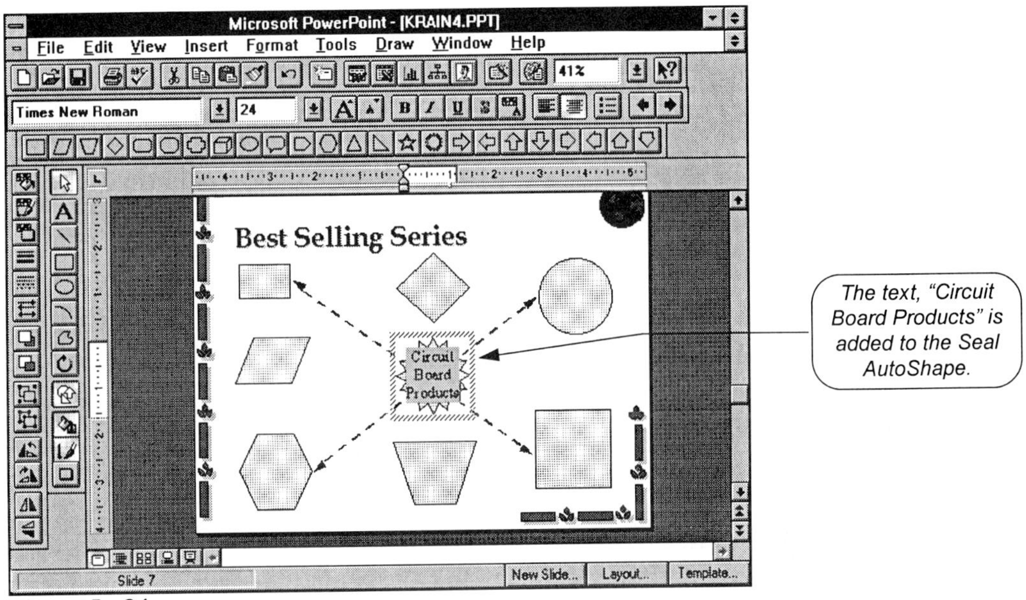

Figure 5 - 34

21. Click on the text border so that handles appear around the border.
22. Click on the **Decrease Font** button on the Formatting toolbar twice to decrease the font size to **18 pt**.
23. Select the rectangle and add the following text:

    Money *(Press* ***ENTER****)*

    Clip
24. Select the parallelogram and add the following text:

    3-Ring *(Press* ***ENTER****)*

    Binder
25. Add the following text to the hexagon:

    Clipboard
26. Add the following text to the trapezoid:

    Earrings

27. Add the following text to the square:

    Desk *(Press **ENTER**)*

    Clock

28. Add the following text to the circle:

    Wall *(Press **ENTER**)*

    Clock

29. Add the following text to the diamond:

    Chess Set

30. Change the size of the text in each of the AutoShapes to **18 pt**.
31. Delete the lines.

    Your Slide 7 should resemble Figure 5 - 35.

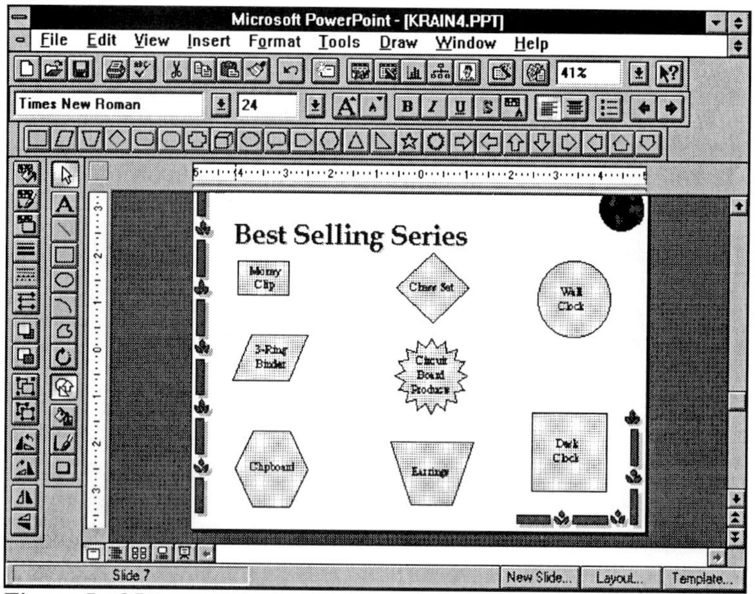

Figure 5 - 35

32. Save the presentation using the same name.
33. Print Slide 7 using the **Black & White** print option.
34. Close the presentation.

SUMMARY

In this lesson, you created a diagram using the *PowerPoint* drawing tools. First you used the Drawing toolbar to add drawing objects to the presentation. Then you edited the drawing objects using the Drawing+ toolbar. Next you added AutoShapes to the presentation using the AutoShapes toolbar. You also added text to two graphs using the Text Tool. You have completed all of the slides in the presentation. In Lesson 6, you will learn how to added transition effects to your presentation and view it as an on-screen presentation or a Slide Show.

KEY TERMS

Arrowheads
Attributes
AutoShapes Toolbar
Crosshair Pointer
Cube Tool
Dashed Lines
Diamond Tool
Drawing Object
Drawing Toolbar
Drawing+ Toolbar
Ellipse Tool
Fill Color
Format Painter
Hexagon Tool
Isosceles Triangle Tool
Line Color
Line Style
Line Tool
Octagon Tool
Parallelogram Tool
Rectangle Tool
Seal Tool
Selection Tool
Star Tool
Text Color
Text Tool
Thin Left Arrow Tool
Thin Up Arrow Tool
Trapezoid Tool

INDEPENDENT PROJECTS

The four independent projects allow you to practice the basic skills involved in drawing objects in presentations. You will add drawing objects to your presentation using the Drawing toolbar, edit those drawing objects using the Drawing+ toolbar, and add AutoShapes to your presentation using the AutoShapes toolbar.

Independent Project 5.1: Drawing a Diagram in the ellis4.ppt Presentation

In this Independent Project, you will add a slide to the end of the **ellis4.ppt** presentation and use the background of the slide to create a diagram that illustrates the data in the table you created in Independent Project 4.1. Use Figure 5 - 36 to place the arrows and text.

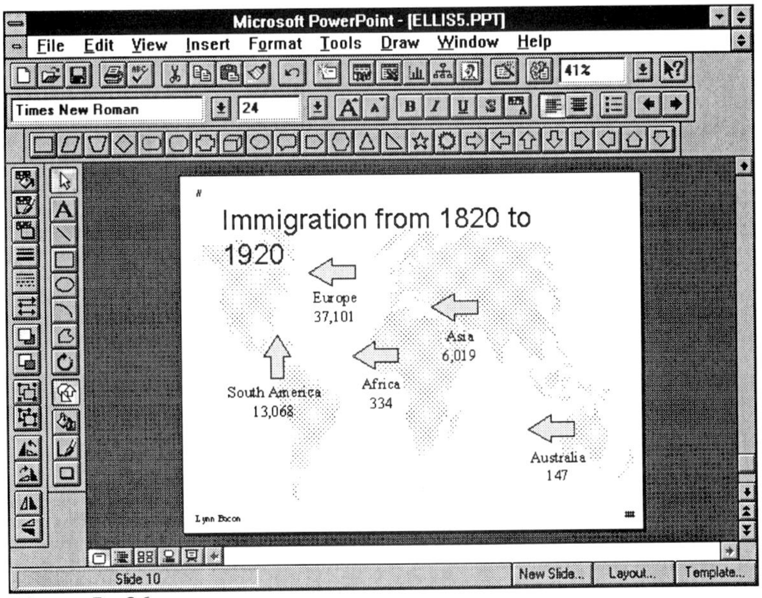

Figure 5 - 36

1. Open *PowerPoint* if it is not already open.
2. Open the **ellis4.ppt** presentation.
3. Move to Slide 9.
4. Add a slide to the presentation with a **Title Only** layout.
5. Add the following title: **Immigration from 1820 to 1920**

You will use the map in the background as part of your diagram. Use Figure 5 - 36 to place the arrows.

6. Click on the **Thin Left Arrow Tool** button on the AutoShapes toolbar and draw an arrow between Europe and the United States.
7. Make sure the arrow is still selected; if not, select it.
8. Click on the **Fill Color** button on the Drawing+ toolbar.
9. If yellow appears in the color selections offered, click on **yellow**. If not, click on **Other Color**, select the brightest shade of **yellow** at the **Other Color** dialog box, and click on **OK**.
10. Click on the **Line Color** button on the Drawing+ toolbar and change the color of the outline to **black**.
11. Click on the **Text Tool** button on the Drawing toolbar and draw a text block under the arrow.
12. Type the following text:

    Europe *(press ENTER)*

    37,101

    *If the text block is not large enough for **Europe** to fit on one line, increase the size of the text block. The text will have too much spacing between lines and needs to be centered.*

13. Select the text block so that handles appear around the border.
14. Choose **FORMAT/Line Spacing**.
15. Type **0** in the **Before Paragraph** text box, then click on **OK**.
16. Click on the **Center Alignment** button on the Formatting toolbar.

    *To add Asia, Africa, and Australia data, you can use **EDIT/Copy** and **EDIT/Paste**. This way you will not need to change the attributes of the arrow or text. You will need to change only the text in the text block.*

17. Select the arrow, and then click on the **Copy** button on the Standard toolbar.
18. Click on the **Paste** button on the Standard toolbar.
19. Move the second arrow over to Asia.
20. Select the text block so that handles appear around the border.
21. Click on the **Copy** button.
22. Click on the **Paste** button.
23. Move the second text block under the second arrow.
24. Delete the text in the text block and type:

    Asia *(press ENTER)*

    6,019

25. Add the arrows and text blocks for Africa and Australia using steps 17–24. The data follows:

Africa	**Australia**
334	**147**

    To add the South America data you will need use the Thin Up Arrow Tool on the AutoShapes toolbar.

26. Click on the **Thin Up Arrow Tool** button on the AutoShapes toolbar and draw an Up Arrow pointing from South America to the United States.

27. Use the **Format Painter** button on the Standard toolbar to copy the attributes from one of the yellow arrows to the Up Arrow.
28. **Copy** and **Paste** one of the text blocks and move the text block under the Up Arrow.
29. Delete the text and add the following text:

    South America *(press ENTER)*

    13,068
30. Print Slide 10 using the **Black & White** print option.
31. Save the presentation as **ellis5.ppt**.
32. Close the **ellis5.ppt** presentation.
33. Exit *PowerPoint* or continue with the next project.

Independent Project 5.2: Adding a Diagram to the brown4.ppt Presentation

In this Independent Project, you will add a slide to the end of the **brown4.ppt** presentation and create a diagram that illustrates Hands-on Activities at the Browning Museum. Use Figure 5 - 37 to place the drawing objects.

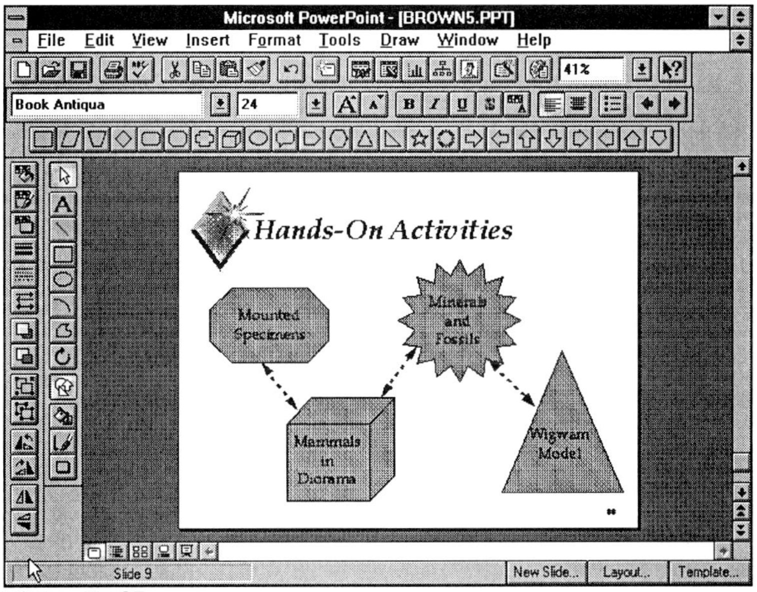

Figure 5 - 37

1. Open *PowerPoint* if it is not already open.
2. Open the **brown4.ppt** presentation.
3. Move to Slide 8.
4. Add a slide to the presentation with a **Title Only** layout.
5. Add the following title: **Hands-On Activities**
6. Click on the **Octagon Tool** button on the AutoShapes toolbar and draw an octagon in the top left corner of the slide under the title.
7. Use the **Fill Color** button on the Drawing+ toolbar to change the color of the octagon to **cyan** (8th column, 1st row in the **Other Color** dialog box).

8. Use the **Line Color** button on the Drawing+ toolbar to change the color of the border of the octagon to **black**.
9. Type the following text in the octagon:

   Mounted *(press ENTER)*

   Specimens
10. Use the **Text Color** button on the Formatting toolbar to change the color of the text to **black**.
11. Use the **Cube Tool** button on the AutoShapes toolbar to draw a cube slightly to right and below the octagon (Figure 5 - 37).
12. Make sure the cube is selected, then type:

    Mammals *(press ENTER)*

    in *(press ENTER)*

    Diorama
13. Use the **Seal Tool** button on the AutoShapes toolbar to draw a seal above and to the right of the cube (Figure 5 - 37).
14. Type the following text in the seal:

    Minerals *(press ENTER)*

    and *(press ENTER)*

    Fossils
15. Use the **Isosceles Triangle Tool** button to draw a triangle in the shape of a wigwam in the bottom right corner of the slide (Figure 5 - 37).
16. Type the following text in the triangle:

    Wigwam *(press ENTER)*

    Model
17. Use the **Format Painter** button on the Standard toolbar to copy the attributes of the octagon to the cube, seal, and triangle.
18. Draw a line from the octagon to the cube.
19. Draw a line from the cube to the seal.
20. Draw a line from the seal to the triangle.
21. Select the line connecting the octagon to the cube.
22. Use the **Line Color** button on the Drawing+ toolbar to change the color of the line to **black**.
23. Click on the **Line Style** button on the Drawing+ toolbar and select the third choice.
24. Click on the **Dashed Lines** button on the Drawing+ toolbar and select the third choice.
25. Click on the **Arrowheads** button on the Drawing+ toolbar and select the **double arrowhead**.
26. Use the **Format Painter** button on the Standard toolbar to copy the attributes to the other lines.
27. Save the presentation as **brown5.ppt**.
28. Print Slide 9 using the **Black & White** print option.
29. Close the presentation.
30. Exit *PowerPoint* or continue with the next project.

Independent Project 5.3: Adding a Diagram to the travel4.ppt Presentation

In this Independent Project, you will add a slide to the end of the **travel4.ppt** presentation and create a diagram using AutoShapes and clip art that illustrates Cruise Locations available at Julie's Travel Agency. Use Figure 5 - 38 to place the AutoShapes and clip art.

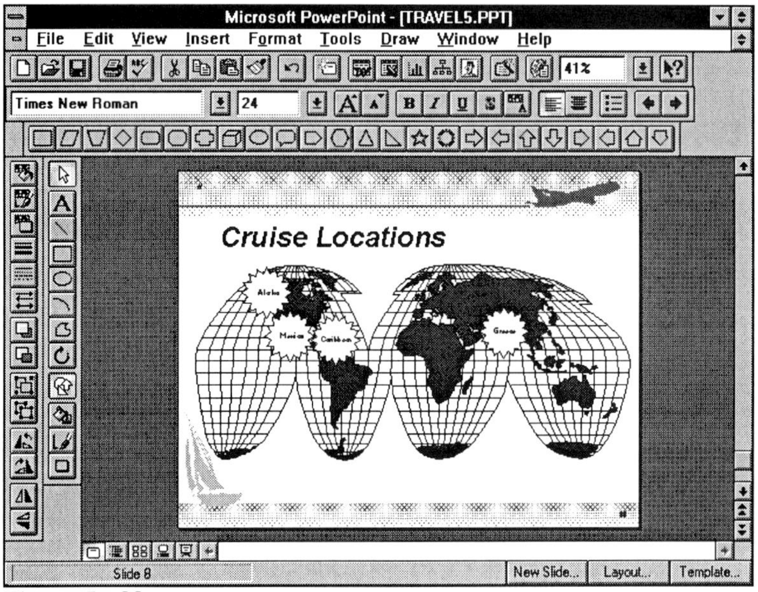

Figure 5 - 38

1. Open the **travel4.ppt** presentation.
2. Add a slide to the end of the presentation with a **Title Only** layout.
3. Add the following title: **Cruise Locations**
4. Use the **Insert Clip Art** button on the Standard toolbar to insert the **World Map** image from the **Maps - International** category.

   The World Map image will be placed in the middle of the slide.

5. Size and move the clip art image as necessary so that it takes up most of the slide space from the title to the ship that is part of the background of the slide.
6. Place a seal AutoShape over the approximate geographic location of the following cruise locations (see Figure 5 - 38 for placement). Press the **SHIFT** key down before releasing the left mouse button so that the seal will be symmetrical.

   Alaska

   Caribbean

   Greece

   Mexico

7. Add the corresponding text to the seal AutoShapes. Size the text to **12 pt**. If the text does not completely fit in the seal at a 12 pt. size, resize the AutoShape.
8. Save the presentation as **travel5.ppt**.
9. Print Slide 8 using the **Pure Black & White** print option.
10. Close the presentation.
11. Exit *PowerPoint* or continue with the next project.

Independent Project 5.4: Adding a Diagram to the train4.ppt Presentation

In this Independent Project, you will add a slide to the end of the **train4.ppt** presentation and create a diagram that illustrates the process of Creating a Presentation. Use Figure 5 - 39 as your reference.

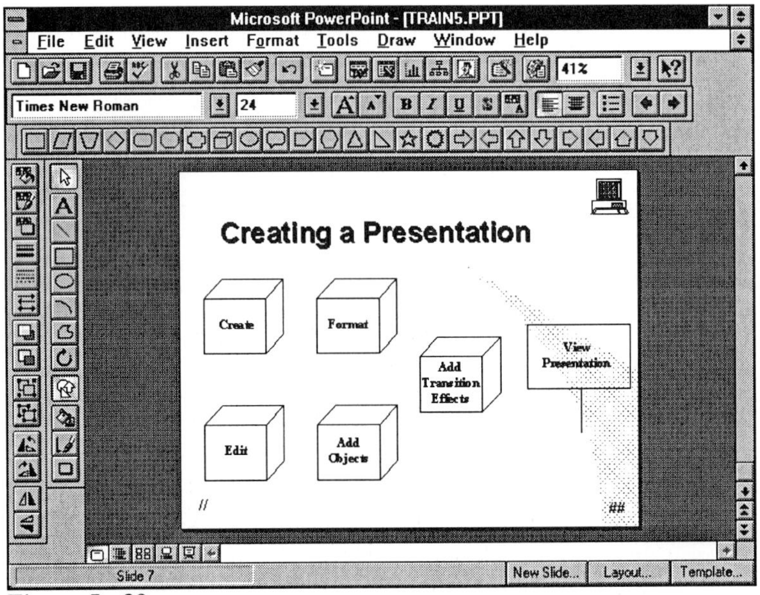

Figure 5 - 39

1. Open the **train4.ppt** presentation.
2. Add a slide to the end of the presentation with a **Title Only** layout.
3. Add the following title: **Creating a Presentation**
4. Use Figure 5 - 39 as a reference for creating the diagram. You can use any AutoShape you want for the objects. As an example, Figure 5 - 39 uses a cube for the first 5 steps and a rectangle and a line for the last step.
5. Make sure you have a shape for each of the following steps:

   Create

   Edit

   Format

   Add Objects

   Add Transition Effects

   View Presentation
6. Save the presentation as **train5.ppt**.
7. Print Slide 7 using the **Pure Black & White** print option.
8. Close the presentation.
9. Exit *PowerPoint*.

Lesson 6

Creating a Slide Show

Objectives

In this lesson you will learn how to:

- Add transition effects to slides
- Add automatic timing to slides
- Add build effects to bulleted list slides
- Hide slides
- View a slide show
- Use the pencil tool to annotate a slide while viewing a slide show
- View a continuously running slide show

PROJECT DESCRIPTION

The final step to creating your presentation is creating a show out of the individual slides. To do this you can add transition and/or build effects, set automatic timing or hide slides. Transition effects are the way the slide is brought onto the screen. They are added to the presentation in Slide Sorter View.

You will also add build effects to bulleted list slides. The build effect creates a slide that shows each bullet one at a time. This effect is an effective way to guide your presentation and keep your audience's attention. You will add automatic timing to your slide show so that the slide show can run on its own.

You can also have the slide show run continuously on a machine. This option is useful if the slide show is giving information to customers while you need to do something else. Continuous shows have been used in trade shows. Julie's Travel Agency in Independent Project 6.3 will use a continuous slide show to give her customers information while the travel agents are seeing other customers.

Another option that is available for slide shows is hiding slides. You can hide slides so that during the slide show you can decide whether or not you want to show the slide. This is useful if you want to keep a reserve of slides for use only if you need them. In this lesson, you will add transition effects and build effects to the **krain4.ppt** presentation. You will add automatic timing to the slides. You will hide slides. Then you will view the effects that you added.

WHAT IS A SLIDE SHOW?

A slide show is an electronically displayed presentation. You can use your computer to display your presentation. When you display the slides, they will take up the full computer screen. The *PowerPoint* program will disappear temporarily while you view the slide show. Your computer essentially becomes a slide projector. You can view the slide show on your computer or you can attach any of the projection devices that are available to project your slide show onto a projection screen. An example of a projection device is an LCD panel that attaches to your computer and sits on an overhead projector. Direct the overhead projector to a screen and your slide show will be projected onto the screen.

There are several advantages to using a slide show instead of slides or transparencies.

- You save the time and expense of creating slides.
- You can use the color options available in *PowerPoint.*
- You can use transition effects to add variety and impact to your presentation.
- You can change your presentation right down to the last second.
- You can annotate your slides as you give your presentation.
- You can hide slides to be used only if you need them.

USING TRANSITION EFFECTS

Transition effects are added to the presentation in Slide Sorter View. You can add transition effects to your slides to effect the way the slide is brought onto the screen. There are a wide variety of effects that can be applied to your slide. Table 6 - 1 illustrates the transition effects that are available in *PowerPoint.*

Transition Effect	Description
No Transition Effect	No transition effect is applied.
Random Transition	*PowerPoint* selects the transition for you.
Blinds	Draws the image in strips, similar to window blinds opening or closing. Two directions are available: vertical and horizontal.
Box	Draws the image from the outside in (Box In) or the inside out (Box Out).
Checkerboard	Draws the image in a checkerboard fashion. Two directions are available: across and down.
Cover	The image appears on the screen from the indicated directions. The directions available are: left, up, right, down, left-up, right-up, and left-down.
Cut	The whole slide is placed on the screen at one time.
Cut Through Black	The whole slide is placed on the screen at one time after a black screen quickly appears.
Dissolve	The image appears in pieces until the whole slide appears.
Fade Through Black	The image fades using shades of black, white, and gray.
Random Bars	The image appears on the screen one line at a time. Two directions are available: horizontal and vertical.
Split	The image appears on the screen from 2 directions. Directions that are available are: horizontal out, horizontal in, vertical out, and vertical in.
Strips	The image appears on the screen in strips from the direction indicated. Directions that are available are: down-left, down-right, up-left, up-right, left-down, left-up, right-down, and right-up.
Uncover	The previous slide is removed from the screen in the direction indicated. The next slide is revealed as the previous slide is removed. Directions that are available are: left, up, right, down, left-up, right-up, left-down, and right-down.
Wipe	The image appears on the screen from the direction indicated in a sweeping fashion. Available directions are: right to left, left to right, top to bottom, and bottom to top.

Table 6 1

To add transition effects to a slide:

- Switch to Slide Sorter View.

- Select the slide to which you wish to add a transition effect.
- Click on the **Transition** button  on the Slide Sorter toolbar.

  *The Slide Sorter toolbar appears only in Slide Sorter View and it automatically appears below the Standard toolbar. When you click on the **Transition** button, the **Transition** dialog box appears on the screen.*
- Select the transition effect from the **Effect** drop-down list box.

  The effect will be applied to the picture that appears in the bottom right corner of the dialog box. The key and the dog switch back and forth so that you can see the applied transition effect.
- Select the desired speed: slow, fast, or medium.

  The speed will be demonstrated using the selected effect with the pictures of the key and the dog.
- Select how you would like the slide to advance. You can select **only on mouse click** so that you control the movement of the slide. Or you can have the slides advance automatically and set the time for advancement.
- Click on **OK**.

  You return to Slide Sorter View. A small transition icon is placed at the bottom left corner of the slide. To see the transition effect applied to the miniature slide, click on this transition icon.

ALTERNATE METHOD: *If you just want to select the transition effect without setting the speed or the method of advancement, you can select the transition effect from the **Transition Effects** drop-down list box on the Slide Sorter toolbar.*

Activity 6.1: Adding Transition Effects to the krain4.ppt Presentation

In this activity you will add transition effects to the **krain4.ppt** presentation.

1. Open *PowerPoint*, if it is not already open.
2. Open the **krain4.ppt** presentation.
3. Switch to Slide Sorter View.
4. Select Slide 1.

5. Click on the **Transition** button on the Slide Sorter toolbar.

   *The Slide Sorter toolbar is below the Standard toolbar. The **Transition** dialog box appears on the screen (Figure 6 - 1).*

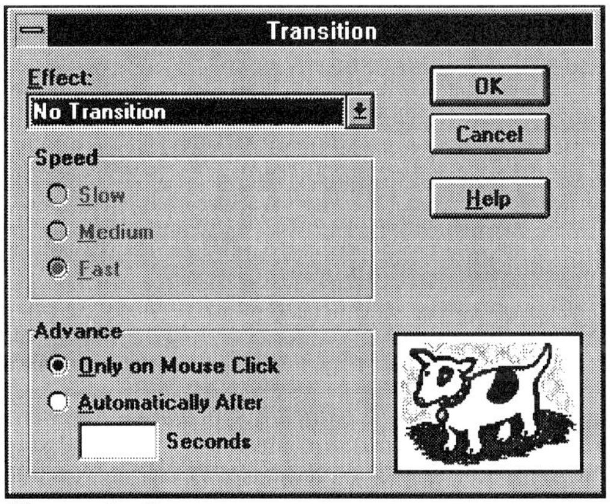

Figure 6 - 1

6. Click on the ↓ on the **Effect** drop-down list box.
7. Select **Blinds Vertical.**

   The transition effect is illustrated in the bottom left corner of the dialog box. The dog will switch to a key or the key will switch to the dog using the transition effect.

8. Click on **Automatically After** in the Advance section, and then type **10** in the **Seconds** text box.
9. Click on **OK**.

   A transition icon and ***:10*** *will appear under the bottom left corner of Slide 1 indicating that a transition effect has been selected and an automatic advance time has been set.* ***Blinds Vertical*** *also appears in the* ***Transition Effects*** *drop-down list box on the Slide Sorter toolbar (Figure 6 - 2).*

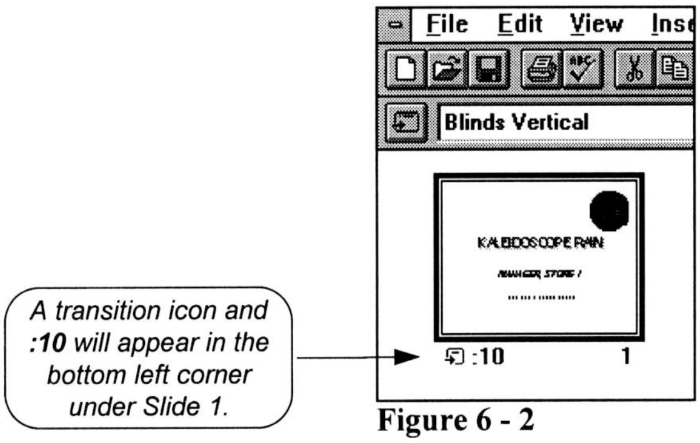

Figure 6 - 2

10. Repeat steps 4–9 to select **Blinds Horizontal** for Slide 2 and set an automatic advancement time of **10** seconds.
11. Click on the transition icon below Slide 2.

    The selected transition effect will be illustrated in Slide Sorter View using Slide 1 and Slide 2. You can also select transition effects from the Slide Sorter toolbar.

12. Click on Slide 3.
13. Click on the ↓ on the **Transition Effects** drop-down list box on the Slide Sorter toolbar.
14. Select **Box Out.**
15. Use the **Transition** button on the Slide Sorter toolbar to set the automatic advance time for Slide 3 to **10** seconds.
16. Use the **Transition** button on the Slide Sorter toolbar to add the following effects to the indicated slides. Also set the automatic advance time for each slide to **10** seconds.

Slide 4	**Checkerboard Across**
Slide 5	**Cover Left-Up**
Slide 6	**Cut Through Black**
Slide 7	**Dissolve**
Slide 8	**Random Bars Vertical**
Slide 9	**Split Vertical Out**
Slide 10	**Uncover Left-Up**

17. Save the presentation as **krain5.ppt.**

    Your presentation should have a transition icon and ***:10*** *in the bottom left corner of every slide in the presentation (Figure 6 -3).*

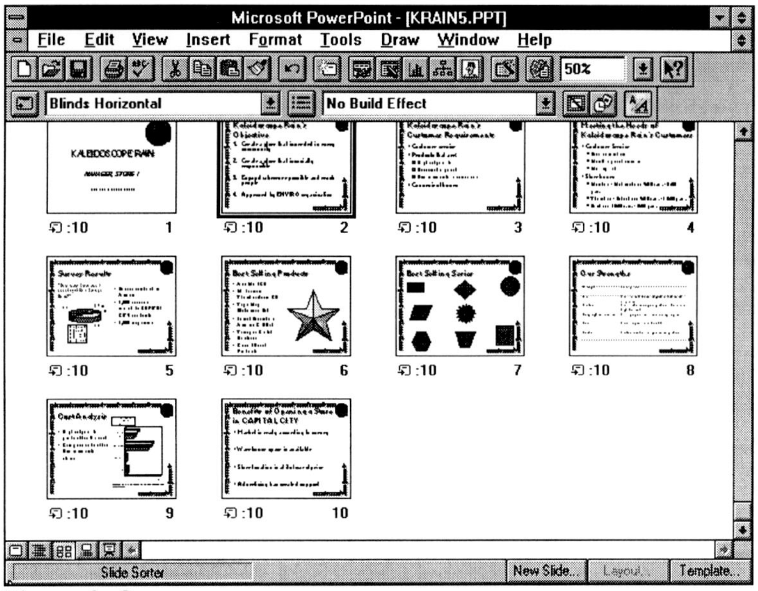

Figure 6 - 3

Adding Build Effects

A build slide is one in which each bullet point in the main text is revealed one at a time during a slide show. Build slides are effective when you want to talk about each point on the slide and you want to make sure your audience knows exactly where you are. A build slide is a slide show tool that you can use to guide the sequence of your slide show.

Just like transition effects for slides, build effects are available for the method of placing the bullets on the slide. Build effects that are available are listed with their description in Table 6 - 2.

Build Effect	Description
No Build Effect	No build effect is applied.
Random Effects	PowerPoint selects the effect for you.
Fly	The bullets fly onto the slide from the direction indicated. The available directions are: from right, from bottom, from left, and from top.
Blinds	The bullets appear on the screen in strips similar to blinds on a window. Two directions are available: vertical and horizontal.
Box	The bullets appear on the screen from the direction indicated. Two directions are available: outside in or inside out.
Checkerboard	The bullets appear on the screen in a checkerboard fashion. Two directions are available: across and down.
Dissolve	The bullets dissolve onto the screen.
Random Bars	The bullets appear on the screen using random bars. Two directions are available: horizontal and vertical.
Split	The bullets appear on the screen splitting from the center of the bullet and moving to the direction indicated. The directions that are available are: horizontal out, horizontal in, vertical out, and vertical in.
Strips	The bullets appear on the screen in the direction indicated in a strip-by-strip fashion. The available directions are: down-left, down-right, up-left, up-right, left-down, left-up, right-down, and right-up.
Wipe	The bullets appear on the screen from the direction indicated in a sweeping fashion. The available directions are: left, up, right, and down.

Table 6 - 2

To add build effects to a slide:

- Switch to Slide Sorter View.
- Select the slide to which you wish to add a build effect.
- Click on the **Build** button on the Slide Sorter toolbar.

  *The **Build** dialog box appears on the screen.*
- Click on the **Build Body Text** check box.

  Clicking in this check box activates the build effect.
- Click in the **Dim Previous Points** check box if you want the previous bullets to be dimmed when you move on to the next bullet.
- You can change the color of the dimmed previous points if you want by clicking on the ↓ of the drop-down list box under the **Dim Previous Points** check box.

  *When you click on the ↓ a pop-up dialog box will appear similar to the pop-up dialog boxes that appear when you click on the **Fill Color** or **Line Color** buttons on the Drawing+ toolbar. You can click on any of the colors that are presented. If you want to choose a different color, click on **Other Color**. Then the **Other Color** dialog box will appear on the screen, giving you a wider selection of colors.*
- Click on the **Effect** check box if you want to select a build effect, and then select the desired effect from the **Effect** drop-down list box.
- Click on **OK**.

  *You return to Slide Sorter View. A small build icon is placed at the bottom left corner of the slide next to the transition icon. To see the build effect applied to the slide, make sure the slide is selected, and then click on the **Slide Show** button above the Status bar.*

ALTERNATE METHOD: *If you just want to select the build effect without setting the dimmed previous points option, you can select the build effect from the **Build Effects** drop-down list box on the Slide Sorter toolbar.*

NOTE: *You can have a transition effect for the slide and a build effect for the bullets applied to the same slide. There are no "rules" about how many effects you should apply to your presentation. It is up to you. However, you can overdo it. So make sure you test out your slide show several times. Test it out with several class members and ask their opinions. The main goals are to jazz up your presentation and keep your audience's attention. You do not want the effects to take away from the information that you want to present.*

Activity 6.2: Adding Build Effects to the krain5.ppt Presentation

In this activity you will add build effects to several of the bulleted list slides. The bullets on a build slide are shown one at a time.

1. After Activity 6.1, you should be in Slide Sorter View.
2. Select Slide 2.

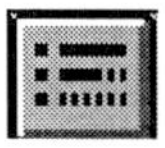

3. Click on the **Build** button on the Slide Sorter toolbar.

   *The **Build** dialog box appears on the screen (Figure 6 - 4).*
4. Click in the **Build Body Text** check box so that an **X** appears.
5. Click on the **Dim Previous Points** check box so that an **X** appears.

   PowerPoint automatically selects a color that will go well with the current color scheme.

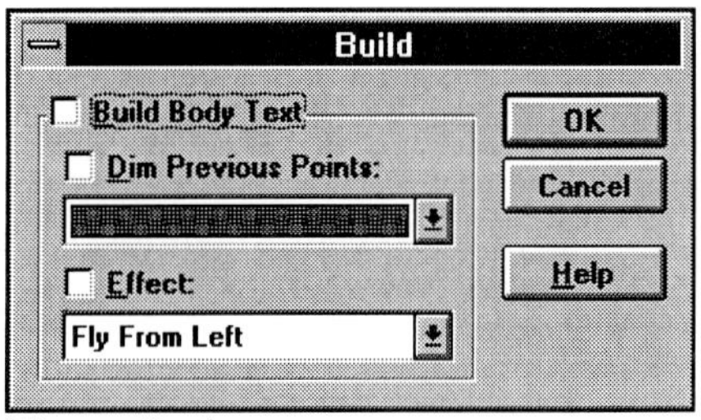

Figure 6 - 4

6. Click in the **Effect** check box so that an **X** appears.
7. Select **Fly From Top** from the **Effect** drop-down list box.
8. Click on **OK**.

   A build icon is placed under Slide 2, next to the transition icon. The build effect appears in the ***Build Effects*** *drop-down list box on the Slide Sorter toolbar (Figure 6 - 5).*

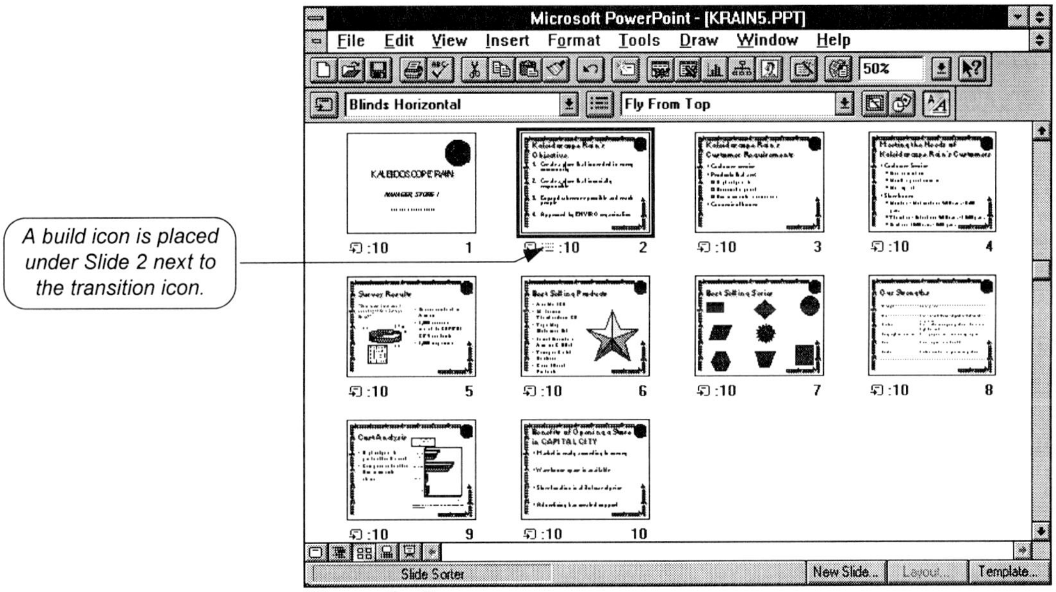

Figure 6 - 5

9. Click on the **Slide Show** button above the Status bar.

   The title for Slide 2 appears on the screen.
10. Click the left mouse button three times to show each of the bullets on Slide 2.

    Bullet 1, 2, and 3 appear on the screen. They fly in from the top of the screen. The previous bullets are dimmed when the next bullet appears on the screen.
11. Press **ESC** to return to Slide Sorter View.
12. Click on Slide 3.
13. Repeat steps 3–8 to add the **Dissolve** build effect to Slide 3. You also want to dim the previous points.
14. View the build effects using the **Slide Show** button.

    As you view the build effects for Slide 3, you will see that bullet 2 and its subbullets are considered one bullet and appear together on the screen.

15. Click on Slide 6.
16. Click on the ↓ of the **Build Effects** drop-down list box on the Slide Sorter toolbar and select **Checkerboard Down**.

    Checkerboard Down *now appears in the* ***Build Effects*** *list box and a build icon appears below the slide.*
17. View the results using the **Slide Show** button.

    As you view the results of the build effect you will see that the previous points are not dimmed. If you want the previous points to be dimmed you will have to use the ***Build*** *dialog box.*
18. Add the **Split Horizontal Out** effect to Slide 10 using the **Build Effects** drop-down list box on the Slide Sorter toolbar.
19. View the results.
20. Save the presentation using the same name.

    Your presentation should resemble Figure 6 - 6.

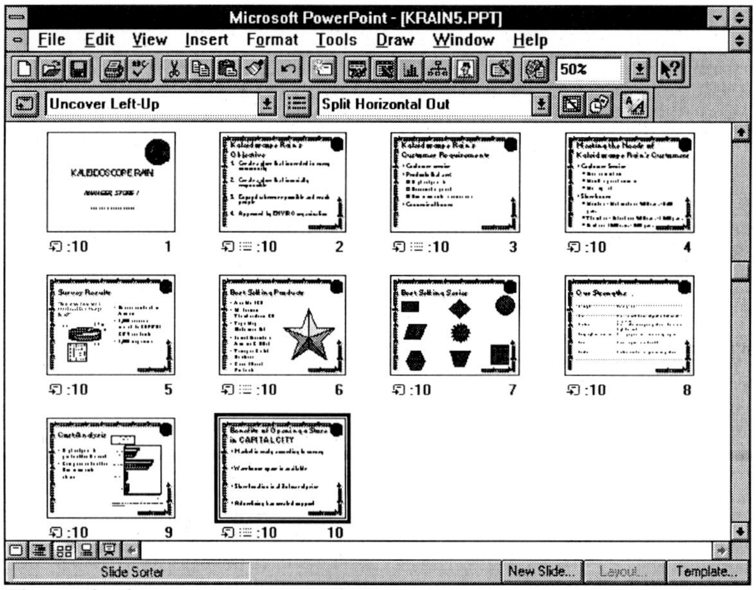

Figure 6 - 6

Hiding Slides

You can select slides to be hidden while you give a slide show. During the slide show an icon will appear on the slide preceding the hidden slide. If you decide to show the slide during the slide show, you can click on this icon to show the slide. This option can be used when you are not sure how many slides you will need during a slide show. You can create backup slides to use only if you need them.

To hide a slide:

- Switch to Slide Sorter View.
- Select the slide you wish to hide.
- Click on the **Hide Slide** button  on the Slide Sorter toolbar.

*The **Hide Slide** button is depressed and a gray box with a diagonal line through it appears around the number of the slide at the bottom right corner of the slide.*

To unhide a slide:

- Switch to Slide Sorter View.
- Select the slide you wish to unhide.
- Click on the **Hide Slide** button  on the Slide Sorter toolbar.

  *The **Hide Slide** button is raised and the gray box with a diagonal line through it is removed from the number below the slide.*

Activity 6.3: Hiding and Unhiding Slides in the krain5.ppt Presentation

In this activity you will hide two slides in the **krain5.ppt** presentation. Then you will unhide one of the slides. The effects of the hidden slides will be viewed in Activity 6.4 when you view your presentation from the beginning.

1. After Activity 6.2, you should be in Slide Sorter View.
2. Select Slide 9.

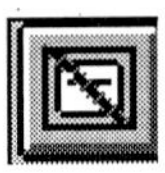

3. Click on the **Hide Slide** button on the Slide Sorter toolbar.

   *The **Hide Slide** button on the Slide Sorter toolbar is depressed and a gray box with a diagonal line appears around the 9 that appears below Slide 9 (Figure 6 - 7).*

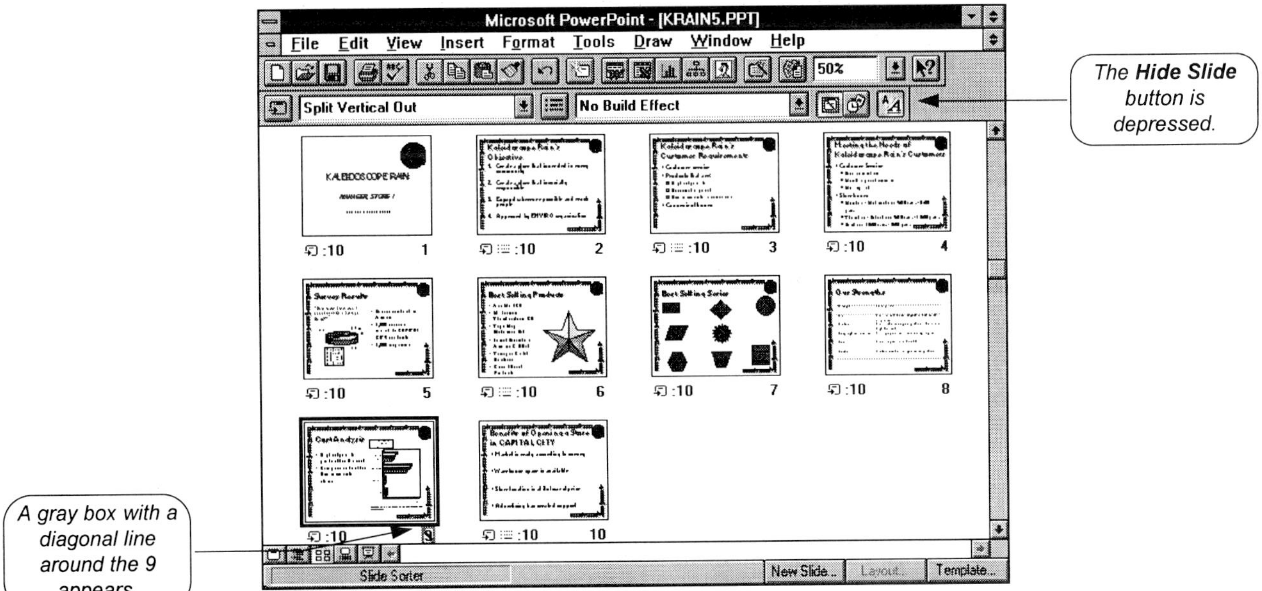

Figure 6 - 7

4. Select Slide 7.
5. Click on the **Hide Slide** button.

   *Again the **Hide Slide** button is depressed and a gray box with a diagonal line appears around the 7 below Slide 7. You will now unhide Slide 9.*

6. Select Slide 9.

7. Click on the **Hide Slide** button.

   The gray box with a diagonal line is removed from the 9 below Slide 9, indicating that the slide is no longer hidden.

8. Save the presentation using the same name.

   Your presentation will resemble Figure 6 - 8.

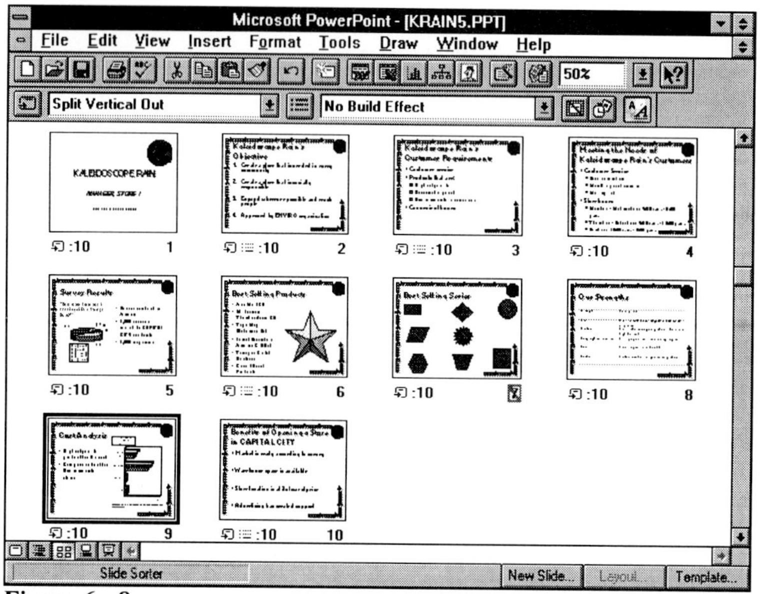

Figure 6 - 8

VIEWING A SLIDE SHOW

Once you have added transition and/or build effects, hidden desired slides in your presentation and set automatic timings for slides, the final step is to view your slide show. While viewing the slide show, you will see the transition and build effects applied to your slide show. You will be able to view hidden slides if you desire. You will also be able to annotate slides using the pencil tool during the viewing of your slide show. Annotations that are added to a slide during a slide show will be erased when you move to the next slide. The annotations are useful for highlighting specific information while you are presenting your slide show.

To view a slide show:

- Choose **VIEW/Slide Show**.

  *The **Slide Show** dialog box appears on the screen.*

- Select the slide range you wish to view. The default is **All**.
- Select how you would like to advance through the slide show.

  The default setting is to advance through the slide show manually, meaning you will control the advancement of slides. You can also set timings for the advancement of slides and let the slides advance automatically.

- Click on **Show**.

  The first slide you indicated will appear on the screen. The slide will fill the whole screen. Your screen essentially becomes a slide projector.

- Move through the presentation.

  There are several ways to move through the presentation. To move to the next slide, you can press ***ENTER****, press the* ↓ *or the* →*, or click on the left mouse button. To move to the previous slide, you can press the* ↑ *or the* ←*, or click on the right mouse button. To end the slide show, press* ***ESC****.*

NOTE: *If you have hidden any slides, a hidden slide icon will appear in the bottom right corner of the slide preceding the hidden slide, next to the pencil icon. To view a hidden slide, click on the hidden slide icon.*

When you have reached the last slide in your presentation, you will return to PowerPoint.

ALTERNATE METHOD: *You can also view your slide show by clicking on the* ***Slide Show*** *button. Using this method, you will view the slide show starting with the slide that is selected.*

To annotate a slide:

While you are viewing the slide show, a pencil icon appears in the bottom right corner of the slide. Click on the pencil icon.

- The mouse pointer becomes a pencil.

  The icon in the bottom right corner becomes an arrow.

- Draw any annotations on the slide.

  Drawing is freehand. Click and hold the left mouse button down as you draw. To draw a straight line, press the ***SHIFT*** *key down before dragging the line.*

- To stop annotating, click on the arrow icon in the bottom right corner.

  The icon changes back to a pencil.

Activity 6.4: Viewing the krain5.ppt Slide Show

Now that the transition effects, build effects and automatic timings have been added to the **krain5.ppt** presentation and you have hidden Slide 7, you are ready to view your slide show.

1. After Activity 6.3, you should be in Slide Sorter View.
2. Choose **VIEW/Slide Show**.

   The ***Slide Show*** *dialog box appears on the screen (Figure 6 - 9).*

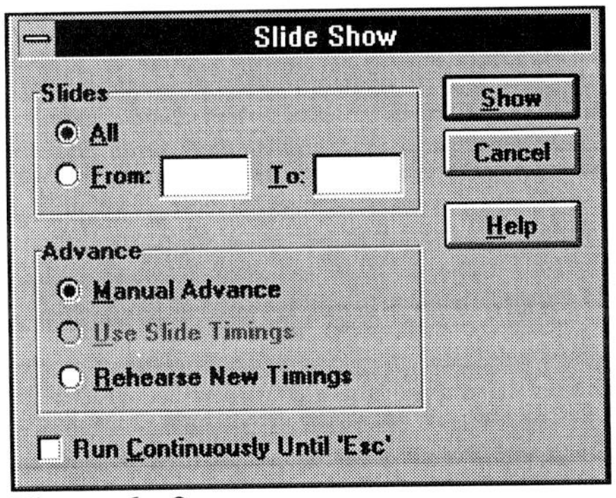

Figure 6 - 9

3. Click on **Manual Advance** in the Advance section if it is not already selected, and then click on **Show**.

   *Slide 1 appears on the screen using the **Blinds Vertical** transition effect.*

4. Click the left mouse button to advance to Slide 2.

   *Slide 2 appears on the screen using the **Blinds Horizontal** transition effect. You have also selected a build effect for Slide 2 so none of the bullets are showing yet (Figure 6 - 10).*

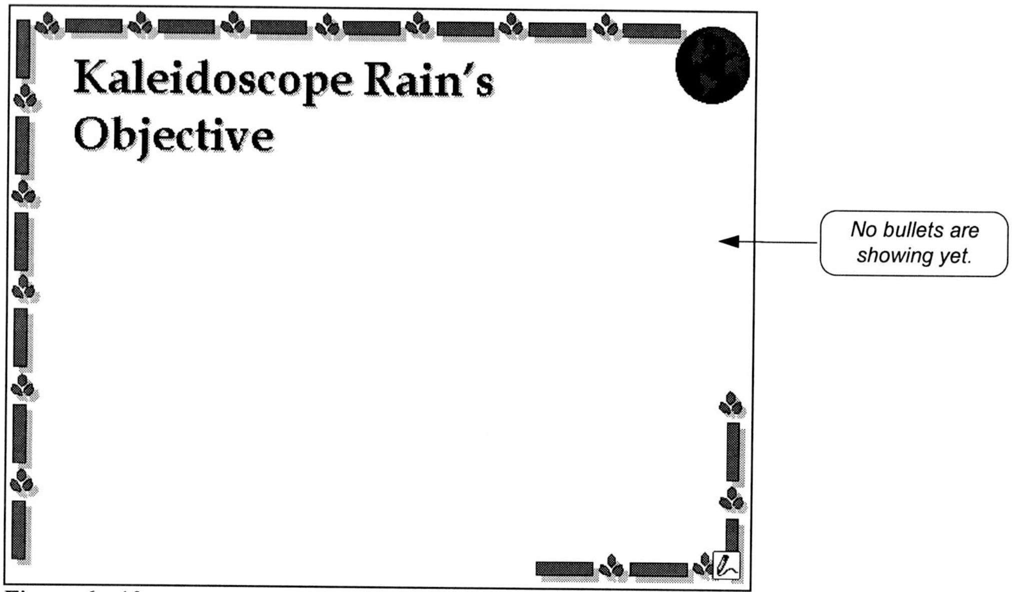

Figure 6 - 10

5. Click on the left mouse button four times to show each bullet on Slide 2.

   *Each bullet appears on the screen using the **Fly Down** build effect and the previous points are dimmed.*

6. Click the right mouse button twice to move back to the third bullet, then the second bullet.

7. Click the left mouse button three times.

   *The third click advances the slide show to Slide 3. Slide 3 appears on the screen using the **Box Out** transition effect. The build effect has also been selected for Slide 3, so only the title appears on the screen.*

8. Click the mouse button three times to view each of the bullets.

   The previous points on Slide 3 are dimmed.

9. Click on the left mouse button to advance to Slide 4.

   *Slide 4 appears on the screen using the **Checkerboard Across** transition effect.*

10. Click on the pencil icon in the bottom right corner of the screen.

    *The mouse pointer becomes a pencil (Figure 6 - 11). You will draw lines below **Customer Service** and **Store hours**.*

PROBLEM SOLVER: *If the pencil icon does not appear on the screen, move the mouse pointer. After moving the mouse pointer, the pencil icon should appear.*

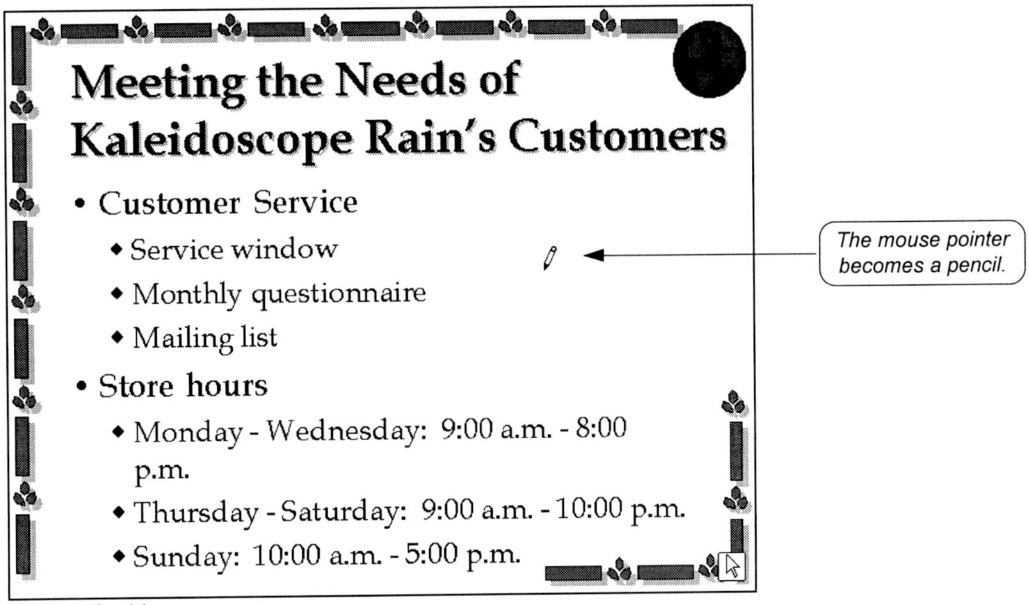

Figure 6 - 11

11. Point to the space below the **C** in **Customer** (Figure 6 - 12).

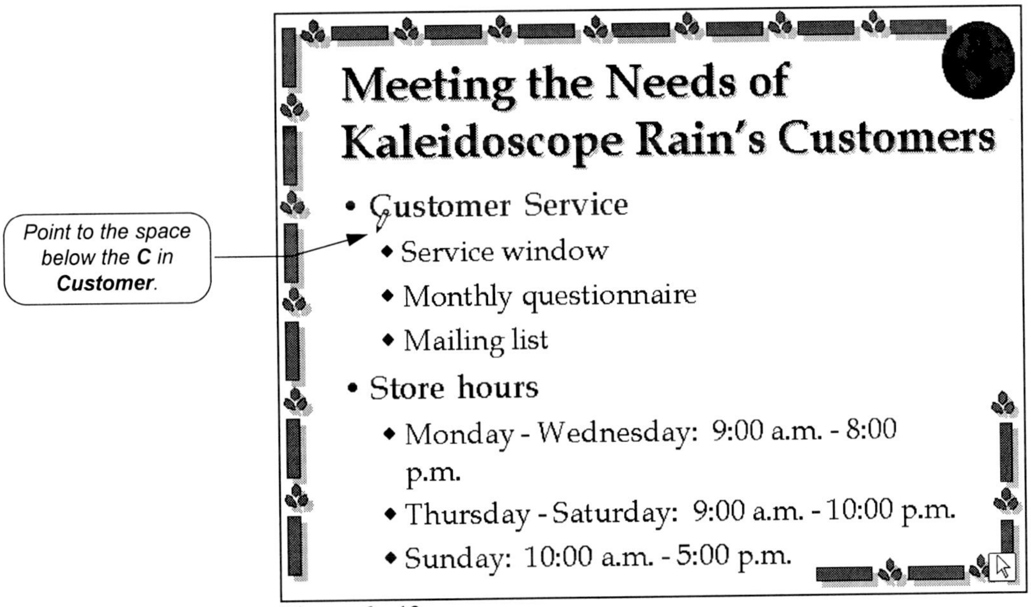

Figure 6 - 12

12. Click and hold the left mouse button down, drag a line to the end of **Customer Service**, and release the mouse button.

    A line is drawn below Customer Service. It is, however, not the straightest of lines. You will draw a straight line next (Figure 6 - 13).

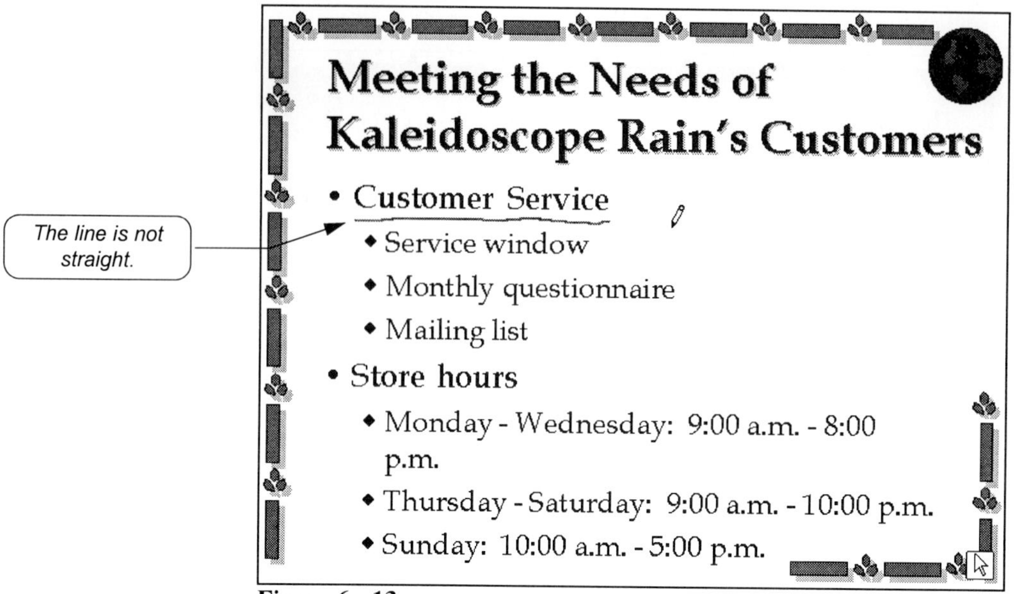

Figure 6 - 13

13. Point to the space below the **S** in **Store Hours**, then press the **SHIFT** key down.
14. Drag a line below **Store Hours**.

    This time the line is straight (Figure 6 - 14).

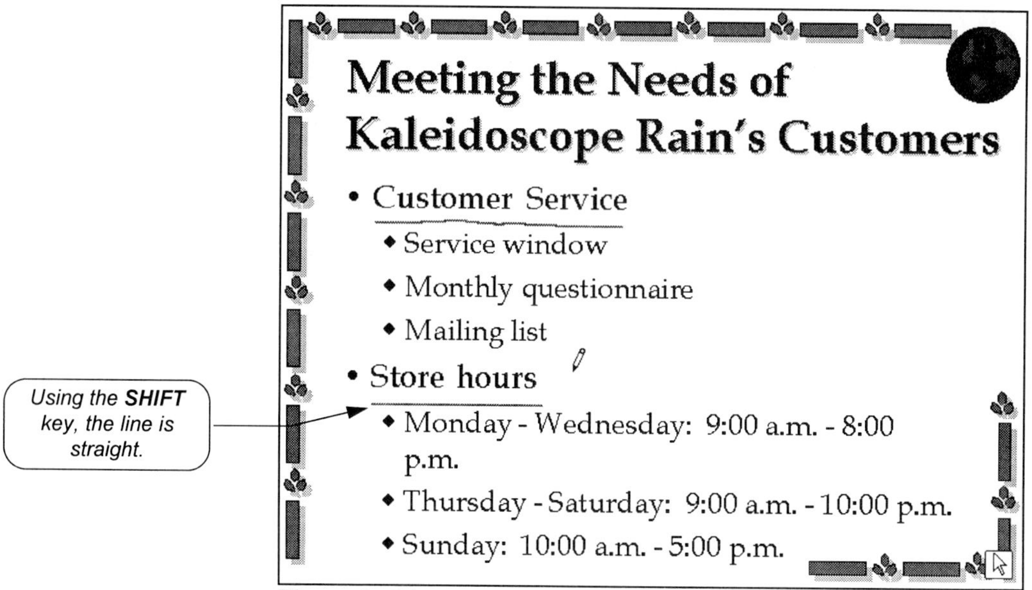

Figure 6 - 14

15. Click on the arrow icon to return the pencil.
16. Advance to Slide 5.

    Slide 5 appears on the screen using the ***Cover Left-Up*** *transition effect.*
17. Move back to Slide 4.

    The annotations have been erased.

18. Advance to Slide 5 again, and then advance to Slide 6 and show each of the 6 bullets in the Build.

    *Slide 6 appears on the screen using the **Cut Through Black** transition effect and the **Checkerboard Down** build effect for the bullets. Notice that the previous bullets are not dimmed on Slide 6. After the sixth bullet appears on the screen, the hide slide icon appears in the bottom right corner of the screen next to the pencil icon (Figure 6 - 15).*

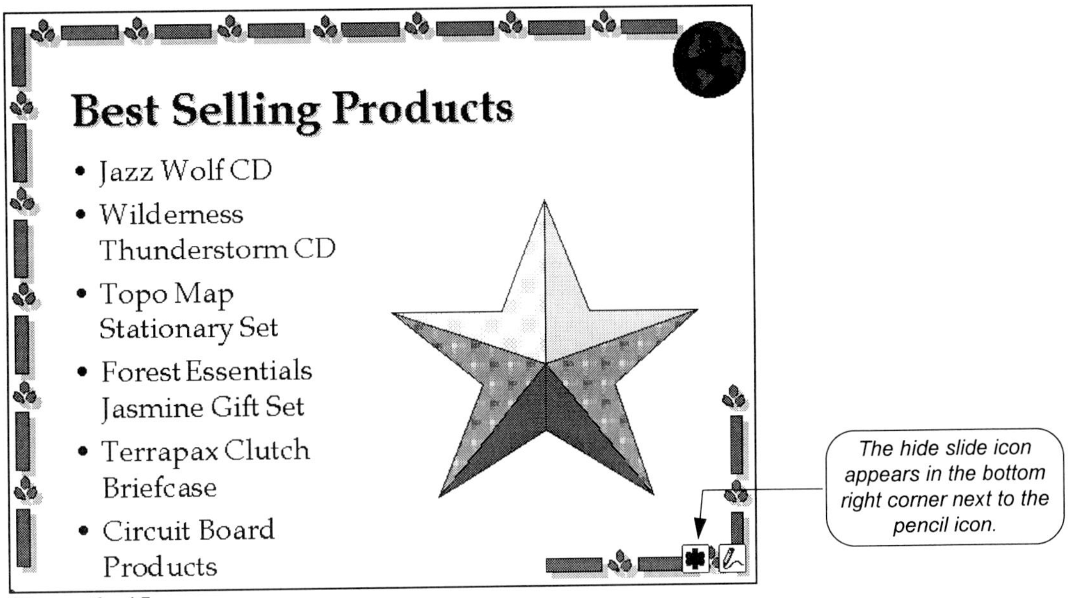

Figure 6 - 15

19. Click on the hide slide icon.

    *Slide 7 appears on the screen using the **Dissolve** transition effect. If you had not clicked on the hide slide icon, and advanced as usual, you would have advanced to Slide 8.*

20. Advance to Slide 8, Slide 9, and Slide 10.

    *Slide 8 appears on the screen using the **Random Bars Vertical** transition effect. Slide 9 appears on the screen using the **Split Vertical Out** transition effect. Slide 10 appears on the screen using the **Uncover Left-Up** transition effect. Each bullet on Slide 10 appears on the screen using the **Split Horizontal Out** build effect. After the last bullet on Slide 10 appears you are returned to Slide Sorter View.*

21. Choose **VIEW/Slide Show** again.
22. Click on **Use Slide Timings** in the Advance section, and then click on **Show**.
23. Watch the slide show automatically advance.

    You will be returned to Slide Sorter View when the slide show is completed.

24. Close the presentation without saving. There is no need to save the presentation again since you only viewed it.
25. Exit from *PowerPoint*.

SUMMARY

In this lesson you created a slide show for the **krain5.ppt** presentation. Creating a slide show is the last step involved in creating a presentation. You added transition effects to each slide and build effects for several of the bulleted list slides. You added automatic timings to the slides. Then you hid two slides and unhid one of those slides. Finally, you viewed the results of the effects you added to the presentation by viewing the slide show.

KEY TERMS

Advance	Dissolve	Slide Sorter Toolbar
Annotations	Fade Through Black	Slide Sorter View
Blinds	Fly	Slide Timings
Box	Hidden Slide Icon	Split
Build Effects	Hide Slide	Strips
Checkerboard	LCD Panel	Transition Effects
Cover	Overhead Projector	Uncover
Cut	Pencil Icon	Unhide Slide
Cut Through Black	Random Bars	Viewing a Slide Show
Dim Previous Points	Slide Show	Wipe

INDEPENDENT PROJECTS

The four independent projects allow you to practice the basic skills involved in creating slide shows and viewing them. You will add transition and build effects to slides, hide and unhide slides, and then view the slide show to see the effects.

Independent Project 6.1: Creating a Slide Show for the Ellis Island Presentation

In this project you will add transition effects to all of the slides. Then you will add build effects to several of the bulleted list slides. You will hide a slide. Then you will view the slide show. While viewing the slide show, you will use the pencil tool to annotate a slide.

1. Open *PowerPoint* if it is not already open.
2. Open the **ellis5.ppt** presentation.
3. Switch to Slide Sorter View.
4. Select Slide 1.
5. Click on the **Transition** button on the Slide Sorter Toolbar.

   *The **Transition** dialog box appears on the screen.*
6. Select **Random Transition** from the **Effect** drop-down list box, and then click on **OK**.
7. Click on the transition icon that appears below Slide 1 several times.

   Each time you click on the icon, a different transition is illustrated.
8. Select Slide 2.
9. Select **Random Transition** from the **Transition Effects** drop-down list box on the Slide Sorter toolbar.
10. Select **Random Transition** for the remainder of the slides in the presentation.
11. Select Slide 4.
12. Click on the **Build** button on the Slide Sorter toolbar.

    *The **Build** dialog box appears on the screen.*

13. Place an **X** in the **Build Body Text** check box, the **Dim Previous Points** check box, and the **Effect** check box.
14. Select **Fly From Top** from the **Effect** drop-down list box, and then click on **OK**.
15. Repeat Steps 11–14 for Slides 5 and 6.

    *When you are finished, The **History of Ellis Island** slides will have the build icon appearing in the bottom left corner of the slides. The previous points will be dimmed for all three slides and the build effect will be **Fly From Top** for all three slides.*

16. Select Slide 9.
17. Click on the **Hide Slide** button on the Slide Sorter toolbar.

    A gray box with a diagonal line is placed over the 9 appearing below Slide 9.

18. Save the presentation as **ellis6.ppt**.

    With the effects applied to your presentation, Slide Sorter View will resemble Figure 6 - 16.

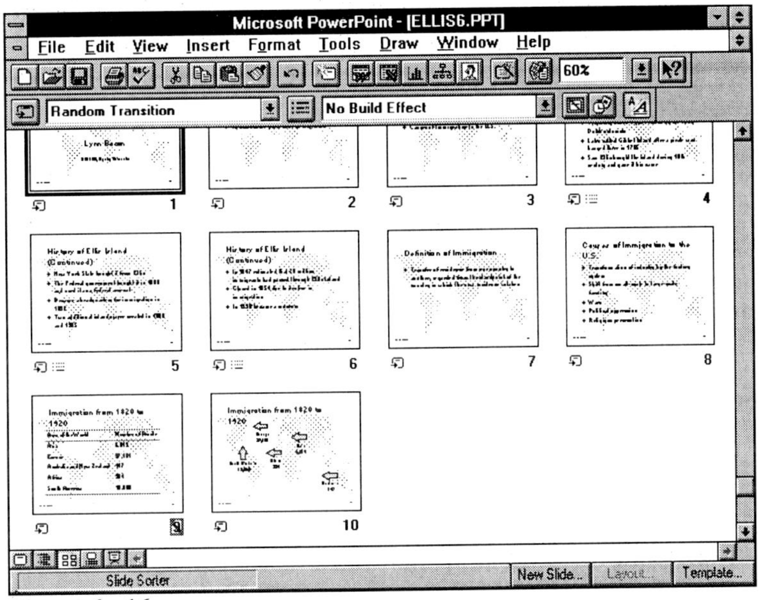

Figure 6 - 16

19. Choose **VIEW/Slide Show**.

    *The **Slide Show** dialog box appears on the screen.*

20. Click on **Show**.
21. View the slide show by pressing the left mouse button to move forward, the right mouse button to move backward, and the **ESC** key to stop the slide show. As you are viewing the slide show:
    - On Slide 8, use the pencil tool to draw a line below **Transformation** in the first bullet. Remember to press the **SHIFT** key down to draw a straight line.
    - Choose not to view the hidden slide by *not* clicking on the hidden slide icon on Slide 8.
22. Close the presentation.
23. Exit *PowerPoint* or continue with the next project.

Independent Project 6.2: Creating a Slide Show for the Browning Museum Presentation

In this project you will add transition effects to all the slides. Then you will add build effects to the **Browning Museum Staff** slide. You will hide the **Hands-On Activities** slide because you are not sure if Susan Whitney wants to use it. Then you and Susan Whitney will view the slide show. After viewing the slide show, Susan wants Slide 9 to appear automatically in the slide show, so you unhide Slide 9.

1. Open *PowerPoint* if it is not already open.
2. Open the **brown5.ppt** presentation.
3. Switch to Slide Sorter View.
4. Select Slide 1.
5. Click on the **Transition** button on the Slide Sorter toolbar.

   *The **Transition** dialog box appears on the screen.*
6. Select **Box In** from the **Effect** drop-down list box, and then click on **OK**.
7. Click on the transition icon that appears below Slide 1.

   The transition effect is illustrated.
8. Select Slide 2.
9. Select **Checkerboard Across** from the **Transition Effects** drop-down list box on the Slide Sorter toolbar.
10. Select the following transition effects for the indicated slides:

Slide 3	**Cover Right-Up**
Slide 4	**Dissolve**
Slide 5	**Random Bars Vertical**
Slide 6	**Split Horizontal Out**
Slide 7	**Uncover Right**
Slide 8	**Wipe Up**
Slide 9	**Fade Through Black**

11. Select Slide 2.
12. Click on the **Build** button on the Slide Sorter toolbar.

    *The **Build** dialog box appears on the screen.*
13. Place an **X** in the **Build Body Text** check box, the **Dim Previous Points** check box, and the **Effect** check box.
14. Select **Dissolve** from the **Effect** drop-down list box, and then click on **OK**.
15. Click on the **Slide Show** button to view the build effects applied to Slide 2.
16. Press **ESC** to stop viewing the slide show and return to Slide Sorter View.
17. Select Slide 9.
18. Click on the **Hide Slide** button on the Slide Sorter toolbar.

    A gray box with a diagonal line is placed over the 9 appearing below Slide 9.
19. Save the presentation as **brown6.ppt**.

    With the effects applied to your presentation, Slide Sorter View will resemble Figure 6 - 17.

20. Choose **VIEW/Slide Show**.

    *The **Slide Show** dialog box appears on the screen.*

21. Click on **Show**.

22. View the slide show. When you get to Slide 8, click on the hide slide icon to view Slide 9.

    After seeing the slide show, Susan Whitney wants to have Slide 9 automatically appear in the slide show. You will unhide Slide 9.

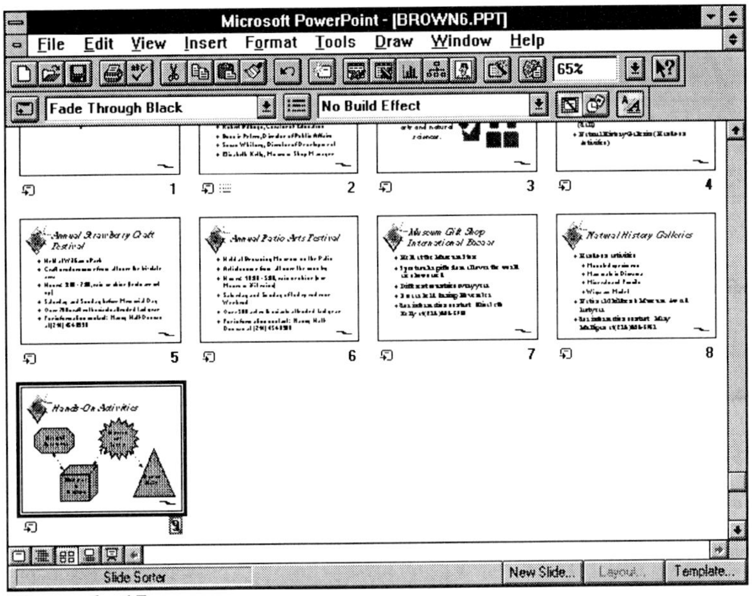

Figure 6 - 17

23. Click on Slide 9.

24. Click on the **Hide Slide** button on the Slide Sorter toolbar.

    *The **Hide Slide** button is raised and the gray box with a diagonal line is removed from the 9.*

25. Save the presentation using the same name.

26. Close the presentation.

27. Exit *PowerPoint* or continue with the next project.

Independent Project 6.3: Creating a Slide Show for Julie's Travel Agency

In this project you will add transition effects to all the slides. Because this slide show will be running on a machine that the customers will be watching, you will set the time for each slide to appear on the screen and have the slide show run continuously.

1. Open *PowerPoint* if it is not already open.
2. Open the **travel5.ppt** presentation.
3. Switch to Slide Sorter View.
4. Select Slide 1.
5. Click on the **Transition** button on the Slide Sorter toolbar.

6. Select **Blinds Horizontal** from the **Effect** drop-down list box.
7. Click on **Automatically After** in the Advance section and type **10** in the **Seconds** text box.
8. Click on **OK**.
9. Add the following transition effects to the indicated slides. While you are selecting the transition effect for each slide at the **Transition** dialog box, also set each slide to automatically advance after **10** seconds.

Slide 2	**Box Out**
Slide 3	**Checkerboard Down**
Slide 4	**Cover Left**
Slide 5	**Cover Left-Down**
Slide 6	**Dissolve**
Slide 7	**Fade Through Black**
Slide 8	**Uncover Right-Up**

10. Save the presentation as **travel6.ppt**.

With the effects applied to your presentation, Slide Sorter View will resemble Figure 6 - 18.

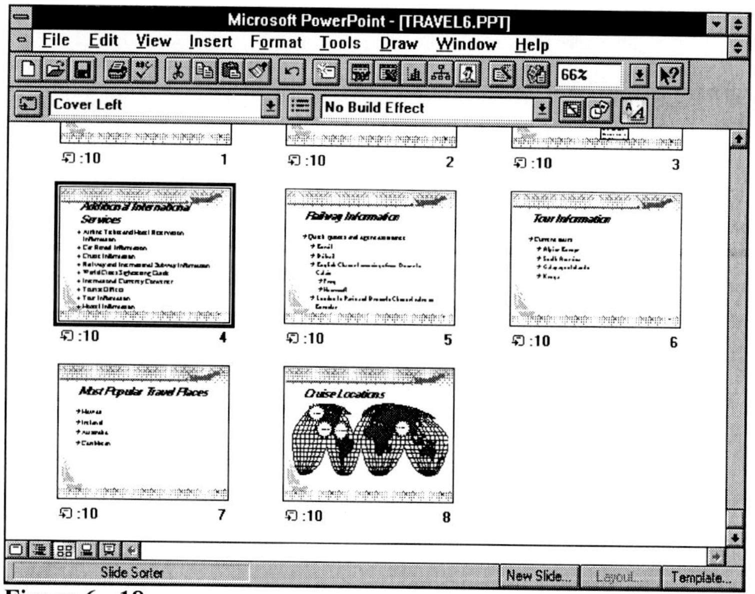

Figure 6 - 18

11. Choose **VIEW/Slide Show**.

    *The **Slide Show** dialog box appears on the screen.*

12. Click on **Use Slide Timings** in the Advance section.
13. Click in the **Run Continuously Until 'Esc'** check box so that an **X** appears.
14. Click on **Show**.

15. The slide show will run by itself. When you see Slide 1 for the second time, press **ESC**.

    You return to Slide Sorter View.

16. Close the presentation.
17. Exit *PowerPoint* or continue with the next project.

Independent Project 6.4: Creating a Slide Show for the PowerPoint Presentation

In this project you will add transition and build effects to the **train5.ppt** presentation. After adding the effects to the presentation, you will view your slide show. While viewing your slide show, you will use the pencil tool to add annotations to Slide 7.

1. Open *PowerPoint* if it is not already open.
2. Open the **train5.ppt** presentation.
3. Switch to Slide Sorter View.
4. Add a transition effect to each of the seven slides.
5. Add a build effect to Slides 2, 3, 4, and 5.
6. Save the presentation as **train6.ppt**.

    With the effects applied to your presentation, Slide Sorter View will resemble Figure 6 - 19.

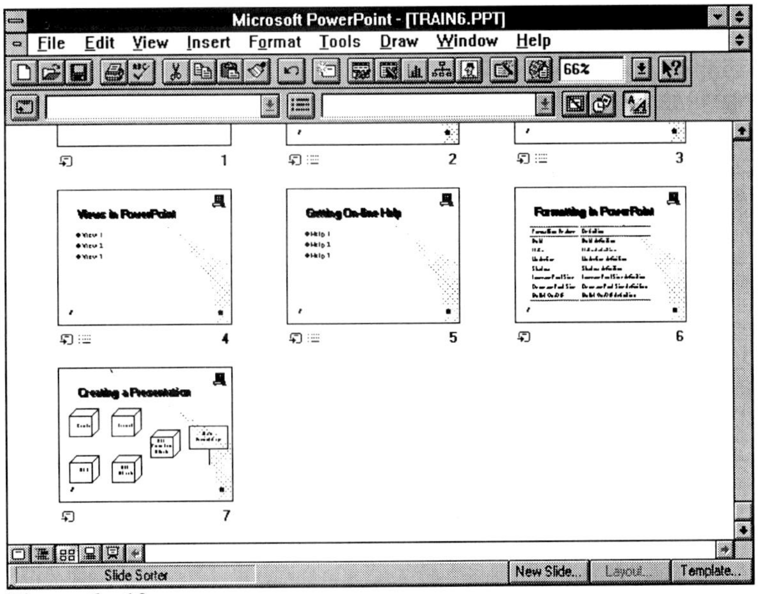

Figure 6 - 19

7. View your slide show. Stop at Slide 7.
8. On Slide 7, use the pencil tool to draw lines between the shapes and the screen indicating the flow of creating a presentation.

    After drawing the lines, Slide 7 will resemble Figure 6-20.

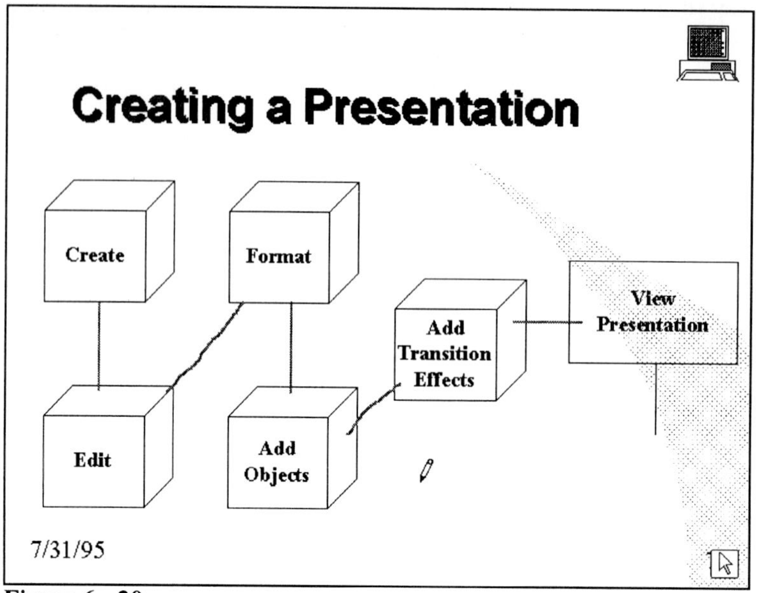

Figure 6 - 20

9. Click on the arrow in the bottom right corner of the slide.
10. Return to Slide Sorter View.
11. Close the presentation.
12. Exit *PowerPoint.*

Appendix: Features Reference

The following table contains a summary of the main features presented in the lessons. As you know, most features in *PowerPoint* can be performed in a variety of ways. Listed mouse shortcuts involve the use of buttons on the Standard, Formatting, Drawing, Drawing+, Outlining, and Slide Sorter toolbars and other mouse techniques. Many features require that the text be selected prior to executing the command. If you need more detail on using these features, the table contains a reference to the lesson describing its use.

Features	Mouse Shortcut	Menu Bar Commands	Shortcut Keys	Lessons
Add a Slide	New Slide button on Status Bar	INSERT/New Slide	CTRL+M	1
Add AutoShapes	AutoShapes button on the Drawing toolbar			5
Add Build Effects	Build button or the Build Effect list box on the Slide Sorter toolbar	TOOLS/Build		6
Add Ellipse	Ellipse Tool button on the Drawing toolbar			5
Add Line	Line Tool button on the Drawing toolbar			5
Add Rectangle	Rectangle Tool button on the Drawing toolbar			5
Add Text without Placeholder	Text Tool button on the Drawing toolbar			5
Add Transition Effects	Transition button or the Transition Effects list box on the Slide Sorter toolbar	TOOLS/Transition		6
Apply a Template	Template button on the Status bar	FORMAT/Presentation Template		1
Arrowhead Style	Arrowheads button on the Drawing+ toolbar			5
Begin New File	New button on the Standard toolbar	FILE/New	CTRL+N	I, 1
Bold	Bold button on the Formatting toolbar	FORMAT/Font	CTRL+B	3
Bullets On/Off	Bullet On/Off button on the Formatting toolbar	FORMAT/Bullet		3

Features	Mouse Shortcut	Menu Bar Commands	Shortcut Keys	Lessons
Center text	Center Alignment button on the Formatting toolbar	FORMAT/Alignment	CTRL+E	3
Change AutoShape		DRAW/Change AutoShape		5
Change Case		FORMAT/Change Case		3
Change Font	Font list box on the Formatting toolbar	FORMAT/Font	CTRL+SHIFT+F	3
Change Orientation of Slide		FILE/Slide Setup		2
Change the Bullet Symbol		FORMAT/Bullet		3
Change the Layout	Layout button on the Status bar	FORMAT/Slide Layout		3
Change the Size of an AutoShape		DRAW/Change AutoShape		5
Close		FILE/Close	CTRL+W or CTRL+F4	1
Copy	Copy button on the Standard toolbar	EDIT/Copy	CTRL+C or CTRL+INSERT	2, 5
Dashed Lines	Dashed Lines button on the Drawing+ toolbar			5
Delete		EDIT/Clear	DELETE key	2
Demote Bullets	Demote (Indent more) button on the Outlining toolbar		TAB key	2
Display/hide the Guides		VIEW/Guides	CTRL+G	I
Display/hide the Ruler		View/Ruler		I
Display/hide Toolbars		VIEW/Toolbars		I
Exit		FILE/Exit	CTRL+Q or ALT+F4	I
Fill Color	Fill Color button on the Drawing+ toolbar			5
Handout Master	SHIFT+Slide Sorter View button	VIEW/Master		3
Help	Help button on the Standard toolbar	HELP/Contents	F1 key	I
Hide Drawing Objects from Slide Master		FORMAT/Slide Background		3
Hide/Unhide a Slide	Hide button on the Slide Sorter toolbar	TOOLS/Hide Slide		6
Insert Clip Art	Insert Clip Art button on the Standard toolbar	INSERT/Clip Art		4
Insert Date		INSERT/Date	ALT+SHIFT+D	3

Insert Graph	Insert Graph button on the Standard toolbar	INSERT/Microsoft Graph		3
Insert Page Number	Insert Microsoft Word Table button on the Standard toolbar	INSERT/Page Number	ALT+SHIFT+P	3
Insert Time		INSERT/Time	ALT+SHIFT+T	3
Insert Word Table		INSERT/Microsoft Word Table		4
Italics	Italics button on the Formatting toolbar	FORMAT/Font	CTRL+I	3
Left align text	Left Alignment button on the Formatting toolbar	FORMAT/Alignment	CTRL+L	3
Line Color	Line Color button on the Drawing+ toolbar			5
Line Spacing		FORMAT/Line Spacing		3
Line Style	Line Style button on the Drawing+ toolbar			5
Move	Cut button on the Standard toolbar	EDIT/Cut	CTRL+X	2, 5
Move to next cell in a table or datasheet			TAB key	4
Move to Next Slide	Next Slide button on the vertical scroll bar		PAGE DOWN key	2
Move to previous cell in a table or datasheet			SHIFT+TAB keys	4
Move to Previous Slide			PAGE UP key	2
Notes Master	SHIFT+Notes Pages View button	VIEW/Master		3
Notes Pages View	Notes Pages View button	VIEW/Notes Pages		2
Open	Open button on the Standard toolbar	FILE/Open	CTRL+O	2
Outline View	Outline View button	VIEW/Outline	CTRL+ALT+O	2
Paste	Paste button on the Standard toolbar	EDIT/Paste	CTRL+V or SHIFT+INSERT	2, 5
Print	Print button on the Standard toolbar	FILE/Print	CTRL+P or CTRL+SHIFT+F12	1
Promote Bullets	Promote (Indent less) button on the Outlining toolbar		SHIFT+TAB keys	2
Save a File for the First Time		FILE/Save As	F12	1
Save a File with the Same Name	Save button on the Standard toolbar	FILE/Save	CTRL+S or SHIFT+F12	1

Features	Mouse Shortcut	Menu Bar Commands	Shortcut Keys	Lessons
Shadow	Text Shadow button on the Formatting toolbar			3
Size of text	Size list box, Increase Font Size button, or Decrease Font Size button on the Formatting toolbar	FORMAT/Font	CTRL+SHIFT+> (Increase Font Size) CTRL+SHIFT+< (Decrease Font Size)	3
Slide Master	SHIFT+Slide View button	VIEW/Master		3, 4
Slide Show	Slide Show button	VIEW/Slide Show		6
Slide Sorter View	Slide Sorter View button	VIEW/Slide Sorter	CTRL+ALT+P	2, 6
Slide View	Slide View button	VIEW/Slides	CTRL+ALT+N	1
Spell Check	Spell Check button on the Standard toolbar	TOOLS/Spelling	F7 key or CTRL+ALT+L	2
Switch to Another Presentation		WINDOW/*(file name)*		1
Text Color	Text Color button on the Formatting toolbar	FORMAT/Font		5
Underline	Underline button on the Formatting toolbar	FORMAT/Font	CTRL+U	3
Zoom Control	Zoom Control list box on the Standard toolbar	VIEW/Zoom		2

Index